SECRETARIAL PRACT

The Made Simple series
has been created
especially for self-education
but can equally well
be used as
an aid to group study.
However complex the subject,
the reader is taken
step by step,
clearly and methodically,
through the course. Each volume
has been prepared by experts,
taking account of
modern educational requirements,
to ensure the most
effective way of
acquiring knowledge.

In the same series

Accounting
Acting and Stagecraft
Additional Mathematics
Administration in Business
Advertising
Anthropology
Applied Economics
Applied Mathematics
Applied Mechanics
Art Appreciation
Art of Speaking
Art of Writing
Biology
Book-keeping
British Constitution
Business and Administrative
  Organisation
Business Economics
Business Statistics and Accounting
Calculus
Chemistry
Childcare
Commerce
Company Law
Computer Programming
Computers and Microprocessors
Cookery
Cost and Management Accounting
Data Processing
Dressmaking
Economic History
Economic and Social Geography
Economics
Effective Communication
Electricity
Electronic Computers
Electronics
English
English Literature
Export
Financial Management
French
Geology
German

Housing, Tenancy and Planning
  Law
Human Anatomy
Human Biology
Italian
Journalism
Latin
Law
Management
Marketing
Mathematics
Metalwork
Modern Biology
Modern Electronics
Modern European History
Modern Mathematics
Money and Banking
Music
New Mathematics
Office Administration
Office Practice
Organic Chemistry
Personnel Management
Philosophy
Photography
Physical Geography
Physics
Practical Typewriting
Psychiatry
Psychology
Public Relations
Rapid Reading
Russian
Salesmanship
Secretarial Practice
Social Services
Sociology
Spanish
Statistics
Teeline Shorthand
Twentieth-Century British
  History
Typing
Woodwork

SECRETARIAL PRACTICE Made Simple

Geoffrey Whitehead, BSc (Econ)

Made Simple Books
HEINEMANN : London

Printed and bound in Great Britain by
Richard Clay (The Chaucer Press) Ltd,
Bungay, Suffolk
for the publishers William Heinemann Ltd,
10 Upper Grosvenor Street,
London W1X 9PA

First edition, September 1977
Reprinted, March 1979
Reprinted (with revisions), September 1981
Reprinted (with revisions), March 1983

British Library Cataloguing in Publication Data

Whitehead, Geoffrey
  Secretarial practice made simple.—(Made simple
  books)
  1. Office practice   2. Secretaries
  I. Title   II. Series
  651.3′741   HF5547.5

ISBN 0 434 98498 1

Foreword

This book carries the study of secretarial duties begun so successfully with an earlier volume, *Office Practice Made Simple*, into the higher level required by private secretaries and personal assistants. It meets the requirements of secretaries studying for the Private Secretary's Diploma of the London Chamber of Commerce and Industry and the Diploma for Personal Assistants of the Royal Society of Arts.

In writing this book I have assumed that the reader already has some knowledge of general office practice at about the level described in the earlier book already mentioned. Readers who find this book more advanced than they had expected are urged to read *Office Practice Made Simple* first.

In preparing this book I have received considerable help from the public relations departments of many firms, who have kindly supplied photographs, line drawings and technical data about their products. A list of the firms concerned is given overleaf. In expressing my general appreciation of this type of assistance I must in particular refer to B. Jane Dickson, of Carson Office Furniture Ltd, Clifford J. Walton, of the Post Office Telephone Public Relations Department, Cambridge, and Godfrey Tyler of Envoy Public Relations Ltd, who all went to considerable trouble on my behalf.

I must also acknowledge warmly the assistance of Susan Drury, who researched the chapter on Sources of Information; John Barker, of Thurrock Management Centre, who kindly appraised the Management Appreciation chapters and Delia Pipe, who acted as a moderator chapter by chapter on the private secretary's duties. Their assistance was invaluable. Finally my thanks to Pamela Maas, for her painstaking and helpful consideration of the completed script, and to Robert Postema for many helpful suggestions and general assistance from an editorial viewpoint.

G. W.

Acknowledgements

BED Business Journals Ltd
Bell and Howell Ltd
Business Aids Ltd
Carson Office Furniture Ltd
Computer Power
  (Compower Ltd, Cannock)
Dictaphone Co. Ltd
Envoy Public Relations Ltd
Hengstler Flextime Ltd
Herman Miller Ltd
ITT Business Systems Ltd
ITT Terryphone
Kalamazoo Ltd
Maclaren Publishers Ltd
Maclean Hunter Ltd
Nashua Copycat Ltd
National Loose Leaf Co. Ltd

Penta Airline Hotels
  (European Hotel Corporation)
The Post Office
Rank Xerox Ltd
Roneo Neopost Ltd
SCM (United Kingdom) Ltd
Sasco Ltd
The Shannon Ltd
Shipton-Telstor Ltd
Sperry Rand Ltd
Sperry Remington Kardex
Spicers Ltd, Office Services
  Division
Standard Telephones & Cables Ltd
Twinlock Ltd
Unitype Printing Co. Ltd
Warwick Time Stamp Ltd

By the same author

In the Made Simple series
  Book-keeping
  Business and Administrative Organisation
  Business Economics (with Ken Hoyle)
  Business Statistics and Accounting (with Ken Hoyle)
  Commerce
  Money and Banking (with Ken Hoyle)
  Office Practice
  Secretarial Practice
  Transport and Distribution (with Don Benson)

From Croner Publications Ltd, New Malden, Surrey
  Elements of Overseas Trade

From George Vyner Ltd, Mytholmbridge Mills, Huddersfield
  Simplified Book-keeping for Small Businesses
  The Simplex Club Accounts Book
  The Teachers' Series of Record Books (for lesson preparation, etc.)
  Working for Yourself is *also* a Career
  Choosing Options for Your Future in the World of Work

From Shaw & Sons Ltd, Lower Sydenham
  Test Yourself on the Highway Code
  Ridley's Law of Carriage of Goods by Land, Sea and Air (Editor)

Contents

FOREWORD   v

ACKNOWLEDGEMENTS   vi

1 THE PRIVATE SECRETARY   1
   What is Secretarial Practice?   1
   The Private Secretary and the Mixed Economy   1
   The Qualities Required of a Private Secretary   3
   What's in a Name?   6
   Summary   7
   Suggested Further Reading   7

2 THE PRIVATE SECRETARY'S WORK AREA   8
   Position of the Secretarial Work Area   8
   Furnishing the Work Area   9
   Summary   15
   Suggested Further Reading   15

3 YOU AND YOUR EXECUTIVE   16
   The Executive–Secretary Relationship   16
   What the Executive Expects from his Secretary   16
   The Efficient Secretarial Partner   21
   Summary   22
   Suggested Further Reading   23

4 THE SECRETARY AND COMMUNICATION   24
   The Nature of Communication   24
   Command of English   24
   Spoken Communication   27
   Written Communication   29
   Summary   38
   Suggested Further Reading   38

5 BUSINESS CORRESPONDENCE—TAKING DICTATION   39
   Methods of Imparting Letter Content to the Secretary   39
   The Dictation Session   40
   Recorded Dictation   43
   Summary   46
   Suggested Further Reading   47

6 BUSINESS CORRESPONDENCE—TRANSCRIPTION   48
   The Art of Transcription   48
   Preparing to Transcribe   49
   The Layout of a Business Letter   50
   Transcribing the Notes   58
   Summary   60
   Suggested Further Reading   61

7 BUSINESS CORRESPONDENCE—TYPEWRITING AND WORD PROCESSING 62
   Recent Developments in Typewriting 62
   What is Word Processing? 63
   Introducing a Word-Processing System 64
   Word Processing Applications 65
   The Equipment Available 67
   Summary 70
   Suggested Further Reading 70

8 TELEPHONE TECHNIQUES 71
   The Secretary and the Telephone 71
   The Secretary's Telephonic Requirements 73
   The Secretary and Switchboards 74
   Other Sophisticated Telephonic Aids 77
   Telecommunication 80
   Summary 83
   Suggested Further Reading 84

9 ROUTINE SECRETARIAL DUTIES—MAIL INWARDS AND OUTWARDS 85
   Mail Inwards Procedures 85
   The Top Secretary and Mail Inwards 90
   Mail Outwards Procedures 91
   The Petty Cash Book 93
   The Top Secretary and Mail Outwards 93
   Summary 96
   Suggested Further Reading 96

10 ROUTINE SECRETARIAL DUTIES—FILING AND RECORD-KEEPING 97
   The Executive Secretary and the Filing System 97
   Departmental Filing *v.* Centralisation of Files 98
   Basic Principles of Filing 99
   Methods of Filing 101
   Filing Aids 110
   Summary 111
   Suggested Further Reading 111

11 ROUTINE SECRETARIAL DUTIES—REPROGRAPHY 112
   The Executive Secretary and Reprography 112
   Basic Principles in Reprography 113
   Systems of Copying and Duplicating 114
   Summary 121
   Suggested Further Reading 121

12 EXECUTIVE SECRETARIAL DUTIES—DIARIES, APPOINTMENTS AND
     RECEPTION DUTIES 122
   The Efficient Secretary 122
   Diaries 122
   'Busy Person' Indexes 125
   Follow-up Systems 126
   Year Planners and Visual Planners 127
   The Working Day 127
   Summary 131
   Suggested Further Reading 132

13 EXECUTIVE SECRETARIAL DUTIES—PUBLIC RELATIONS   133
    The Public Relations Department   133
    Protocol   137
    Summary   138
    Suggested Further Reading   139

14 EXECUTIVE SECRETARIAL DUTIES—MEETINGS   140
    The Importance of Meetings   140
    Activities Preliminary to a Meeting   141
    Activities on the Day of the Meeting   143
    The Conduct of a Meeting   144
    Taking Minutes   146
    Secretarial Duties Subsequent to a Meeting   147
    Summary   148
    Suggested Further Reading   149

15 EXECUTIVE SECRETARIAL DUTIES—CONFERENCES AND FUNCTIONS   150
    The Importance of Conferences and Functions   150
    Facilities for Conferences and Functions   151
    Preparing for a Conference or Function   152
    Activities During the Event   153
    Follow-Up Operations   155
    Social Functions   156
    Hostess Duties   156
    Summary   158
    Suggested Further Reading   159

16 EXECUTIVE TRAVEL   160
    The Importance of Executive Travel   160
    The Objectives of the Overseas Visit   160
    The Itinerary   161
    Practical Travel Details and Documents   163
    Covering the Executive in his Absence   165
    Departure Day Minus One   165
    Summary   165
    Suggested Further Reading   167

17 MANAGEMENT APPRECIATION—MANAGEMENT IN THE
      FRAMEWORK OF PRODUCTION   168
    The Secretary and an Appreciation of Management   168
    The Meaning of Production   168
    Types of Business Organisation   173
    The Development of Management Thought   175
        (a) The Doctrine of 'Laisser Faire'   175
        (b) Scientific Management   176
        (c) The 'Human Relations' Movement   177
        (d) Modern Influences and Styles of Leadership   178
    Summary   179
    Suggested Further Reading   179

18 MANAGEMENT APPRECIATION—MANAGEMENT AND PLANNING   180
    Objectives and the Formulation of Policies   180
    Planning   181

	Forecasting	182
	Management by Objectives	183
	Summary	184
	Suggested Further Reading	184
19	MANAGEMENT APPRECIATION—ORGANISATION AND DIRECTION	185
	Principles of Organisation	185
	Committees	187
	Direction	190
	Social and Economic Responsibility	192
	Summary	193
	Suggested Further Reading	194
20	MANAGEMENT APPRECIATION—CONTROL TECHNIQUES	195
	The Problems of Control	195
	Progress Control (Production Control)	197
	Critical Path Analysis (Network Analysis)	197
	Stock Control	198
	Quality Control	199
	Statistical Controls	199
	Budgetary Control	200
	Management Information	201
	Computer Appreciation	203
	Summary	205
	Suggested Further Reading	205
21	MANAGEMENT APPRECIATION—PERSONNEL MANAGEMENT	206
	The Personnel Function	206
	Personnel Planning	207
	Selection and Recruitment	207
	Staff Development and Training	209
	Management Training and Development	210
	Wages and Conditions of Employment	211
	Flexible Working Hours	212
	Industrial Relations	213
	Personnel Records	214
	Summary	217
	Suggested Further Reading	217
22	SOURCES OF REFERENCE	218
	Introduction	218
	English Language and Correspondence	218
	Post Office Services	218
	Meetings	219
	People	219
	Trade and Industry	219
	Travel and Conferences	220
	The Press and Public Relations	221
	General and Current Affairs Information	221
	Consultancy and Advisory Services	221
	Office Equipment	222
	Other Sources of Information	222

APPENDIX 1: Questions 223

APPENDIX 2: Professional Organisations for Executive Secretaries 231

APPENDIX 3: Examinations for Private Secretaries 233

INDEX 235

1

THE PRIVATE SECRETARY

What is Secretarial Practice?

Secretarial Practice is a term used to describe the procedures and methods of work adopted by private secretaries. It is similar to, but at a higher level than, Office Practice. A person performing clerical duties needs to have an understanding of Office Practice. A person performing secretarial duties needs to understand the higher level of activities described by the term Secretarial Practice. A companion volume, *Office Practice Made Simple*, contains a wealth of information on the routine office activities that form the basis of the private secretary's procedures. This book extends the study of Office Practice into the higher levels of secretarial work, where the private secretary who is already familiar with the more routine techniques faces further problems.

These problems include the preparation and mailing of impeccable correspondence; the maintenance and supervision of an error-free desk diary; the presentation to the executive in concise form as a neat package everything that may be needed for each interview, report or other item of work in the daily round; the organisation of meetings, including the preparation of agendas, their distribution to those concerned, the seating in the meeting room; the minuting of the meeting itself and the following up of decisions are matters to which the secretary will largely attend. It may be necessary to organise conferences or functions; to arrange for appropriate invitations to guests, and look to their reception; to book accommodation, arrange executive travel, and perform countless other activities. This book is intended to give guidance and assistance on all these matters.

The term **private secretary** should not be confused with **company secretary**, an important executive who is charged with supervising the legal implications of company status and keeping the register of shareholders and other statutory books. This type of executive is usually anxious to distinguish the post from ordinary secretarial work, and therefore uses the terms 'Company Secretary' and 'Company Secretarial Practice' to describe the position, and the procedures.

The Private Secretary and the Mixed Economy

We live in a system of society known as a **mixed economy** because it produces the wealth that we need in two ways: partly by private enterprise and partly by nationalised industries. Wealth, of course, does not mean money, it means goods and services. Everything we need is either a good—furniture, fruit, typewriters and cosmetics are typical examples—or a service. Dentistry, stenography, hairdressing and entertainment are typical examples of services. Goods and services are the wealth of nations, and they are produced either by the free enterprise activity of private citizens or by nationalised industries run by employees who are the servants of the general public. The latter are

1

usually employed by an organisation set up by the law-making body—Parliament in the United Kingdom—such as a Regional Hospital Board or an Atomic Energy Authority.

Whatever the system of organisation adopted—free enterprise or nationalised industry—the key element in the organisation will be the **head office**. From head office the instructions will be issued which start the activities that create wealth. Once programmes have started, there will flow into the head office streams of information on the progress being made, the output being achieved, the patients being treated, the problems that have developed. This will enable head office to take action where necessary; to chase up the missing part required for a machine; to advance plans if work is proceeding faster than expected, etc. All such action is called **executive action**. The word 'executive' comes from two Latin words (*sequi secut*) meaning 'to carry out the next activity needed'. When we talk about top managers we usually use the word 'executives' because the management at head office is particularly charged with the responsibility of deciding what the next step will be, and issuing the orders to carry it out.

Behind every executive there is a first-class **private secretary** who acts as the executive's *alter ego* or 'other self'. Traditionally the executive was male and the secretary female, but we live in a changing world; there are now many female top executives and the male stenographer is not unknown. To avoid the use of 'he/she' too frequently I have, with apologies to the sensitive, consistently written of the executive as 'he' and of the secretary as 'she'.

The private secretary—or, if you prefer, the 'executive secretary'—has a vital part to play in the whole process of head office executive action. To many people she *is* the top executive, for they will never get in to see him. She filters off the callers, taking their packages and their messages and freeing them to go about their other business without disturbing him. She takes notes at his departmental meetings and records the decisions about action to be taken. She probably initiates many of these actions by typing letters of a routine nature on a mere verbal instruction. 'Write to Jones at Terminal 5 and tell him to start production on Monday,' the executive may say. On more important matters, where a precisely worded letter is required, the executive will dictate it, and in many cases they will wrestle together with the wording until it is exactly right. Such activities call for the exercise of those special qualities which distinguish the private secretary from the shorthand typist; tact and charm may be necessary if the executive is weak on grammar and syntax.

The private secretary is the power behind the throne in many executive situations. As a group they probably do more to promote the efficiency of the nation than any other single occupation. Not a wheel turns until the head office memo arrives to start the machinery, and a call from the production manager's personal secretary can shut down a plant in an emergency in minutes.

It follows that the work of the private secretary is of enormous national importance. She is to be found in every type of private enterprise, from the small family concern to the multi-national company. In the traditional state activities like the Army, Navy and Civil Service and in the newer state-controlled industries like electricity, gas, atomic energy and transport, the private secretary has her vital part to play. In universities, colleges, schools, hospitals and social and welfare bodies of every sort she is the key link between the executive, board, panel or committee charged with responsibility for the service and the ordinary employees who will carry the plans into operation for the general public who require the services.

It follows that the private secretary must be a person of responsibility and even dedication, qualified by training, experience and temperament to perform these vital duties efficiently and enthusiastically. Like other experts she tends to be 'always on tap, but never on top'. This book is designed to contribute towards the training of those who aspire to be top secretaries. Let us begin by examining the qualities needed by such personnel.

The Qualities Required of a Private Secretary

The private secretary requires many qualities and skills, as well as a wide knowledge of business in general and her own firm in particular. These qualities are tabulated in Table 1.1. They come under four main headings.

Table 1.1.   Qualities Required by the Private Secretary

General education	Secretarial skills	Business knowledge	Personal qualities
University degree *or* at least 2 A levels *or* Higher National Diploma in Business Studies *or* the widest possible educational background especially in English. Other languages may be helpful	Shorthand, 100–140 w.p.m. Typing, 50–75 w.p.m. Accurate spelling Sensitive display Sound knowledge of filing, reprography and telephone techniques	A basic understanding of economics, commerce, book-keeping and law is very useful A really comprehensive understanding of her own particular firm and its personalities, products and markets is invaluable	Commonsense Tact Discretion Initiative Adaptability Honesty Trustworthiness Loyalty Neat appearance Careful grooming Good humour Understanding Helpful attitude Reliability Punctuality Imagination Dedication Hostess qualities Self-control Good health Pleasantly spoken Well organised Methodical Good memory

Since each of these is as important as the others it is difficult to decide in which order to list them. In Table 1.1 the order is:

(*a*) Wide general education
(*b*) Mastery of the secretarial skills
(*c*) Business knowledge (including in-firm experience)
(*d*) Personal qualities

We must now examine each of these in turn, in an introductory way; some of them will be the subjects of major chapters later.

Wide General Education

The top secretary works at the very highest secretarial level in her organisation. She will meet and take dictation from the topmost people in that field, probably from all over the world. She will meet celebrities in all walks of life. The publisher's private secretary will meet authors who are perhaps politicians, generals, captains of industry, explorers, television personalities, etc. The oil executive's secretary will meet the leading chemical engineers, rulers of oil-producing nations, government representatives arguing about concessions, and so on. To deal successfully with this wide variety of encounters the top secretary must have a good general education. Ideally she should have a university degree; as a minimum she should have been educated at least to the age of eighteen, with what in the United Kingdom is called GCE Advanced Level or equivalent qualifications. If you are aspiring to reach one of these top secretarial jobs and your own education is inadequate you should do something about it at once. It is possible to acquire education to the required level by evening study at almost any further education college, or even by correspondence from a reputable correspondence college. Many firms will gladly pay tuition fees and stationery costs for staff proposing to extend their general education in this way; others pay lump sum bonuses to staff who have successfully completed a course of study.

The secretary who proposes to qualify herself for a top position by extending her general education may not be sure which studies to pursue. The type of employment she proposes to take up will to some extent determine which subjects she should study, but the universal requirement is a really good standard of English. This is a basic need for the secretary, who must speak, write and type perfect English. Foreign languages are very important in many firms, particularly those engaged in international trade. While French, German, Italian and Spanish are the most common languages studied, Dutch, Portuguese and the Scandinavian languages are also important, while Arabic, Russian and Chinese offer increasingly lucrative opportunities to the limited number of secretaries who opt to study them.

A secretary can extend her understanding of the business world by studying one or more of the subjects which are directly related to business. The best of all perhaps is Economics, but Law is very important to all types of businessmen, and Accountancy, Economic Geography and many other subjects of a more specialist nature may be appropriate to your particular firm. They can all be studied over the course of a few years. Some of the best preparation comes from the Business Education Council's National and Higher National certificates in Business Studies. Over a period of four years it is possible to achieve degree-equivalent status in a wide range of business subjects. With the right secretarial skills combined with this good general education a secretary can achieve membership of the top secretarial organisations described in Appendix 2 (see page 231).

Mastery of the Secretarial Skills

It is assumed by employers that the applicant for a top secretarial post will have mastered completely the secretarial skills which are the essential tools of her trade. The very minimum qualification is 100 words per minute shorthand and 50 words per minute typing, but most top secretaries will have speeds of at least 120 w.p.m. and 60 w.p.m. respectively. A secretary must also have a flair for display, and must spell and punctuate accurately. She must be able to present impeccable work for signature, except in those circumstances where only a rough draft is called for.

Other secretarial skills include filing, reprography, ability to answer the telephone (often two or three at the same time), to receive visitors and to deal calmly with emergency situations.

Business Knowledge and In-firm Experience

A secretary should have a good background knowledge of business, whatever her general education. Thus a graduate in English Literature, or an accomplished linguist, may display a literacy which is invaluable to her employer and yet be at a disadvantage when dealing with the Accountant or the Company Secretary because she has no knowledge of either book-keeping or law. While business knowledge does not necessarily have to be learned in the classroom—indeed, the Made Simple series of books is designed especially for self-study—some subjects are most easily assimilated with the help of a gifted teacher. Others may be read up discreetly in quiet moments during business hours, or by private study at home.

A general understanding of the economic framework of the business world can be achieved simply by painstaking perusal of the daily press, particularly the business pages. The journey to work and home again can be partly spent in reading this type of article, and if pursued over a working lifetime it amounts to an education. The secretary who spends the last ten minutes of her journey to and from work reading business articles is spending—over the course of twenty years—as much time on these matters as a full-time degree student would spend in a three-year full-time course.

Perhaps the most important background knowledge that the secretary can acquire is in-firm experience. This can chiefly be acquired by watching what is going on around you; who are the key figures in any particular field of business activity; who are the strong personalities; what are the important products and markets, etc. To this knowledge, which inevitably accumulates as part of the hurly-burly of business life, can be added less obvious background knowledge available from house magazines, staff notice boards and the Annual Report if the firm is a public company. Even historical details about the foundation of the firm and its growth over the years may be available. Such information may be of service at almost any time. A confident quotation from the Annual Report or an accurate statistic from a sales conference report in the house magazine may settle an argument or clinch a decision to the amazement of less well-informed staff.

Personal Qualities

The most intangible qualities of the private secretary, and the most important ones, are the personal qualities she displays. The employer considering a candidate for a top secretarial post is entitled to assume that she has the first three attributes of Table 1.1: a good general education, a mastery of the tools of her trade and a reasonable business background. All that is left are her personal qualities. Will she be cooperative or obstructive? Will she be absent when he needs her most? Will she be a credit to him, and to the organisation, with visitors and business associates? Will she be at loggerheads with other staff?

It might be thought that some qualities are innate; one is born with them, or without them. This is of course partly true, but it is even more true that qualities which are poorly developed or even totally absent from our personalities can be developed. Equally, we can control and play down aspects of personality which are adverse in the business situation.

These personal qualities must be such that they enable the secretary to do a really good job for the firm and the executive she serves. They must therefore be such that they achieve the following aims:

(*a*) Actually get her to work, and on time, so that she can play her part. She must cultivate good health, so far as that is possible, by regular, abstemious habits, personal hygiene and prompt medical attention when necessary. She must develop systems of behaviour which get her up in the morning, on to her transport and into the office in time.

(*b*) Promote the efficiency of the office by fostering a sense of helpful cooperation with other departments. This includes assisting young staff to develop by a courteous, helpful attitude towards them; the avoidance of confrontations with other secretaries or centralised servicing departments like typing pools and reprographic departments, and exercising self-control at times of extra pressure to ensure a calm atmosphere. By thinking ahead, advantage can be taken of lulls in business activity to advance routine reorganisation or intermittent activities like mailings which cannot be carried out easily at really busy times.

(*c*) Establish a sound, friendly working relationship with the executive by a combination of desirable attitudes and necessary activities. These include the establishment of good personal relationships by personal hygiene, the cultivation of dress sense, careful grooming, the cultivation of a pleasant speaking voice and the avoidance of mannerisms which manifestly irritate him. She must anticipate his needs, fortify his strengths and disguise his imperfections. A personal secretary must understand what makes her executive 'tick'. Even the highest secretarial qualifications will be of little use if she cannot anticipate his reactions and does not know how his mind works. She must give him an honest opinion when he asks for one, for if she is right he will remember it and if she is wrong it will do no harm.

(*d*) Finally, we must remember that he himself is only an employee in many cases, so that the good of the firm is in the long run the yardstick by which she must judge his position and her loyalty to him. If he is manifestly at variance with the firm's stated policy the greatest loyalty she can show him is to point this out, and thus ensure that he does not get too far off the rails.

If it appears that a private secretary must be a veritable angel to achieve all these desirable—and sometimes contradictory—ends, it remains that many top secretaries do achieve them. Their salaries, and the esteem in which they are held, reflect the ability they show in doing so.

What's in a Name?

When Juliet protested that a name was of little importance—'That which we call a rose, by any other name would smell as sweet'—she voiced a feeling that wins little support today. It is an almost universal practice these days to seek higher status by using a more imposing name. Dustmen have become refuse collectors and ratcatchers are rodent operatives. Copy typists and shorthand typists call themselves secretaries, and even personal secretaries if they work chiefly for one person, be he merely a foreman. It is not surprising therefore that the best-qualified secretarial staff seek to adopt titles which reflect their greater responsibilities and higher skills. The terms 'top secretary', 'personal secretary', 'private secretary', 'executive secretary', 'personal assistant'—abbreviated to 'p.a.'—and 'management aide' are all commonly used. Sometimes the status of the executive confers the best status of all on his secretary, and we have 'Principal's secretary', 'Chairman's secretary', etc.

To support the name you choose to use you should preferably have paper qualifications, and the best of these in the United Kingdom is the London Chamber of Commerce Private Secretary's Diploma. The Royal Society of Arts Diploma for Personal Assistants is very similar. A full description of both these examinations is to be found in Appendix 3. Other comparable examinations have roughly similar syllabuses but may use the terms 'personal secretary' or 'executive secretary'. Armed with these qualifications it is then possible to obtain membership of the professional organisations already referred to, and featured in Appendix 2.

Summary

1. Secretarial practice is an extension of general office practice to cover those activities performed by the private secretary in serving top executives. These include the organisation, minuting and following up of business meetings; the organisation of conferences and functions; public relations; executive travel; hostess activities and many more.

2. The private secretary has an important part to play in private enterprise firms, and in the Civil Service and nationalised industries.

3. She must possess many skills and qualities. She should have a wide general education, high speeds in shorthand and typewriting, a background of business knowledge and personal qualities which include commonsense, tact, imagination, adaptability, discretion and loyalty.

4. In this book the term 'private secretary' has been used to cover the whole range of top-quality secretarial and 'personal assistant' jobs, which constitute the top ten per cent of secretarial positions.

Suggested Further Reading

Almost a Marriage, Vera Sugg, Frederick Muller, 1966.
How to be a Successful Secretary, Marilyn C. Burke, The World's Work Ltd, 1961.

2

THE PRIVATE SECRETARY'S WORK AREA

Position of the Secretarial Work Area

In the majority of cases the private secretary will be in a room adjacent to that of the executive she serves. This is in many ways the best situation. If the secretary is to keep on top of her work she must press ahead with it, and if this involves a clattering typewriter or a whirring photocopier the executive will clearly be disturbed if his secretary is seated in the same room as himself. He may frequently need to ask her to stop work because a long-distance telephone call is indistinct. It also happens that in many senior positions some personal problem which the executive must discuss with an employee, or some matter of high policy which he is not at liberty to discuss in front of his secretary, makes it necessary for him to ask her to leave the room. The secretary then necessarily falls behind with her work and is both frustrated and imposed upon.

There are many other situations where it is better for them to be apart. Frequently a fellow secretary will take a poor view of the arrangements made by an executive, and will want to protest about them to his secretary. A conciliatory arrangement may be easily arranged between them which would not be possible if the executive shared an office with his secretary. Similarly, a secretary who has her own office can protect her executive much more easily from intrusive undesirable visitors. The little white lie that he is engaged, which will send them about their business, can hardly be told if he is in the room manifestly doing very little that cannot be interrupted. Against these points it may be argued that a secretary who is in the same room as the executive will learn his views, methods and reactions to situations more quickly than if she is in an ante-room. To a middle management executive whose promotion may be accelerated by the efficiency of his secretary it may make more sense therefore to have her physically present at all times. At higher levels this becomes less important and her ability to act as a filter through which visitors must pass becomes more vital.

The private secretary's work area should therefore be located convenient to the executive's own office, preferably in an ante-room, or in that corner of a general office most convenient to his door. In an open-plan office her desk should be closer to the traffic flow than his, and if screening is used he should be to some extent screened off from routine visitors.

The work position should be carefully considered. She will probably get up to go into his office fifty times a day. Even a small detour to avoid a filing cabinet or squeeze past a hat stand will become irritating after a while. The access should be direct and unobstructed; the floor covering such that she is not impeded; the door itself should open freely and close quietly.

Lighting can be of great importance; both natural and artificial lighting should be taken into account.

Acoustics can play an important part in a secretary's life. Nothing is more tiring than to work in a room with bad acoustics, where hard surfaces reflect sound from wall to wall and every scraped chair reverberates endlessly. The modern office has acoustically designed ceilings, display panels, partitions and pin boards which absorb sound, and also add warmth and texture to the environment. Noise can also be reduced by siting noisy machines in annexes or cubicle rooms separate from the open-plan offices. The use of screens, faced on both sides with acoustic material, reduces disturbances caused by conversation. The secretary's own typewriter can in many cases be fitted with a cover which significantly reduces noise.

Even small conference areas, such as the one shown in Plate 2, will not disturb other members of staff and therefore assist the acoustics. The meeting (or chat) area is separated from the rest of the office by tall screens 2 metres high. The acoustic panels absorb sound so that the chat is barely audible outside, while the transparent screens give visibility without surrendering privacy. The visibility enhances control of staff in the outer office, and enables them also to see who is in the meeting without disturbing it by the need to enter the conference room. A hat and coat hook unit is mounted on one section of the screen.

Extremes of temperature drastically reduce output in any office. Blinds are essential for windows which are liable to receive bright sunlight, air-conditioning may be necessary at certain times of the year, and draughts should either be excluded or screened from employees.

A secretary who is about to take a post is often asked 'Have you any questions?' A good reply is to ask if you may see the work position you will occupy, since your present work position is a very comfortable one and you would like to feel that in this new post you will be equally well placed. A prospective employer can hardly refuse, and it gives you the chance to say at once that you feel it is unsatisfactory in some way. The promise to re-arrange it to your liking will benefit you greatly when you take up the post.

Furnishing the Work Area

Not everyone can plan her work area and spend money to purchase exactly the type of furniture and equipment that suits her best. We all have to make do, especially at the commencement of employment. As time passes the opportunity usually arises to select items of equipment which suit you better, and you can usually speed up the process if you try. If a particular item of furniture or equipment is totally unsatisfactory, because it makes the work more tiring or reduces your efficiency, make a formal complaint about it and get it changed.

The Desk Configuration

The style of desk and the desk arrangement must be such as to suit the secretary's personal characteristics. This does not mean that she must be given a free hand to purchase exactly what she would like, but it does mean that within limits she is entitled to rearrange it until she is happy with it. In general the business will benefit if her movements are quick and natural, and she is comfortable and contented. Modern office furniture is produced in such a way that is is versatile, and rearrangements to suit individuals are easily managed. It generally consists of standardised units of attractive design which

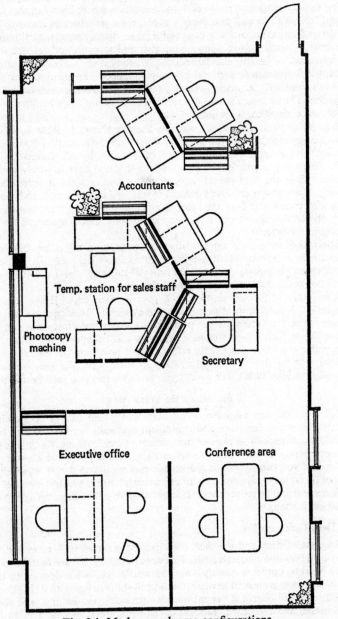

Accountants

Temp. station for sales staff

Photocopy machine

Secretary

Executive office

Conference area

Fig. 2.1. Modern work area configurations.

(Courtesy of Carson Office Furniture Ltd)

can be fitted together in a variety of configurations. The work-area configurations illustrated in Fig. 2.1 show typical linked units. The older style centre-well desks and drophead typewriter desks, although still useful where space is limited, have been replaced by L-shaped configurations which give the secretary a permanent typewriting area, and at right angles to it a working space which is also continuously available. Because of the cheapness of mass-produced standardised units the two working areas can be provided at about the same cost as the older types of desk, and the labour of changing from one activity to another is saved.

The private secretary in particular has the problem of changing frequently from one activity to another and the L-shaped configuration is of great advantage to her.

Fig. 2.2. A desk organiser.

(Courtesy of Twinlock Ltd)

The effective working area of the desk can be increased by a well designed set of drawers in the pedestal. By fitting out a set of drawers with suitable drawer dividers, stationery racks, rubber stamp racks, card index racks and hanging file frames, it is possible to remove from the top of the desk the assorted paraphernalia which clutters the desks in most antiquated offices. A hanging file frame used as a work organiser can keep each activity separate, the secretary putting away each group of work she performs into the filing system as she completes it, until it is called for. This is particularly useful where a secretary is doing work for more than one executive.

Plate 1 shows a suitable set of drawers, and Fig. 2.2 shows a typical work organiser which can either stand free on a desk or be based in a deep drawer. The provision of these types of drawer frees the office desk for the few items which are essential to it: a telephone—preferably seated on a non-slip telephone mat—and an intercom unit, the typewriter, and perhaps a desk light together with some in, out and pending trays. Plate 1 shows a typical work station which has been laid out to meet the personal preferences of a busy secretary.

Chairs

The desk and typist's chair should be regarded as a single unit, and should be matched so that in the normal working position the secretary's arms can be held in the correct typing position while at the same time her feet are comfortably positioned either on the floor or on a footrest. The lighting must be adequate, and well positioned to illuminate the desk and the typewriter.

A secretary may spend two or three hours a day in total actually typing. The rest of the time she is walking about the office, going in to see her boss, greeting visitors, filing and finding documents. The trouble is that the two or three hours of actual typing is done in intermittent snatches, not in sustained periods. She must therefore have a chair which is appropriate to her needs. This means that it must be a revolving chair so that she can swing herself round to free her legs from the 'under the desk' position to a position where she can walk away from the typewriter. It must also be fully adjustable. Never accept a chair until you have really tried it out. This does not mean merely sitting on it, but also deciding whether the seat and backrest can be positioned to suit your particular figure.

Senior secretaries and supervisors should watch for inadequacies in the seating of staff under their control and be ready to offer suggestions when replacement furniture is being purchased. The standard reference book is given in the Suggested Further Reading to this chapter.

Where the work area is not an L-shaped configuration, but is more spread out, it is helpful to have two revolving chairs to save moving one about. This type of layout is adopted where the secretary has much of her time involved in other activities than typing—perhaps proof-reading, pasting up artwork, collating and stapling reports. The extra space is often advantageous, as are work surfaces, storage shelves and filing racks supported on free-standing screen walls. Some of these features are illustrated in Plate 1. Note particularly the screen-hung shelf and lighting fittings above the typewriter, the screen-hung filing unit for wallet files, which also supports the filing trays, and the well designed set of drawers in the desk. The accessories tray in the top drawer is subdivided for the storage of such items as pencils, rubbers, paper clips, etc. The lower shelves hold stationery, card indexes, rubber stamps and many other items. The secretary's electric Olympia typewriter is on a Link 900 free-standing typist extension table which fits under the screen-mounted desk, but can be pulled out to give extra working area. Her Grundig Stenorette audio dictating machine is conveniently situated near her typing position, while she has two telephones, one of which is a press-button intercom for internal use. The telephone directory is a Shannostrip flipover unit of one-line visible records, with 780 strips bearing names and telephone numbers.

A secretary frequently has to entertain visitors for a few minutes while her 'boss' completes the previous appointment. If space permits in the secretary's office, it is agreeable to arrange a small entertaining and reception area, with perhaps two or three unit armchairs, a coffee table with a shelf for magazines, and a few pot plants or flowers. A wardrobe for visitors' coats and bags is also useful. A nice picture on the wall and—where appropriate—a small display of the firm's products or a model of its plant layout help to create a good impression. Even a drinks cabinet or a permanently hot coffee facility may be included in cases where a reasonable amount of cosseting of visitors is desirable.

The Typewriter

A secretary is only as good as her typewriter. A top secretary must have a top-quality typewriter if her correspondence is to be well presented. It is false economy for an office to persist in using antiquated machines with typefaces which lack style. Once a letter is typed and signed it represents the company to the reader. The company commands respect to the extent that its correspondence commands respect. She should therefore insist upon having a modern machine, with at least some of the modern features. A list of desirable features would include:

(a) The typewriter must be an electronic machine with the latest facilities, such as **interchangeable 'daisy-wheel' type faces, line-display facilities** so that errors can be corrected before typing takes place, etc.

(b) An adjustable **'impression control'** which regulates the striking force applied to the typeface, to give the right amount of power for different kinds of work and for numbers of copies required.

(c) **Proportional spacing**, which gives a wide character more space on the line than a narrow character. This gives the line of typescript an appearance similar to a line in a printed book, making it particularly easy to read.

(d) **Automatic repeat keys**, which save time and effort when underlining or inserting decorative effects, space fillers, etc.

(e) **Correction keys**, which either re-position exactly over an incorrect character or, in conjunction with a **lift-off ribbon**, enable the incorrect character to be cleanly removed from the paper, ready for re-typing.

(f) A **justified right-hand** margin is desirable for certain types of work, and can be achieved on some machines relatively simply.

(g) **Ribbon cartridges**, which are easily and cleanly inserted, and may also be changed for preparing special items such as hectograph spirit masters, are convenient.

(h) Also useful is a machine which, with the flick of a switch, can change to carbon ribbon, producing good style letters, and to ordinary ribbon for drafts, internal memoranda and less important correspondence.

(i) Some machines have **space-expand devices** which enable words to be spread out evenly for special display purposes, or for statistical tabulations.

Servicing is vital when sophisticated typewriters are being used, and it is therefore essential to insist upon an 'immediate service' arrangement whenever new machines are supplied. The frustration and delay that results from slow service can be annoying and expensive.

A fuller description of executive typewriters is given later in the chapter on typewriting, but as an element in the secretarial work station the typewriter is clearly of great importance.

Associated with good style on the typewriter keyboard is the question of stylish letterheads and stationery. The letterhead is the key feature of any piece of stationery, to which the executive secretary adds her own high-quality work. However perfect the typing she does, a shoddy letterhead and a cheap envelope will prevent a good impression being created. The executive secretary must play her part in raising objections to poor stationery.

The Telephone and Intercom

The secretarial work station is always equipped with both telephone and intercom equipment. It may have more than one telephone, depending upon the business concerned. Telephones may have intercom switches as well as the usual facility to receive and make calls. The secretary will often have these telephones so that she can switch a call through to her 'boss'. Alternatively, she may have an actual switchboard. Her duties will require her to receive calls on behalf of her executive, to filter off routine matters to avoid wasting the executive's time, and to act as a buffer between him and the important calls for just enough time to allow him to collect his thoughts or for her to find the relevant data so that he can answer the call efficiently.

There are many business occasions when it is most convenient to deal with a telephone call without holding it in one's own hands. It is easier to find documents, locate references, make notes or collate papers if the telephone is a **loudspeaking type** which will amplify the call from the normal earpiece into a loudspeaker. In these days of subscriber trunk dialling the secretary often dials for an external line without the assistance of a switchboard operator. The time wasted holding on to a telephone while it rings in the queue at destination can be considerable. The secretary can carry on with her normal work if she has a loudspeaking instrument, and the consequent savings will more than pay for the hire charge or purchasing price of the equipment. The chapter on 'Use of the Telephone' contains a description of this type of equipment and the uses to which it can be put. It also includes a full account of other time-saving devices such as **card call makers** which automatically dial out numbers, and **'Terryphones'** which can locate staff around a building in as little as five seconds.

A telephone which slips is a great nuisance when dialling. Telephone non-slip mats are inexpensive and will help to prevent mis-dialling.

Filing Cabinets

Every senior secretary will have filing cabinets to look after. Even in an office where centralised filing systems are used it is usual to keep most of the live and confidential correspondence available in the local area where it is certain to be called for. Most top correspondence is of vital importance to the whole organisation and must be kept in security according to some well-understood system of filing so that it can be retrieved at once if required. In many cases total security will be called for, to prevent industrial or commercial espionage, or to safeguard personal details relating to staff. The secretary must not only know the basic principles of filing, but must be familiar with the system used in her particular firm. She must ensure that supplies of file covers, tabs, etc., are available so that correspondence can be filed at once. If filing is delayed due to a shortage of such items it will often result in correspondence being lost or misplaced temporarily. If stocks have to be drawn from a central point on a particular day she must ensure that her supplies are adequate but not excessive, and keep a note of items needed ready for the day when re-stocking is permitted. This rule also applies for all items of office stationery.

The types of equipment available vary enormously. The business equipment industry is constantly developing new equipment and procedures which should be evaluated and considered. Most firms have a special Purchasing Department which performs this function, but the secretary will often have a point of view to express about the adequacy of items in use and the alternatives available. Exhibitions such as the International Business Exhibition held in Birmingham present opportunities for inspecting new equipment and you should visit them whenever an opportunity occurs.

Smaller Office Equipment

Besides the major items of equipment a secretary should be supplied with a wide variety of office aids appropriate to the work she performs. You should use these aids as economically as possible to reduce business costs, but bearing in mind that the appearance of your work is always the prime consideration. The odd moments of time available to you can be usefully employed browsing through the office supplies catalogue and ordering up items which will be useful. Such items as staplers, punches, paper knives, date stamps, correction fluid, paper clips, desk and wall calendars, year-planners, paste, cellulose tape, etc., are all very inexpensive compared with the advantages obtained by their use. It is false economy to walk about the office to borrow, for example, a two-hole punch when they cost a trifling sum. Plate 3 shows a selection of smaller office aids of use to a top secretary.

Summary

1. The private secretary should be positioned close to the office of the executive she serves. Her access to his office should be direct and clear of obstructions.

2. She should have her furniture and lighting arranged to suit her personal preferences, since the business will benefit if she is comfortable and her movements are natural.

3. A top secretary must be supplied with an electric typewriter which incorporates those modern devices which are appropriate to her own field of work, and enable her to present impeccably typed reports and correspondence.

4. She must have telephone and intercom equipment appropriate to the work station she is manning, with sophisticated loudspeaking and other devices where these will increase her productivity.

5. Her work station must include a secure filing system appropriate to the volume and importance of the work she is doing, and she must have adequate supplies of filing software, stationery and minor office aids.

Suggested Further Reading

Specification for Office Desks, Tables and Seating, British Standards Institution, BS 3893. 1965.

Business Equipment Guide, B.E.D. Business Journals Ltd, published annually.

The EMGEE Office Aids Cataloque, Gutteridge Sampson, published annually.

The Vanguard Office Aids Catalogue, Royal Sovereign Group, published annually.

3

YOU AND YOUR EXECUTIVE

The Executive–Secretary Relationship

Every executive has been appointed to play some useful part in his company or institution. He is part of a team, and the success of the firm depends upon the proper functioning of the whole team. If it works well together then the firm will be profitable—a matter of some interest to those who have invested money in it. Even more, its future will be secure, which is of vital interest to all employees from top management downwards, as well as to the firm's customers and suppliers. It follows that your executive has responsibilities to the team of which he is a member. If he occupies a key rôle he must see that the objectives set in the Board Room are achieved in practice. He will look to you to assist him. You are his aide in fulfilling the part of the plan allocated to him, and he will expect your willing cooperation in any activity which will promote the success of the venture.

The relationship between an executive and his secretary is therefore one of partnership in the office. That partnership can be an exciting adventure, giving enormous job satisfaction, and leading to the advancement of both the executive and the secretary. Your personal self-development in this essentially creative activity depends a great deal upon the executive, but it depends even more on your ability to manage him and influence him into passing on some of the interesting work to you. It is not enough to offer the secretarial skills which all executives need, or even those personal attributes such as punctuality, reliability, discretion and tact which the good secretary displays. You have to become a valuable part of the management team, knowing as much about the policies of the firm as your executive, able to play a vital and active part in his work.

At the very highest levels the secretary becomes a **personal assistant**, often with her own secretarial and clerical staff. In these circumstances she will do a great deal of preparatory work on those matters which will eventually come up to her principal for decision. She may call for reports and discuss proposals with executives at the very highest levels, so that the smooth functioning of top management is ensured.

What the Executive Expects from his Secretary

The executive expects his secretary to play a full secretarial rôle. This involves the use of the normal secretarial talents which led him to select you as his personal assistant. These are:

ir secretarial skills of typewriting and shorthand
command of English
organising ability

cretarial skills other attributes almost certainly played some

16

part in your selection. Unless you were the only applicant for the post, which is unusual in a top secretarial position, he probably selected you for indefinable qualities which led him to suppose that you would be the sort of secretary he required; a person who would cooperate with him in his type of work, get to know and understand his methods and his attitudes, and support him generally in his endeavours. We must therefore add to (*a*), (*b*) and (*c*) above, one further item:

(*d*) Your instinct for cooperation in achieving his executive objectives.

Let us take a detailed look at these aspects of secretarial activity.

Using Your Secretarial Skills

Whilst these are dealt with in detail in the chapters on Typewriting, Dictation and Transcription, we must make the point here that from the executive's point of view the final products of your secretarial skills are evidence bearing witness to his own efficiency. Well-typed reports and correspondence, sensitively displayed and lucidly worded, bring credit to both parties, while poorly phrased and poorly typed pieces of correspondence reflect incompetence just as clearly. If you aspire to top secretarial status you must ensure that your secretarial skills are at the necessarily high level required. You must surround yourself with reference books which will enable you to sort out little problems of spelling, grammar and syntax. Never type a sentence that does not make sense, even if he dictated it. Lift the intercom and query it with him. Even if he is right in what he has dictated, your failure to understand the sentence may lead him to suspect that others will fail to understand it too. He may therefore choose a simpler wording.

Every executive has his personal idiosyncracies about dictation, typing and display. You must get to know his foibles and abide by them. Some men cannot stand the slightest errors in their correspondence, no matter how trivial the subject matter. Others are so cost-conscious that they will never let you retype. Whilst we circumvent idiosyncracy where we can, it must be discreetly done; the wise secretary cooperates where she can and appears to cooperate most of the time.

Naturally you will use your secretarial skills better if you have plenty of time. If you are not under pressure mistakes will be less likely to occur. If you have plenty of time you will be able to read through work before submitting it for signature. This will eliminate any 'literals' (errors in typing), check for accurate spelling and punctuation and may even detect unclear passages. To ensure that you have plenty of time train him to dictate early in the day, and to sign letters that are ready in convenient odd moments. This will help the post department and speed up communications, since letters posted early in the day are more likely to be cleared by the Post Office and reach their destinations sooner. Another way to save time on correspondence is to train him to use a portable dictation machine. The cassette type is the best, since the cassettes can be removed for transcription and a new cassette inserted at once so that the machine is readily available. This is helpful to you, and of enormous benefit to him since it clears his brain of unnecessary items. An executive who tries to remember things to tell his secretary will forget half of them, and develop nervous exhaustion trying to remember the rest. With his portable machine he simply opens his briefcase, gets out the microphone and says, 'By the way, Mary, I must write to the Chairman's wife and thank her for the invitation. Usual wording will do. Thanks.' This clears his brain for other problems.

Using Your Command of English

Every executive expects his secretary to have an excellent command of language and to use it wherever possible to promote their mutual endeavours. Apart from the use of English in dictated correspondence and reports there will be many occasions when you can use this ability on your own intiative. If you train him to expect that you will answer all routine letters as a matter of course—for example, sending off brochures in response to casual requests—you will relieve him of much routine work and free him for more exacting labour. Similarly, you should read everything that arrives on his desk except items manifestly labelled 'Top Secret' or 'Highly Confidential'. If you know what all his correspondence is about you will find it easier to take dictation, easier to file items correctly and find them more readily. You may even get him to allow you to mark up lengthy reports, underlining the most important phrases or sentences, and perhaps marking with an 'A' in the margin any points which require action on his part. Get him to tell you which periodicals, trade papers, etc. he likes to have checked for important news items. Clearly this will depend on the type of work entirely; a change in vehicle test regulations or the opening up of a new service on the short-sea routes to Europe may be of consuming interest to a transport manager. He may receive regular up-dating services like Croner's 'Road Transport Operation' manual. If you bring such manuals up to date each month as the up-dated pages arrive, draw to his attention any vital passages which he may need to know about. Sometimes house journals and even office notice-boards bear messages which are of vital interest to senior staff. For example, an announcement of a staff outing may need to be drawn to his attention.

The general rule is this: **use your command of English effectively to promote the general partnership effort**; to make him aware of things he needs to know; to do on your own initiative things that you know he will approve of, to handle run-of-the-mill matters which he need not be bothered with; and even to tell him about things that annoy you or are unsatisfactory. In the whole process of up-dating your own knowledge by reading the current literature about your firm and your industry you are bound to come across new equipment, new systems of work and gadgetry which makes the office more efficient, more secure, less tiring, etc. It is up to you to draw his attention to these items and to arrange for a budget that will cover their purchase.

Using Your Talent for Organisation

A talent for organisation is essential to a top secretary. You must be able to organise yourself, and the executive you serve, and anyone else who impinges upon your partnership in the office. This is not a talent which is born into individuals, though we often say 'She is a born organiser'. Rather it is a talent that can be learned, and improved upon as time passes. Certain aspects of the secretarial rôle are vital elements in the executive's organisation.

The maintenance of **an accurate diary** is essential. This may require a dual system, an executive diary on the executive's desk to keep him fully informed, and a secretarial copy in your own possession. It is vital to compare the two regularly, since both of you may make alterations at any time. A regular enquiry about any changes in the programme, especially with regard to his whereabouts at any given time, will ensure that the two programmes do not deviate. These matters are dealt with more fully in the chapter on 'The Working Day'.

Some executives keep a pocket diary and jot down odd appointments in it whilst away from the office. These can seriously interfere with arrangements if they are not coordinated with the main diary. A regular request for information on such diary entries is essential if his programme is to run smoothly.

Where the executive's diary is completely controlled by the secretary it is a good idea to type him out a copy each Monday, showing the week's programme as at present arranged. Tucked into the corner of his blotter it is an ever-present reminder of his next appointment.

A year planner is a useful extension of the diary system. Such planners are very inexpensive and can be started at any time by purchasing one from a stationer and pinning it up on a pinboard or screen in your work area. It enables you to record items which recur regularly—like quarterly sales conferences—and one-off arrangements like an induction meeting to deal with a new piece of legislation. A secretary who gets into the habit of keeping a year planner will find many occasions when it reminds her to draw the executive's attention to events recorded on it. Every executive has controlling and planning functions. A year planner pinpoints times in the year when he should call for reports from staff under his control, or submit reports to those above him. Routine maintenance schedules, inventory checks, reappraisals of insurance policies, and countless other activities may be implemented in good time if the year planner calls them to mind and the secretary then inserts them in the current page of the desk diary.

A further aid to efficiency is a 'follow-up' or 'tickler' system (see page 126) which tickles the memory about important little items which would otherwise be forgotten. Whatever system is adopted, it is important to add items to the follow-up system immediately you are asked to do them. Perhaps ten or twelve points might be listed for you to follow up at the end of a dictation session. You must record them on your pad at once, and either deal with them immediately—ticking them up there and then—or put them into your follow-up system for attention later in the day.

An awareness of priorities is essential to good organisation. The top secretary must not raise a mass of points if times are so busy that only the most urgent can be dealt with. Important things first. Not the least of these is the organisation required to see that the executive is in the right place, at the right time, with the right documents and figures. You must act as his memory, not only for the actual appointments but also for key facts. Who else is going to be there? What are the vital points of Mr A's proposals and Mr B's objections? What points of protocol must be observed and what is he going to say for the 'Vote of Thanks'?

Perhaps the most important aspect of organising ability as far as a secretary is concerned is a talent for detailed administration. It is for the executive to sit back and ponder general policy; you will be more concerned with the real details. There are countless moments during the working day when you can, and must, exercise this talent. The office cannot really come to life until you are in, the mail is opened and sorted, and the desk diaries have been compared and synchronised. Then the filing cabinets must be unlocked and the morning's appointments and meetings be prepared for, by extracting the files required and putting them into the work organiser (see page 11) in correct sequence. A quick check round his office to see if there is anything out of place, any clutter that should have been cleared, any messages from night staff or the telex, and you have time to snatch a quick cup of coffee. By the time he arrives you have dealt with three or four routine items and are free to take dictation before his first meeting at 10.30 a.m.

Using Your Instinct for Cooperation

If the executive–secretary relationship is one of partnership, each partner brings to the relationship different attributes which will make it a success. The executive's chief attribute is his position on the Board, or whatever other level at which he operates. This enables him to discover what is required of the partnership, to negotiate elbow-room within which his team can operate, etc. Your chief attribute is your ability to cooperate in achieving the desired results. Once again the nature of your cooperation will depend upon the industry, the firm and the status of your executive within the firm. In expecting your cooperation the executive will look to you to use your talents of observation and judgment. Get to know him really well. By watching him closely you will find out where you can pitch in and help. If you know his problems with his superiors, with those below him, with customers, bankers and lawyers, and with his wife and family, you will at once see areas where you can help him. At times it must be discreetly done, at other times he may ask directly for help, or you may offer it. Initially on taking up an appointment, the best kind of help is to be absolutely efficient with any job you are given. This will inspire confidence and lead to the offer of further tasks. You can gradually assume routine chores, and get him to induct you into more complex procedures. Within a short while you will have brought the partnership into existence. Before much longer you will be indispensible.

Executives vary, and the boundary lines of authority they give range from a pernickety, close control to a bountiful open-handedness. Whilst the former can be tedious in its restrictions, the latter has its pitfalls for the less experienced. In the end partnership requires a degree of freedom of action if job interest and job satisfaction are to be maintained. An open discussion of the relationship may extend your field of activity. Asking him what his attitude is to you opening confidential mail, or to the exclusion of visitors who have not made an appointment, or to the use of personal names, may lead to an extension of your partnership rights and duties.

The executive expects his secretary to identify herself with him and get to know his attitudes to people, to situations and events. This poses the problem that the executive may be at odds with those around him; a difficult man to get on with other people; unyielding in confrontations. A secretary who loyally supports such an executive inevitably becomes estranged from other people in the firm, and may feel that this is unfair and disadvantageous to her own career. The ideal solution to the problem is to influence him into more reasonable attitudes. It may be possible to make your executive a more reasonable fellow—if not, it may regrettably be necessary to seek a change. When applying for a transfer in such situations, a record of **reasonably dogged endurance of adverse circumstances** will be a recommendation.

The Efficient Secretarial Partner

The executive looks for efficiency above all in his secretarial partner. Efficiency may be shown in countless ways; many of them have already been referred to above. A few further points may be listed as follows:

(*a*) Get to know everyone in the firm on your executive's behalf, and develop trust in them by your unfailing courtesy and helpfulness. The secretary who rebuffs a junior, or scores off another secretary of similar rank to herself, does her executive a disservice. Some vital whisper on the grapevine may never reach her; some reciprocal act of kindness which she could have expected had she behaved more generously will not be offered in a future emergency. It is part of secretarial efficiency to be kind, courteous, cooperative and helpful to staff at all levels.

(*b*) Develop a friendly liaison with key personnel such as departmental heads, administrative officers, reprographic technicians, the staff of Personnel Department, and anyone else whose activities may affect your executive. Ask them to keep you informed of all events which affect him. Such matters as bereavements, hospitalisations, happy events, industrial injuries, examination successes and completion of apprenticeships may call for congratulations, condolences, or some similar action. It is important that an executive appears human to those below him. A kind enquiry or generous gesture may one day bring a warm return in the form of greater cooperation by the individual concerned.

(*c*) During his absence there is a great temptation to sit back and take life easily for a few days. While this may indeed be possible it is important not to let the department decline in efficiency so far as it can be maintained. Don't let mail pile up. Open the mail; deal with all the routine items yourself and consider the degree of importance of the rest. If they are items which can wait for your executive's return, then type a short letter to each correspondent acknowledging receipt and explaining the reasons for the delay. Then put the correspondence in the 'pending' tray, with the carbon copy of your 'holding' letter. If there are items which cannot wait and require decisions, take them to the next in line, explain the urgency and outline what you feel will be your chief's approach.

During the absence of your chief the partnership rôle which you have developed comes into its own. You will now answer all his calls, and will have to take action on his behalf. Senior staff who normally speak directly to him will be forced to speak to you instead. Clearly this is no time to be away from your post. If the telephone operator is forced to tell the managing director that Mr A is at the Dresden Fair, and you are at the hairdresser's, it will reflect no credit on you. Liaise with the telephone operator each time you leave your post and if you are taking well-deserved time off see that you have cleared it with senior staff.

(*d*) In more normal times the battle for efficiency includes a certain amount of control over what your chief is doing and how he is doing it. You must defend your executive's time by dealing tactfully with those who would interrupt him. The rest of the office will gladly leave things in your hands if they find they can trust you to get them in to see your executive sooner or later. Knowing his timetable you can say, 'Well, after 3.30 he should be free. I'll try to get you in then for a few minutes.' You may in fact have left yourself ten minutes before that time to get your chief's signature on some urgent letters and acquaint him with the nature of his 3.30 p.m. visitor.

The secretary can do much to see that her executive uses his time effectively. If he has a short interval between appointments, give him that file about tomorrow's urgent meeting. If he takes papers home make sure you know which files he has taken and record them on an 'Out' marker in the filing system. Comb through the 'Out' markers and chase up those that are overdue. This includes a little gentle bullying if he leaves anything at home. Condition him into accepting that you can

(i) make a greater proportion of his routine telephone calls for him;

(ii) take care of his papers better than he can and have them available in apple-pie order when he requires them again;

(iii) handle his affairs better if he keeps you more fully informed about business matters in general and his own movements in particular;

(iv) take over some of his organising responsibilities. These vary from job to job, but such matters as rotas for staff duties, collecting and collating records prior to writing reports and similar matters are burdens easily lifted from his shoulders.

The Cost-Effective Secretary

A secretary is usually paid her salary on a weekly or monthly basis. She is not paid by results, so much a letter or so much per 1,000 words. She is rarely dismissed if her output falls in a particular month, and she is rarely paid more when she has been through one of those 'rush' periods that are met with from time to time in every business. For this reason it is easy for the secretary or personal assistant to feel remote from cost calculations, which appear to be more relevant to a factory or distribution network than to office life. In fact, of course, nothing could be farther from the truth. Every penny of total cost has to be charged to the customer eventually if the business is to continue. Every executive must justify the cost of his department, and every activity must be viewed from the standpoint of its cost-effectiveness.

Cost-effectiveness is a relationship between output and input. If the total value added to a business by its employees' efforts exceeds the cost of the raw materials, components, general supplies and labour being used, then it is cost-effective. Cost-effectiveness is therefore increased by punctuality, accuracy, neatness, speed of performance, thoroughness and economy of operation. It is reduced by lateness, absence from work, laziness, incompetence, tittle-tattle and uncooperative behaviour. Every executive hopes for a cost-effective secretary, who on clearing her desk at night can look back upon a host of little activities conscientiously performed; on one or two major projects which have made useful progress during the day; on adequate preparations put in hand for the morrow; and a diary, year planner and follow-up system up-dated to ensure that nothing is forgotten in the weeks, months and even years ahead.

Summary

1. The executive–secretary relationship is one of partnership in the office.

2. The executive expects his secretary to use her secretarial skills, her command of English, her talent for organisation and her instinct for cooperation to further the objectives of management.

3. Important aspects of secretarial participation include the maintenance of accurate diaries and year planners, the relief of the executive from all types of routine duties and administrative details, and the discreet supervision of the executive to ensure that he works effectively, keeps to his schedules, is in possession of the fullest information, and observes protocol.

4. The executive hopes for a cost-effective secretary, whose output in terms of letters typed, documents processed, problems solved and arrangements concluded justifies the expenses incurred in her accommodation and salary.

Suggested Further Reading

What is a Secretary?, Hilary Reynolds, The Industrial Society, 1979.
The Senior Secretary, Rhona Brand, The Industrial Society, 1978.

4

THE SECRETARY AND COMMUNICATION

The Nature of Communication

The secretary is vitally involved in communication. She spends her entire day greeting people either in person or on the telephone, passing messages, instructions and explanations. She takes dictation and transcribes it into correspondence which is at once dispatched to its business destination. This correspondence includes orders, quotations, acceptances, contractual terms and conditions, invitations, etc. Each of these items will invoke a response from the addressee, who will perhaps order materials, proceed to manufacture, insure cargoes, book hotels or engage in some other expensive activity which forms part of the intricate network of business life.

The nature of communication is that two parties are brought either directly (spoken communication) or indirectly (written communication) into contact with each other, so that the needs or views of the first are made clear to the second, who reacts in such a way as to satisfy the needs or take account of the views expressed.

The term 'communication' is very widely used in business today, particularly in the field of industrial relations, where a failure to communicate properly is usually blamed for confrontations between management and managed. The pattern of communication for modern offices is given in Fig. 4.1.

In this chapter, although many readers may indeed seek employment in the 'mass media' fields, the subject of communication has been narrowed down to include only the personal forms of spoken and written communication where individuals or small groups of people are brought into communication with one another.

Whichever means of communication you are concerned with at any given moment, there are certain basic rules of communication which you should observe.

Rule 1. The important party in any communication activity is the recipient, not the communicator. It is what the recipient *thinks* you mean that matters. You must therefore use words the recipient can understand. Speak or write clearly and develop your argument consistently.

Rule 2. The correct form of communication must be used. A memo is appropriate to draw a colleague's attention to a small point that has arisen; it would not be appropriate for the circulation of detailed proposals to the Board of a public company.

Rule 3. The timing of a communication affects its impact. Do not raise matters on impulse; plan your communication so that it arrives at a time when it can be dealt with calmly and be given proper attention.

Command of English

Secretarial communication depends upon the use of language. The English language is particularly rich, by which we mean that it has a great many

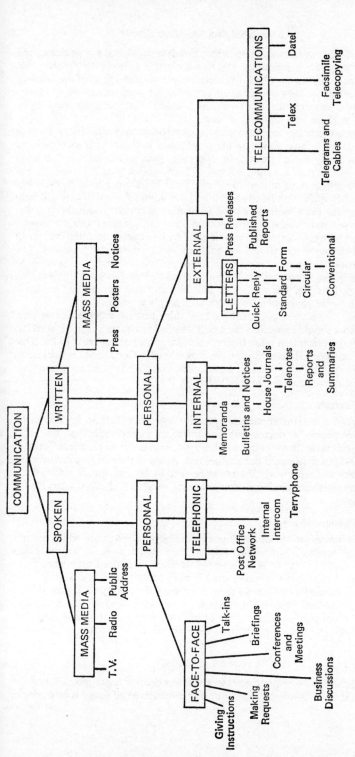

Fig. 4.1. The pattern of business communication today.

words. If these words are well used they can describe almost any situation, and convey very subtle meanings. Unfortunately this richness also means that there are many words which ordinary people do not know. If we want to communicate we must use simple words wherever possible, and avoid specialist words, or words that are rarely used, unless we are actually speaking or writing to those who understand them.

The good secretary therefore tries to extend her own vocabulary as much as possible, but in writing letters or memos uses a vocabulary which will be understood by the addressee. In extending your own vocabulary a good dictionary (see page 218) and a *Roget's Thesaurus* (see page 218) are essential. (The word 'thesaurus' means 'treasury'. Peter Mark Roget died in 1869, but his treasury of English words and phrases is up-dated regularly. It will help you find the exact word you need to express almost any idea. With a dictionary you start with the word and find out what it means; with a thesaurus you start with the idea, or the meaning you wish to convey, and find the word.)

Well-chosen words should be built into well-constructed sentences. The parts from which sentences are constructed are called clauses. It is possible to write very long sentences made up of several clauses, but generally speaking this is undesirable. The reader has difficulty retaining the ideas in his head.

Try to write your letters and memos in simple sentences.

Finally, the writer's personality should shine through any piece of writing. The reader should appreciate the writer's **sincerity**, and believe in his **veracity**. The great French naturalist Buffon coined a memorable phrase in his 'Discourse on Style'. He said 'Style is the man himself'. Good style involves using simple words in well-structured sentences so that both your meaning and your personality are conveyed to the reader.

Use of Jargon

'Jargon' is a term applied to specialist words unlikely to be known by ordinary people. A doctor may use the term 'chiropomphyllax' but other people call them 'bumps on the hands'. An accountant understands 'order of liquidity' but the general public does not. Avoid the use of jargon in correspondence and reports which have to be read by laymen, and if writing for a mixed readership include a glossary of terms which will clarify matters for the uninitiated.

Use of Slang

Slang words are words developed in ordinary conversation which are not generally accepted as standard English even though they are widely understood. The word 'boss' is an example. Derived from the Dutch word *baas*, meaning 'master', it was widely used in both America and South Africa, and came to be used in Britain as slang from both these sources. It has still not become standard English although used very widely, and is often avoided in formal correspondence or written in inverted commas. The 'boss'–secretary relationship becomes the executive–secretary relationship when writing formally.

Use of Clichés

A cliché is a stereotyped phrase which has become hackneyed with use. A phrase such as 'Assuring you of our best attention at all times' is an example.

The criticism of clichés arises from their stale repetitiousness, and in the case of business clichés the lack of sincerity that accompanies a trite phrase often repeated.

Spoken Communication

Spoken communication, sometimes called verbal or oral communication may be face-to-face communication or it may be conducted over the telephone. We are just entering an era when the television camera is making it possible for people in telephonic communication with one another to see the person speaking to them, but it will be some years before this new system is widespread. In both types of oral communication, as distinct from written communication, language is informal and words are less carefully chosen than in letters and reports. This is permissible, because we can reinforce the actual words with voice inflections, facial expressions and gestures. In many business situations a verbal exchange of views is essential, because we can talk much more quickly than we can write. A long and detailed criticism of a report, for example, might require hours of dictation and transcription if it was to be adequately phrased in a letter. If the author of the report can be called in for a discussion about its limitations he can at once defend the report and justify it, or accept the criticisms where they are justified.

Giving Instructions

In giving instructions it is essential to have the attention of the person under instruction. Once secured, this attention can best be held by a quick explanation of the purpose of the work in hand and how it fits into the pattern of business activity. This should be kept brief and clear. Then the processes to be carried out should be described and demonstrated, and the individual should be allowed to try them personally. This will reinforce the instruction given. Finally, it is a good idea to give the individual a job-card which you have previously prepared, and which is returnable to you. In preparing such a job-card you will think through the instructions you are to give, which will improve your delivery, and on future occasions your card index of job-cards will assist you in instructing the next junior employee who is asked to perform that particular task.

Receiving Instructions

For every person giving instructions there are one or more persons at the receiving end. If you receive instructions you must give the instructor your fullest attention; you must follow closely what is being said and raise any queries at once. You should try to perform the activity if given the opportunity, or at least offer to recapitulate the instructions. If you are not supplied with a job-card or other written record of the instructions given, then it is sound practice to make a note of them as soon as you are left alone, and keep it by you for future reference. In this way you can build up a manual of office procedures which will be useful to you in future, either to recap the method to be used, or as a basis for instructing someone else. It may even serve as a proof to your superior that what you have been doing was in fact the prescribed procedure laid down to you. It is frequently necessary to take down notes at briefing meetings for future events and functions, so that you can play your full part on the day.

Making Requests

An executive secretary will frequently have staff under her direct control, or have staff attached to give assistance at particularly busy periods. While it is often necessary to give instructions to such staff, it is not always appropriate to give formal orders. Sometimes greater cooperation and effort can be achieved by requesting assistance, or by treating the activity as a joint project. 'What we have to do in the next two weeks, etc., etc.' implies at once that this is a team effort. Only participation by all concerned will achieve the desired result.

Discussions and Debates

Oral communication enables the speaker's personality to become apparent much more easily than written communication. It is important when answering the telephone to convey your interest in the other party, and your concern to answer the query quickly and helpfully. Telephone techniques are dealt with more fully in Chapter 8. Similarly, meetings and conferences are the subject of later chapters in this book (see Chapters 14 and 15). Here we will consider only the 'communication' aspects which arise in face-to-face business discussions. Any sort of contribution to a discussion or debate, or any part to be played in a public relations exercise, should be carefully prepared. Such preparatory work will reduce the chances of making slips, or of placing incorrect emphasis on a particular point.

A secretary may be required to put forward suggestions relating to her work. As a personal assistant she may have to announce press statements on behalf of the senior executive she serves. The following rules will help such presentations:

(a) Collect your ideas before speaking, and assemble detailed facts, statistical data and an orderly account of any incident or event to be covered in the talk.

(b) Distinguish in the statement between facts and opinions. If the views to be expressed are only tentative ones, because the full facts have not yet come to light, make this clear in the statement.

(c) Be careful to give a rounded view of the situation. Before speaking ask yourself whether you have unintentionally avoided any unpleasant aspects.

(d) In the actual presentation

(i) State your proposition clearly in a few words.
(ii) Argue your case logically to justify the proposition.
(iii) Concede any weaknesses graciously, and justify your attitude by demonstrating that they are not crucial.
(iv) Anticipate objections, and prepare counter arguments to support your proposals.
(v) Keep the statement brief, and end with a clear re-statement of your proposals.

If this sort of careful preparation is made the aim of good communication—a meeting of minds—is more likely to be achieved. You will have said what you wanted to say, and those listening to the statement will know what you said and have understood your reasons for saying it.

Verbal communication has its advantages but it has disadvantages too.

The chief of these is that there is no written record of what is said. In business the majority of binding contracts are probably made verbally. They would be difficult to prove in court unless witnesses could be produced to testify about what was said. For this reason it is usual to confirm verbal contracts in writing, except in those very high level institutions like the London Stock Exchange and Lloyds, where the rule 'My word is my Bond' makes the verbal contract absolutely binding on both parties, whether or not witnesses are available.

Written Communication

Written communication takes many forms. The business letter is the most commonly recognised form of written communication, and countless business conversations end with one party saying to the other, 'Well, if you will just put that in writing in a brief letter to me, we can proceed without any difficulties.'

Pressures of business have led to the devising of numerous short-cuts to the problems of written communication, such as quick-reply forms, standard-form letters, circulars, etc. Instantaneous written communication is possible through such devices as the tele-note (see Plate 5). Near-instantaneous transmission, as with facsimile copying—which sends air waybills and similar documents anywhere in the world in four minutes—enables businessmen to keep ahead of other technologies. Concorde hopes to reach Australia in $10\frac{1}{2}$ hours, but the air waybills will have preceded the goods and have been cleared through their administrative processes before the supersonic plane arrives with its cargo.

The majority of these types of written communication are described below.

Conventional Business Letters

Business correspondence is still the chief basis of arrangements between businessmen. It has the merit that it is in permanent written form, and can be used as evidence in any dispute about the arrangements. Ideally correspondence should be drawn up carefully and checked for compliance with a number of well-known rules. A useful memory aid here is the Seven C's mnemonic. This memory aid is given in Fig. 4.2.

> A business letter must be neat,
> Clear, concise, correct, complete,
> Consistent, courteous, cautious — these
> The correspondent's Seven C's.

Fig. 4.2. The seven C's for correspondents.

Letters must be **clear,** so that the reader understands the message from the sender, and can act upon it. Any ambiguity or lack of clarity may involve expense which otherwise would be avoidable.

A **concise** letter will come to the point at once, pinpoint the salient features of the matter under discussion briefly and evoke a prompt response or prompt action to implement the wishes of the sender.

A letter must be **correct,** particularly in such details as dates and times of meetings, delivery dates for the fulfilment of orders, prices quoted, etc. All such items should be checked carefully before the letter is dispatched. A wise secretary calls such details back wherever possible with the help of a colleague.

A letter which is not **complete** can be the cause of considerable expense and irritation, particularly a circular letter sent to a number of correspondents. Imagine a circular sent to five hundred salesmen to announce a conference. The letter gives all the details except the date. Not only will a corrected letter need to be sent out, with all that involves in terms of labour, stationery and postage charges, but before that can be done the switchboard will be jammed with expensive telephone calls asking for the missing information. It is important to think through the whole process of running a conference or similar function to ensure that the complete information is included in any correspondence.

Consistency in written correspondence requires us to ensure that one part of a letter does not contradict another part. We cannot reject a point of view in one part of a letter and then use it to prove our case in another part.

Letters should be **courteous**; that is, polite and considerate. Business activity confers mutual benefits on the parties who engage in it, and therefore flourishes best in an atmosphere of mutual respect. Even the strongest points of view can be expressed in moderate language, which impresses upon the other party that you rely as much upon his high principles as upon the force of your arguments for the redress of your grievances.

Finally, it is advisable in business communication to be **cautious.** The law of contracts recognises four types of statements: puffs, representations, warranties and conditions. Only the first of these carries no contractual obligations. I can say 'This is the finest little car in the world' without fear of being sued by the buyer because he has found a better one. It is a mere puff, an exaggerated statement which everyone knows is not meant to be taken seriously. By contrast, a misrepresentation, or a breach of a clause in a contract which is a warranty, or a condition, can lead to action in the courts. If I say that a car is a 1981 Ford Cortina when it is really a 1979 Ford Cortina, that is a misrepresentation and may lead to an action in the courts. It is unwise to write confidently about things when you are really not sure. To say 'This product will not catch fire' is a less cautious statement than 'In fifteen years of manufacturing this product we have never heard of a case where it has overheated'.

Preparing a Letter

Bearing in mind the rules outlined above, the preparation of a letter should be thorough. Decide what you have to say and arrange in your own mind the best sequence for the points you have to make. Devise a heading to the letter which will enable it to be directed to the correct department, and also familiarise the recipient with the general nature of the contents. Paragraphing breaks up the subject matter of a letter into its separate aspects. Short paragraphs are most easily understood, and they should be punctuated carefully. The test is: 'Does the punctuation make the paragraph easier to understand?'

The conclusion and signature on a letter are important. A correspondent who begins to read under the impression that he is receiving the letter from a particular executive may be disconcerted to find in the end that the letter is signed p.p. (per pro). It is better to explain this discourtesy in the body of the letter with a short paragraph which may be a suitable conclusion to the letter.

For example, he might say 'To avoid delay I am asking my secretary to sign this letter, since I shall be absent from the office later today.' Another useful type of conclusion reserves any social remarks to the end of the letter: 'Thank you again for an enjoyable lunch.'

The layout of letters is discussed in detail in Chapter 6 on transcription. It is, of course, a very important part of the secretary's duties to lay out letters stylishly.

Quick-Reply Letters

A quick-reply letter is a letter laid out in a simple way, with space provided for answers to a number of questions. It is usually pre-printed, with space for

```
        Megalopolis City Council, Town Square, Megalopolis
                Quick-Reply Letter    Form 25C
 To                                    Date .............
                                       Our Ref. .........

 Dear Sir,

             re .......................
        The above-named person has applied for employment and has
 given your name as referee. Will you please answer the questions
 below and return this letter in the stamped window envelope
 supplied.                                         Reply
 1.  How long have you known the applicant?    .................
 2.  In what capacity did you have dealings
     with him/her?                             .................
 3.  Would you describe the applicant as
     (a)  Honest?                              .................
     (b)  Trustworthy?                         .................
     (c)  Punctual?                            .................
     (d)  Regular in attendance?               .................
 4.  Do you know of anything to the
     discredit of the applicant?               .................
 5.  If an employee, why did the applicant
     leave your service? ....................................
 6.  If you wish to make any special observation about the
     applicant please do so here. ...........................
     .........................................................
     .........................................................
        Thank you for your assistance,
                       Yours faithfully,

                             Personnel Officer.
 Return to:
        Megalopolis City Council,
        Town Square,
        Megalopolis.

 (Please fold your reply so that this address is visible through
 the window of the envelope.)
```

Fig. 4.3. A 'quick-reply' letter.

the insertion of reference numbers and other details referring to the particular matter in hand. Often the sender's address is printed conveniently so that re-folding is all that is needed for the 'reply' address to appear in the window of an envelope. A typical quick-reply letter is shown in Fig. 4.3 (see page 31).

One disadvantage of quick-reply letters is that copies are usually not available for the records of the person replying. This can be overcome by using a three-part NCR set similar to the memo-set illustrated in Fig. 4.5 (see page 34). This is, of course, more expensive and many firms do not use them for routine enquiries. Where a copy is required for a third party this can be provided by using a four-part NCR set and indicating at the bottom 'c.c. ABC' (the name and address of the person to whom the copy is to be sent).

Standard Form Letters

Standard form letters are letters which deal with a problem that recurs regularly and endlessly. For example, in mail order it is often the case that cheques received from customers are unsatisfactory for a variety of reasons.

```
                    Megalopolis Trading Co. Ltd.
                         7, The Quay,
                         Megalopolis.

To .....................            Date:
   .....................
   .....................            Our Ref. Order No.12175

Dear Sir/Madam,

      Your cheque is returned herewith, as it is unsatisfactory for
the reason ticked below.  Would you please correct the error in an
appropriate way and return the cheque to us with this letter.  We
shall then have great pleasure in fulfilling your order.

                    Yours faithfully,

Reason for return.                  The reason is ticked below.

A.   The cheque has not been dated                ........
B.   The cheque has not been signed               ........
C.   The payee's name is incorrect. Please change
     it to Megalopolis Trading Co.Ltd. and initial
     the alteration                               ........
D.   The word 'pounds' has been omitted from the
     written sum of money to be paid              ........
E.   The sum of money in words is not the same as
     the sum of money in figures. The correct
     amount is .....................              ........
F.   Other reason ...............................................
     .................................................................
```

Fig. 4.4. A 'standard form' letter.

They may be unsigned, or undated, or for the wrong amount. A standard form letter like the one shown in Fig. 4.4 above may be used to deal with this situation.

Another type of standard letter is the type prepared for a particular occasion.

For example, applications to attend a conference may exceed the seats available and it may be advisable to prepare several types of standard letter. One will be the ordinary acceptance letter to go to those whose applications are accepted, with the admission tickets and agenda. Another may be addressed to a limited number of applicants who cannot be offered a firm place but will be borne in mind should any cancellations become available. A third type will be letters of regret, to be sent to those whose application money must be returned. Standard letters can be prepared well in advance and are thus available when required.

Circulars

A circular letter is an unsolicited letter sent out to a wide circle of contacts who may be interested in the contents. A great many sales campaigns start with a circular letter. Some are sent to the entire population of a district; others are more selective. They may be addressed to a particular age group, or to a particular income group. They may be sent to past customers, or to members of a particular trade union, professional body or voluntary organisation. They are usually carefully written and strikingly designed, so that the recipient reads the contents and is encouraged to complete the application form or order form.

Frequently circular letters are given the appearance of personal letters by the use of 'word-processing' techniques. These are described more fully in the chapter on Typewriting, but the individuality they give to the letters arises from the use of a programmed electronic typewriter. This will reproduce automatically any letter fed into it by magnetic tape or other device, stopping at appropriate points so that a typist can type in personal details such as the names and addresses of individual addressees. Since the automatic typing is at very high speeds—a recent addition to the range types at 300 words per minute —this type of individual letter can be reproduced reasonably cheaply. Even so, they are used only where the circular is to a limited number of contacts.

Memoranda

A memorandum, or 'memo' for short, is an informal written communication which is used within an organisation to convey information, request advice, give instructions, etc. It passes between head office and departments or branches, or from individual to individual within departments. It is usually short, and deals with a specific point of detail, though longer memos are sometimes circulated as part of the procedure prior to a discussion of general policy. A memo is more permanent than a verbal message, and more effective since it is less likely to be forgotten. It is often typed on specially printed memo paper, and different colours are sometimes used to pinpoint memos from the more important members of staff.

A particularly effective type of memo-set, illustrated in Fig. 4.5, is the three-part NCR (**no carbon required**) memo-set. Here the sender addresses the memo to its recipient and sends him two copies, retaining one copy for himself. The recipient writes his reply, which duplicates on to the lower copy. He then returns one copy and retains the other. Both parties thus have a copy of the original message and the reply. Such a memo-set ensures that memos are not forgotten. It will be obvious to the sender that he has not received a reply, since his original will not be matched up with a second copy returned from the recipient.

MESSAGE	TO: Alan Brown Engineering Dept.	Pink Copy
		DATE: 27·4·19..

FROM: John Cope, Projects Dept. via Susan Milburn

MESSAGE	FROM: Alan Brown Engineering Dept.	Yellow Copy
		DATE: 27·4·19..

TO: John Cope, Projects Dept. via Susan Milburn

MESSAGE	TO: Alan Brown Engineering Dept.	White Copy
		DATE: 27·4·19..

FROM: John Cope, Projects Dept. via Susan Milburn

I understand that you have agreed by telephone with Smith and McIlroy to expedite fabrication of the intermediate platform by June 30th. Will you please confirm that this is so, and that you have made the necessary arrangements with Miles Ltd for part B of the deckhouse to be delivered in time, and for transport as and when required.

REPLY REQUIRED   YES/NO   SIGNED *S.M.*

REPLY		DATE:
		SIGNED

ORIGINATOR: Send White & Yellow Copy
RECIPIENT: Retain White & Return Yellow

PRINTED BY UNITYPE PRINTING CO LTD
01 874 5645

Fig. 4.5. A three-part NCR memo set.

(Courtesy of Unitype Printing Co. Ltd)

Bulletins and Notices

In medieval times the popes of Rome issued 'papal bulls' which contained rules for the guidance of the faithful throughout the Roman Catholic world. The word 'bulletin' is a diminutive of 'bull', and announces events, alterations of policy and other matters to all persons who are interested. It is therefore an effective form of communication, since the mere exhibition of the bulletin in a public place constitutes notice to members of staff. Many firms print sufficient copies to give one to every member of staff. There is thus no excuse for failing to perform some activity if the order was given in the bulletin. The bulletin also gives an opportunity to all members of staff to announce events of a social nature which they are organising, or to report back to staff on any matters of general interest. A well-organised 'bulletin' system requires a clear procedure to be laid down for the bulletin format, deadlines must be set for the submission of copy, pigeon-holes or trays for staff must be provided, and failure to read the bulletin and be aware of its contents should be a matter for reprimand.

A bulletin is often several pages long. A notice is usually shorter, and announces a particular event. Both bulletins and notices are exhibited on notice-boards, which should be large enough to hold all current announcements without becoming cluttered. One notice-board to every 25 employees is usually enough, and it is desirable to appoint one individual in charge of each board. If this person's name appears on the notice-board it is easy for all staff to contact her, and arrange for the display of notices. Generally this procedure ensures a neat, attractive display of accurate notices, sectioned off under appropriate subheadings by strips of coloured tape. Obsolete material should be removed and retained for a short while in case some query arises as to what was actually displayed.

House Journals

The house journal is similar to a bulletin, but appears less frequently and has sufficient space to include articles of general interest to staff, news items from various regions, a diary of events, etc. It is often used as a public relations medium as well, free copies being given to members of the public who write in about topics which have been featured in the journal. Secretaries often assume responsibility for subediting material destined to appear in the journal, and for submitting news items and calendar events for inclusion.

Reports

A report is a formal communication which gives an account of events or situations which have been investigated or considered by an individual or a committee. They vary from short statements, prepared within the firm by an individual, to long and detailed accounts of complex situations prepared after months of evidence by interested parties and published in book form. Such reports may be several volumes long, and contain transcripts of all the evidence.

The style of presentation follows general lines, but the degree of formality will vary with the purpose and scale of the enquiry. The secretary who prepares a report will know to whom it is directed and why it is required and will therefore be able to choose the vocabulary and the content to suit the reader. For example, a report of the same incident addressed to a police officer and a safety officer might call for quite different contents. When a report is called for, the terms of reference will usually be laid down quite specifically and they should be strictly adhered to both in the investigation and the final report.

The basic principles underlying a report may be listed as follows:

(*a*) The report should have a clear title which is self-explanatory.

(*b*) It should be addressed to the individual who called for the report, or who is entitled by his official position to receive it.

(*c*) It should bear the name of the individual submitting the report, or of the chairman of the committee who produced it. The names of other members should be listed, and their functions or status.

(*d*) Unless it is a routine report the terms of reference should be stated. This is often done as part of the salutation, in the form:

Sir,
   We were appointed on December 1st, 19 . . ., to investigate . . . .
. . . . under the following terms of reference, etc. etc.

(*e*) The body of the report follows, in good sequence, explaining the nature of the investigations made, the individuals examined, the opinions heard and the committee's view of those opinions. Headings, subheadings, paragraphs and more detailed subdivisions and numbering should be used to help the reader follow the report.

(*f*) The conclusions drawn, and the **specific recommendations** made, should then follow as a separate section of the report. This section is very important, since it will give rise to action to implement the report.

(*g*) Finally the report should be signed and dated. It often happens that appendices follow the report giving statistical tables, charts and diagrams, and a voluminous report should have both an index and a table of contents.

Some of the best reports available to the public are the official reports published by Her Majesty's Stationery Office. They are in excellent style, and it is worthwhile obtaining a typical report from a library if you are called upon to prepare a report so that you can follow the pattern set by HMSO.

Plate 4 shows a typical selection of modern aids to the production of small reports. An almost professional appearance can be added to reports by using the punches and plastic ring binding available on the market. Up to 250 booklets per hour can be punched and bound even by inexperienced staff.

Summaries

The art of summarising business information is an essential skill for the executive secretary. So much written material comes into a busy office nowadays that it is impossible to deal with it in its raw state. A certain amount of pre-digestion is necessary to reduce the bulk of reports, and bring them down to manageable size for the decison-making process. There are four processes in preparing a summary. They are:

(*a*) The first read-through
(*b*) Note-taking
(*c*) The rough draft
(*d*) The final summary

Before explaining each of these items, it is important to realise that a summary in business should be as brief and as eye-catching as possible. It is not the same as a précis, which tends to be a polished piece of English in a specified number of words. A summary makes the fullest use of headings and subheadings, it employs concise language so far as possible, while at the same time conveying the full information contained in the source.

The **first read-through** is made to catch a general impression of the subject matter. At the end of the read-through you should try to choose a title for the summary, which describes the contents of the report in general terms. This will act as a reference point in deciding what points to note down in the next stage.

The **note-taking** stage requires us to note down all the salient features of the report, including all the important facts, the topics discussed, the points of view expressed and the reasons for holding them. Anything that is irrelevant from the main body of the report should be excluded.

The **rough draft** is a first attempt to turn the notes into a readable and comprehensive summary. It is often difficult to choose the best words first time, and it is desirable to leave the rough draft for an hour or two and turn to other work. The second attempt will improve upon the first, and from the finally digested draft you can then type a fair copy.

It is only fair to say that some publications are almost impossible to **summarise.** If the pamphlet or report has itself been the result of long and detailed examination, so that it includes only the absolute skeleton of facts required, it is very difficult indeed to summarise. Some government publications are of this type—notably the various Notices with regard to Value Added Tax. Any attempt to summarise such documents usually results in things being left out so that the full content of the original is not included in the summary.

Telenotes

Telenotes (see Plate 5) enable written messages to be sent over the ordinary telephone network, either internally within the firm or externally over the ordinary public telephone network.

The system is based upon three telenote units: a transmitter, a receiver, or a transceiver which performs both functions. Writing, or drawing, with a ballpoint pen on the transmitter is automatically transmitted any distance to give an instantaneous copy on the receiver. Thus, for example, two engineers with transceivers could discuss details of an electrical circuit, drawing a diagram as they do so and amending it during the discussion, in such a way that each can see what the other has drawn and is left with a permanent copy at the end of the discussion. Similarly, any number of hospital doctors linked to a pharmacy could leave written instructions for prescriptions they wish to be made up. There would be no possibility of error such as exists with the use of an ordinary telephone message. A police message could be relayed simultaneously to all substations in an area, giving an instantaneous documentary authority to stop a particular vehicle if sighted. The telenote is clearly a communication aide of great importance.

Press Releases

A press release is an announcement made to the press and other mass media organisations about important developments affecting an industry, or new products becoming available. Since the mass media cater for a very wide range of public tastes and interests, press releases usually secure for those who issue them a certain amount of free publicity.

It is usual to prepare the press release well in advance, so that carefully worded textual material, photographs and other visual and aural aids are available to give maximum impact to the announcement. The preparation and presentation of this material frequently falls to the public relations officer of the firm, but personal assistants and top secretaries often play a major part not only in the preparation but also in the follow-up activities. These require telephones to be manned, additional copies of the release to be mailed, repetition of the original announcement and elucidation of the details, etc.

Telecommunications

Telecommunications systems are dealt with in Chapter 8 on telephone techniques since they are closely related methods of communication.

Summary

1. Communication is the bringing together of two parties by speech, or writing, so that each understands what the other means, and is able to act accordingly.

2. An essential element in communication in the English-speaking world is a sound mastery of the English language, its vocabulary, sentence construction, punctuation and spelling.

3. Good communication conveys not only the ideas but also the personality of each party to the other.

4. Spoken communication is direct, less formal than written communication and may be supported by facial expressions, gestures and intonations. In addressing meetings, discussion groups, etc., careful preparation is advisable.

5. Written communication takes many forms and secretaries must master the essential features of the memo, the business letter, the report and the summary. They should suggest the introduction of, and help design, standard form letters, quick-replies and other time-saving forms of written communication.

Suggested Further Reading

Collins New World Thesaurus, Charlton Laird, Collins, 1979.
The Complete Plain Words, Sir Ernest Gowers, Penguin Books, 1970.
Effective Communication Made Simple, E. C. Eyre, Heinemann, 1979.
English Made Simple, A. Waldhorn and A. Zeiger, Heinemann, most recent edition.
Modern English Usage, H. W. Fowler, Oxford University Press, 1965.
Pitman Business Correspondence, G. Whitehead and D. H. Whitehead, Pitman, 1982.
Roget's International Thesaurus, P. M. Roget, Harper and Row, most recent edition.

5

BUSINESS CORRESPONDENCE—TAKING DICTATION

Methods of Imparting Letter Content to the Secretary

A major function of the executive secretary is to produce impeccable correspondence for signature and subsequent mailing. Her ability to take dictation accurately at high speeds ensures that dictation by the executive will be the favourite method of imparting to her the business letters she is to type. However, it will not be the only method used, and accordingly a preliminary word about other methods is desirable. They may be listed as follows:

(a) Brief verbal instructions
(b) Outine notes
(c) Manuscript draft
(d) Recorded dictation
(e) Direct dictation

Brief Verbal Instructions

Many letters call for perfectly routine replies, and are repeated endlessly as a succession of correspondents writes in with the same request or query. The executive usually disposes of these by handing them over to his secretary at the start of the dictation session, giving a few verbal instructions if a particular point has to be emphasised in a particular letter. The secretary should note down these points, with the name of the addressee to whom each point refers. She should then take the group of letters and place them face down on the desk beside her, so that by the end of the dictation session she will have all the letters to be answered in the correct order.

Provided the secretary has the necessary linguistic skill this type of correspondence presents few problems and is very economical of the time of both parties.

Outline Notes

Sometimes an executive will draw up outline notes on a particular matter and leave it to the secretary to compose the actual letter—or perhaps a first draft. This is a more time-consuming method as far as the executive is concerned, but it may be useful to him in thinking out the salient points of the matter in hand. His outline notes can be changed and altered until he has the chief features in the best order, and he does not have to waste the secretary's time as he would do if this rearrangement process took place in a dictation session. The secretary then uses her linguistic skills to produce a first draft, or perhaps a final letter based upon the outline. In this activity she will be greatly helped by her knowledge of the firm and its general policy, and by the understanding she has of the executive's personal preferences in language. Sometimes a secretary will write letters which mirror so cleverly the executive's own choice of words that he will have difficulty deciding who did write the letter should any query on it arise later.

Manuscript Draft

The word manuscript means 'written by hand'. Where an executive writes out letters in longhand he does of course waste a tremendous amount of time. Normally he would only do so with particularly difficult letters or reports. For example, a report of a technical nature, full of mathematical formulae, might be very difficult to dictate and require such precision of language that it would be difficult to hit the best words and phrases at a first attempt. Another situation where a secretary might be given a great many letters in manuscript form is where she works for a number of executives. This frequently happens in colleges and universities where the ratio of secretarial staff to executive staff is low. An executive who wants to clear his in-tray might write out his letters at convenient times and leave the bundle in the secretary's tray to be typed at her convenience.

One difficulty with manuscripts is the writer's handwriting. A secretary should appeal to the executive she serves to write all his letters 'in a big round hand', like W. S. Gilbert's ruler of the Queen's Navy. Another difficulty is that the executive may be less literate than his secretary, and the manuscript consequently be less well presented than a dictated letter.

Recorded Dictation

Recorded dictation has only developed in the last fifteen years, but it has to be accepted by almost every secretary that some part of her work will be transmitted to her in this way. In particular, the refined hand-dictating machines which came into use in the late seventies are so convenient that every top executive will find this time-saving method of use to him. Although the top secretary, rather naturally, is reluctant to see her vital shorthand skills by-passed by the dictation machine, it is a fact that she is more capable of using the dictation machine than other staff. Audio-typing requires a real grasp of spelling, punctuation, sentence structure, etc., which many audio-typists do not have. The top secretary has no such difficulties and can therefore produce her usual top-quality work however the subject matter of her letters is imparted to her.

The variety of machines available, and the advantages and drawbacks of recorded dictation, are dealt with in the latter part of this chapter.

Direct Dictation

Sometimes an executive dictates to his typist as she is typing. The resulting end-product is immediately available, but the system is less satisfactory than most other systems. Unless the typist is absolutely excellent she will cause delays with the odd error—which interrupts the flow of dictation and wastes executive time. Some executives find it almost impossible to dictate while the typewriter is clattering away, and the system is therefore most appropriate for correspondence which has to be dispatched immediately.

The Dictation Session

A dictation session is a time when the executive and his secretary work together to clear correspondence that has accumulated in his in-tray, and deal with any other matters that have arisen, or which are envisaged in the future. Both parties are therefore involved in the activity and unable to give attention to other matters. It follows that a **business-like approach** is required to reduce the length of the session as much as possible, without overlooking any item or postponing it to a later date. This approach requires that both parties make preparation for the session beforehand and thus ensure an immediate start on the work, concentrated activity during the session and a prompt conclusion.

Executive Preparation

A secretary should try, for her own convenience as well as for his, to organise her executive to be ready to start at once when he calls her in for a dictation session. It is a great waste of the secretary's time if he proceeds to search the drawers of his desk or turn out his pockets to find odd scraps of information which he needs. If he is not the most organised of people she should tactfully suggest he prepares for his dictation session in the following ways:

(*a*) It is a good idea to keep a special **tear-off memo pad,** preferably with a distinctive cover, in his briefcase or even in his wallet if it is a slim pad. This will be available at all times for the quick pencil jotting—'Write to Lever & Johnson re insurance up-dating'. This will ensure that matters of importance are not forgotten, and get the whole day's work cleared up in one session.

(*b*) He should keep files and correspondence by him which are due to be answered, perhaps in a **desk organiser** of the sort illustrated in Fig. 2.2. This enables him to pass over the letters as he deals with them, and saves dictating names and addresses, reference numbers, etc.

(*c*) Before the dictation session he should make notes of the points he wishes to deal with in each letter, minute, memorandum, etc., and also how many copies he requires and who is to receive them. Sometimes an extra note is dictated to the secretary to be added to the other copies—but not to go on the original. The signal 'NOO' item ('not-on-original') will alert her to the need to ensure that only the copy receives this extra note. Some copies are 'blind'—that is, they are not allowed to show particular parts of a letter for security reasons. For example, the despatch manager's copy need not necessarily include the contract price. At the point where a copy is to be 'blinded' the typist will turn up a few lines and insert a sheet of plain paper between the carbon and the copy, so that the plain paper receives the impression and not the copy.

If the letter is so intricate that dictation is not really appropriate he should write the manuscript letter before calling in his secretary—or at least make a note to warn his secretary that he has a difficult manuscript letter to write which she will be given later that day.

(*d*) He should prepare the room for the secretary so that she can sit comfortably in a good light, have a firm surface to work on if she prefers this, and have the best chance of hearing what is said by being seated face to face.

Preparation in the ways described will ensure that the actual dictation session proceeds at a good pace, suffers a minimum of interruption since it will be concluded with reasonable speed, and is sufficiently well organised to be a pleasurable contact between executive and secretary. A secretary who finds that she is forced to waste precious time with a disorganised and rambling dictation session must take steps to see that her executive's efficiency is increased.

Secretarial Preparation

The secretary must be in a state of continuous preparation for dictation, since she may be called upon at any time, but particularly at those times of the day when she knows it is customary to deal with correspondence. The tools of the trade are shorthand notebooks with stiff covers, and pens, or pencils with fairly soft leads. Experienced secretaries usually develop their own ways of noting down alterations to the text and instructions for dealing with the letter, so that they rarely bother to draw margins or divide the page down the middle as suggested in many theory books. The shorthand pad should be readily available, with a rubber band encircling the pages already used. This can be used also to hold the pen or pencils on to the pad, so that one quick hand movement will pick up the whole collection when the secretary is called in for a dictation session.

Pencils should be soft, but not too soft, and it is good to have a couple of spares available. The inconvenience caused if a pencil is dropped and the point broken can interrupt the dictator's flow of words. If the notebook and pencils are kept always in the same place they can be picked up quickly whenever they are required. It is always advisable to take them with you when called into the executive's office, even if dictation is not anticipated, since it gives you somewhere to write down notes of any instructions you are being given.

The dictation session is the ideal time to take up with the 'boss' any queries or difficulties you have. It is also a good moment to discuss the diary, and any possible changes he may have made—perhaps in his private diary overnight. Part of your preparation should include a quick note of any such queries. At the end of the session you can turn to the appropriate place in the pad, raise the matters you have noted there and put down a note about any instructions he issues about dealing with them.

Other requirements are a spare pad if you are getting near the end of your current pad, and a manilla folder for correspondence. This folder is useful to contain all the letters and other slips of paper he gives you in the course of the dictation session.

The Art of Taking Dictation

When a secretary is called for dictation she should go in immediately. However tempting it is to finish the task in hand it is more cost-effective to go at once. The executive is more highly paid than his secretary and if he is kept waiting the time that is being wasted is more valuable. Enter briskly and take up your usual position. This should be facing him, preferably with a flat surface to work on and room to rest your elbows. As soon as you are seated, open your dictation book at the next clean page and write the date, and if necessary the initials of the executive, on the *bottom* line of the pad. This will help you find the correct place at a later date, should it be necessary, by simply flicking over the pages of the pad at the bottom. To open the pad easily a thin elastic band of a suitable size is put round the used part of the pad, so that it can be opened at once to the next clean page. If you write shorthand notes with your right hand you should raise the edge of the notebook page with your left hand and get a grip on the paper. As the letter proceeds you gradually move the page upwards so that the line you are writing on is always at roughly the same position on the pad. When you get to the bottom of the page a quick flip will turn the page over and you are away on the top line of the next page.

Letters succeed one another fairly rapidly and it is important to give a clear indication of where one ends and another begins. Therefore at the end of each letter draw a clear horizontal line across the page.

Executives vary in their voices, speeds and mannerisms. Some speak distinctly and slowly, others speak poorly and too fast. Some dictate every piece of punctuation, others show by the expression in their voices when they expect punctuation to be inserted. The secretary must make the best of her executive. If he is slow and hesitant she should use the odd seconds to write in longhand any outlines that she feels may be difficult to recall later. If he is dictating well and within your capacity keep up with him and if you miss a word ask him about it at the end of the letter while he can still recall what he said. If he forgets your limitations and speaks at 250 w.p.m. you must stop him. To go at that pace when you are limited to 120 w.p.m. means he might as well be talking to himself.

As each piece of correspondence is dealt with the executive should either hand it to his secretary, or place it face downwards on the table beside him. This gives a neat pile of correspondence which will be in the same order as the letters on the secretary's pad. It may then be necessary to indicate to the secretary any letters which are particularly urgent, so that she does them first and presents them for signature in time to catch the first available post.

It is quite usual in a busy office for dictation to be interrupted by telephone and intercom calls. The executive cannot fail to lose concentration at such times and may repeat himself or use similar phrases which he would have avoided if uninterrupted. It is useful to point these out, or to develop a working relationship which permits you to tidy up any such matters which become apparent during the transcription of the dictated material. For example, the executive who refers to a 'pleasant occasion' and then to a 'pleasant chat' will usually not mind his secretary changing the wording to an 'interesting chat'.

If the executive changes a paragraph of a letter—perhaps after hearing it read back—the page must be marked with a quick code—an asterisk or perhaps a number—which is then repeated at the end of the letter where the corrected paragraph has been taken down.

The alert secretary will soon invent her own short forms peculiar to the firm for which she works. Thus a secretary in a chemical works required frequently to write about cyclohexane will soon develop a short form which she knows refers to that word.

Recorded Dictation

Recorded dictation inevitably plays some part in the office experience of top secretaries, and the more sophisticated machines now becoming available are both more appropriate for, and more acceptable to, the executive secretary. Recorded dictation is prepared for the secretary in one of four possible ways. The devices used are:

(a) the desk-top machine
(b) the portable machine

(c) the 'thought-tank' system

(d) the multi-bank system

Because the engineers who devise dictation machines are continuously reappraising their systems and improving their engineering and electronic skills, the industry is not static and a wide variety of applications to suit particular industries and firms is available. However, the four pieces of equipment listed above constitute the standard units from which any individual firm's requirements can be met.

The Desk-Top Machine

This is an executive machine, produced by most dictation machine manufacturers, and a typical unit is shown in Plate 6. It uses standard 'C' cassettes, which are in world-wide use and are relatively cheap. The cassette can be recorded and played back on office machines to be found everywhere, or on domestic cassette equipment. The machine shown has excellent sound reproduction, and can even be used for playing background music for the occasional office function, cocktail party, etc. The equipment rejects background noise so that only the executive's voice is recorded, giving excellent sound quality for the secretary. She does not therefore waste any time going back over badly recorded words. The moving indicator passing over the paper pad on the machine enables the dictator to give some idea of where one letter ends and another begins. This helps the secretary to judge her layout, and ensures that correspondence will have a good appearance. It also enables him to indicate any corrections he may have made.

Where the executive wishes to use the dictation machine to give instructions to his secretary or ask her help in tracing files or information, he must be careful to call her attention to the special nature of the next part of the tape. The easiest way is to use her name:

'Margaret, I seem to have lost the file for Robbins & Murgatroyd. Do you think George could have returned it? Would you please find out and get it back for me. Mr Murgatroyd is coming in tomorrow, isn't he?'

Using her name is much more likely to arouse her from her trance if she has been doing a heavy spell of dictating.

The Portable Machine

The portable machine has great advantages for the executive who travels, or likes to work at home in the evening. The machine illustrated in Plate 6 again uses standard 'C' cassettes, with a capacity of up to 90 minutes' dictation time. These can be posted in to the office for transcription.

The 'Thought-Tank' System

It is this system, illustrated in Plate 7, which is of greatest interest to the executive secretary. It provides a link between the executive and his secretary of a very personal type. The 'thought-tank' unit contains an endless belt of tape led in a double U formation over a recording machine and a transcription machine, either of which can be in use at any time. As the executive switches on his recording machine tape begins to feed past the recorder where it picks up the dictation and feeds back into the body of the large container as loose tape not wound on any spool. This forms the first U shape in the tape.

As the secretary switches on her transcription machine, the tape is fed over an intermediate pinion to form the second U shape in the tape, and up into the transcription machine. It then feeds down into the body of the machine again.

As the executive starts to speak his secretary gets a red light warning that work is coming through and can listen to his dictation just 12 seconds after he started, even while he is still speaking. This direct-link dictation principle eliminates the secretary's nightmare—a build-up of work on the 'boss's' machine presented to her late in the afternoon on a cartridge full of work to be transcribed. It also means that the executive can dictate whenever he likes, knowing that his work will be done as quickly as if he had dictated it to the secretary personally.

The 'thought-tank' has one hour's dictation capacity, to which is added capacity released by the typist as she transcribes, since the endless tape loop becomes available for further dictation as soon as it has been transcribed. There is a facility to link up to three 'thought-tanks' together. Six executives can be connected to the system and up to four typists can be connected, via a selector panel, to each of the 'thought-tanks' transcription channels. This type of installation includes a work indicator, the **dictatimer.** Fixed to her desk control unit, this indicates to her how much dictation is in the 'thought-tank'. As she types she can see the minutes figure go down. As her 'boss' dictates it goes up. When the typing and dictating take place together, the figure will tend to go up more slowly (unless she can type faster than her 'boss' can speak!). She now knows exactly how much work there is for her to do, without, as with traditional separate machine arrangements, having always to allow for whatever unknown quantity is still with her 'boss'. The executive benefits too in knowing how far behind his dictation she is whenever an urgent item crops up.

Also on the 'thought-tank' is the point of furthest advance lock. Usually found only on large centralised dictation systems, this lock means that an executive can playback to an earlier part of his dictation to check on what he said and then replace his handset. The 'thought-tank' will continue to wind forward until the end of his dictation is reached. When the executive reverses the tape for playback it does not affect the minutes figure on the typist's dictatimer.

Most users are finding that 'thought-tanks' are ideal for jotting down verbally all sorts of odd notes, instructions, appointments and so on, including priority items. These items can now be taken out of sequence by the addition of a **priority switch.** Even though there may be several letters in the 'thought-tank' awaiting transcription, a word from her 'boss' will allow the secretary to tackle the last item dictated and return to the other material in sequence later. This type of installation does away with one major secretarial objection to recorded dictation, that it divorces the girl from the executive she serves and reduces her to an audio-typist working in a remote typing pool. The 'thought-tank', while setting both parties free from the necessity to be together during the dictation session, still preserves the more individual executive–secretarial relationship which is so useful to the executive and so much more interesting for his secretary.

Multi-Bank Systems

Multi-bank dictation systems are large-scale systems using banks of recorders which serve the entire staff of a firm. Executives wishing to dictate are connected automatically to any recorder which is free. The transcription is arranged by a supervisor in the typing pool, who routes the completed correspondence back to the executive for signature. This type of installation is therefore remote from the executive secretary's control, and reduces very considerably the number of secretaries required by a firm. However, the secretary playing a senior rôle as personal assistant to a top executive may use the multi-bank system for non-urgent correspondence and reports, but as a dictator, not a transcriber.

Using the Dictation Machine

In the capacity of dictator the secretary will be able to practise herself what she preaches to executives about good dictation. Some of the chief points may be listed as follows:

(a) The dictator must introduce herself by stating her name and department. This facilitates the return of her correspondence.

(b) She must give the details of the work required, particularly the number of copies required, and some indication of the length of the letter. This will assist the typist to select the right size paper to start with, and to judge what layout to adopt. Since delay inevitably occurs in multi-bank systems she should state the date she wishes to appear on the letter. She should specify the enclosures to accompany it, and the references of both the addressee and her own department.

(c) She should speak in a clear, deliberate voice, in phrases of about six words, using the recommended 'letter analogy' alphabet for spelling out names and addresses or specialised technical words.

(d) She should use the recommended method for paragraphing and punctuation, as laid down in the in-house training sessions.

(e) With multi-bank systems an endless succession of dictation overloads one typist and prevents the even distribution of work which is the chief advantage of the system. Normally the dictation of one long report or five short letters is a suitable package of work. By disconnecting, and after a short pause, re-connecting, the dictator gives the supervisor her chance to allocate work among her staff.

Summary

1. Letter content may be imparted to the secretary in a variety of ways. These include brief verbal instructions, outline notes, manuscript form, direct dictation, recorded dictation, and oral dictation which makes use of her shorthand skills.

2. The executive must prepare for a dictation session by collecting the necessary correspondence, memos, etc., and marshalling his thoughts before the secretary is called in.

3. The secretary must similarly prepare by organising her note pad appropriately, having pencils and other aids ready, and drawing up a list of items she wishes to query with the executive when the opportunity arises.

4. The art of dictation must be learned. The secretary must make the best of her executive; ask again on any points that are unclear and use spare moments to go over difficult outlines.

5. Recorded dictation inevitably plays some part in the work of all secretaries, and need not be an impersonal barrier between her and her executive. On the contrary, it can fill in the gaps between their respective performances and thus reduce frustration and raise efficiency.

Suggested Further Reading

How to be a Top Secretary, Mary Bosticco, New English Library, 1975.
Office Practice Made Simple, G. Whitehead, Heinemann, most recent edition.
The Art of Dictation, Eva Roman, Gower Press, 1971.
Typing Centres, L. G. Harvey, Philips Electrical, 1975.
You and Your Secretary, E. M. Pepperell, O.B.E., The Industrial Society, 1970.

6

BUSINESS CORRESPONDENCE—TRANSCRIPTION

The Art of Transcription

Transcription is the conversion of dictated material into finished correspondence ready for signature. It requires a complex series of decisions which start with the choice of the correct size and style of letterhead and the right number of carbons for copies. Then the secretary must choose appropriate margins and line-spacing, decide correctly about paragraphing and punctuation, type accurately and quickly, proof-read carefully and correct any errors as swiftly—and invisibly—as possible.

The secretary can only transcribe quickly and accurately if she has complete mastery of the skills of shorthand, typewriting and audio-typing. Transcription speed can never be as high as dictation speed, and will normally be about half that speed. Better than average performance will be achieved by those whose mastery of the use of English is complete; whose shorthand notes are well formed and easy to read back even when 'cold'; whose typing accuracy is high and whose facilities for the correction of errors are modern and therefore time-saving. Perhaps the greatest factor in a high transcription speed is the courtesy of the executive who dictates in the first place. If he is negligent in his preparation, leaving the secretary to find out vital details like initials, qualifications and addresses of addressees, then she will be slowed down by a necessary pre-transcription research period.

Those aspiring to the position of executive secretary must therefore strive during training to master the following aspects of the secretarial function:

(a) *Complete mastery of the typewriter.* This includes both speed and accuracy, but also skill in the correction of errors.

(b) *Complete mastery of shorthand.* This includes especially the formation of clear outlines. Constant practice during the training period in reading back notes which have long grown cold will pinpoint poor outlines and help to overcome future difficulties with transcription.

(c) *Complete mastery of the use of English.* Whichever way dictation is perceived, through reading the shorthand outlines or hearing the tape recording, the secretary has to make instant decisions about capitalisation, punctuation, spelling and presentation. For example, the phrase 'the minister's ten objections' might be rendered:

> The minister's ten objections
> the minister's ten objections
> the Minister's ten objections
> The Minister's 10 objections
> the Ministers' ten objections

and in several more ways. It is extremely important therefore to take training in the use of English seriously when undergoing secretarial training.

Included in this mastery of the use of English is the ability to spell correctly. It has now been clearly established by painstaking research that actual practice in spelling is necessary if young people are to spell well. This requires us to learn the shapes of words, and the patterns of letters within words. If the young secretary keeps a spelling notebook, indexed A–Z, in which she writes down any word that she finds she has to look up in the dictionary, she will by regularly reviewing these words quickly reduce the number of times she needs to turn to the dictionary for a decision.

To these basic skills mastered during the training period must be added further aspects of the secretarial function after employment has commenced. These are:

(*d*) *A comprehensive understanding of the work of the executive and the firm.* This cannot be achieved in a day, but it is essential to efficient transcription. A secretary who knows her 'boss', his business contacts and fields of interest, will quickly resolve many problems in transcription by an intelligent appraisal of the subject matter of the correspondence. She will keep on file, close to her work position, details of all his correspondents. She will know the projects being handled at present and the general drift of developments taking place. She will understand the firm's situation within the industry generally, and its point of view in controversial matters. This knowledge will assist her recall of dictated material.

(*e*) *Adequate provision of facilities.* The top secretary cannot work with outdated equipment and techniques. She must up-date her equipment whenever the opportunity arises. For example, the correction of errors is a time-consuming business, but modern equipment renders it practically instantaneous. The secretary must do her best to raise transcription speeds by ensuring that she is adequately provided with the tools of her trade. A description of the most modern equipment is provided later in the chapter on 'Word Processing' (see pages 68–9).

Preparing to Transcribe

During the dictation period an executive may have indicated to his secretary that some letters are more important than others. With tape-recorded dictation he may have marked on the indicator slip the position of a particularly important letter. The secretary must obviously transcribe such letters first and present them for signature at an early opportunity. The procedure for transcribing letters is as follows:

Pre-Transcription Preparatory Work

If the executive habitually dictates without giving the full information it is important to read through the letter first to ensure what the required data is and assemble it. This may mean turning-up addresses, initials, etc. It may involve checking with other departments, or telephoning for reservations to airlines and hotels. Clearly this is time-consuming but essential.

Selecting the Paper and Carbon Pack

Economical use of paper is important. By judging the length of the letter the secretary can select a size and weight of paper that is appropriate. For example, air mail letterhead may be required for some letters. A4 may be necessary for a lengthy letter but A5 adequate for a short acknowledgement. Her notes will tell her how many copies are required and she can then assemble the pack for insertion into her machine.

Since the development of NCR paper (no carbon required) many firms no longer use carbon paper. Letterhead paper is coated on the reverse side with encapsulated globules of chemical. When struck by the typewriter keys these globules burst, and mix with another chemical on the copy paper, which is coated similarly. A wide range of NCR papers is now available, since the original patent expired, including types coated with globules which will reproduce on ordinary copy paper. As a result of these developments the tedious interleaving of carbon papers can be avoided.

The Layout of a Business Letter

Business correspondence is extremely important because it forms part of a relationship between the correspondents which is nearly always contractual in nature. This means that the two parties undertake certain responsibilities in return for certain rewards. They may agree to supply goods in return for a payment called the price, or to give services in return for fees or emoluments. If any dispute arises the documents and correspondence can be produced as evidence in court, and written evidence is always regarded as very convincing, because presumably people do not write letters unless they really intend to carry out the promises made in the letter. Whenever a letter is written, therefore, we should bear in mind its important nature, and should be aware of the importance of each part of it. That is why we must now look at each separate part of the letter.

The Letterhead

One of the essential parts of any documentary evidence, whether it is a letter or a document like an invoice, is that it should have the names and addresses of both parties to the correspondence. By having a printed letterhead a firm ensures that the necessary details about its own name, address and telephone number are recorded on every letter. Then, when the typist types in the name and address of the addressee (see 'The Internal Address', page 52), the letter will contain the names and addresses of both parties to the correspondence. Because of the importance of correspondence as evidence it is vital that blank copies of letterhead stationery should not be allowed to fall into the hands of outsiders. The issue of headed notepaper should be closely controlled and if some new piece of legislation or change in the letterhead details renders stocks of stationery obsolete, the surplus stock should be cut up and used as scrap, or even shredded for packing material.

Certain Acts of Parliament—the European Communities Act, 1972, and the Companies Acts, 1948–81—require certain items to appear on the official stationery of Limited Companies. The European Communities Act requires that the following items appear:

(a) The place of registration of the Company and its registered number, as shown on the Certificate of Incorporation.

(b) The address of the Company's registered office.

(c) The expression 'limited liability' if the Company is one that is excused from putting the word 'Limited' at the end of its name.

Plate 1. A secretarial work-station.

(Photograph and furniture by courtesy of Carson Office Furniture Ltd, Files and Shannostrip flipover unit by courtesy of The Shannon Ltd)

Plate 2. A screened 'chat area' which may also be used for the reception of visitors.

(Courtesy of Carson Office Furniture Ltd)

Plate 3. Smaller office aids for the executive secretary.

Plate shows: Velos non-slip telephone mat; swing telephone stands for one, or two, telephones; a desk organiser filing system; Spicers stationery and typist's aids.

(Products supplied by Spicers Ltd, Office Services Division)

Plate 4(a). Aids to the production of booklets and reports.

(Courtesy of Business Aids Ltd)

Plate 4(b). The Sperry Remington LeKtriever 600E.

(Courtesy of Sperry Remington Kardex)

Plate 5. The 'Telenote' system for instantaneous transmission of diagrams and written instructions.

(Courtesy of Standard Telephones & Cables Ltd)

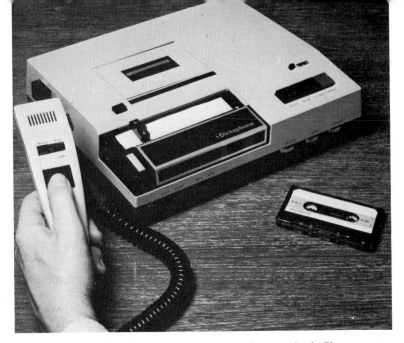

Plate 6(a). A desk-top dictation machine, using standard 'C' cassettes.

(Courtesy of Dictaphone Co. Ltd)

Plate 6(b). A portable dictation machine, which also uses standard 'C' cassettes.

(Courtesy of Dictaphone Co. Ltd)

Plate 7. A 'thought-tank' executive-secretary link.

(Courtesy of Dictaphone Co. Ltd)

Plate 8(a). An Electra II portable electric typewriter, for the secretary who needs to travel.

(Courtesy of SCM (United Kingdom) Ltd)

Plate 8(b). The SR 101 dual-pitch single-element typewriter.

(Courtesy of Sperry Remington Ltd)

(*d*) If there is any reference to the amount of capital of the Company it must be the paid-up capital, and not the authorised capital (because authorised capital may not actually be available if it has not yet been called for).

The Companies Act, 1948, requires that the names of all the directors shall appear, with their Christian or other forenames (initials may be used), but also details of any other forenames that have been used previously. Details of the director's nationality, if not British, must also be given.

Sometimes a letterheading is incomplete to the extent that the phrases 'Our reference' and 'Your reference' may be left to be completed, and the telephone number may include a space for the executive's extension number to be inserted by the typist.

Letterheadings sometimes include a printed request reading 'All correspondence to be addressed to the General Manager [or some other official] and not to individuals.' This is used in circumstances where the management reserves the right to open all correspondence.

The References

As mentioned above, the letterheading often includes lines reading 'Our reference' and 'Your reference'. Depending upon the size of the organisation concerned, references may simply pinpoint particular executives and their secretaries. WSG/AL would perhaps refer to the executive W. S. Gilbert and his secretary Alison Laker. Government correspondence often pinpoints the Department and File Number holding the correspondence, as those who correspond with the Inland Revenue authorities will know.

The Date

Dates should always be typed with the month clearly stated in words. This avoids confusion, since in the USA it is usual to specify the month first. In the United Kingdom the day is usually specified first in an all-number date. Thus 4.12.82 means the 4th December, 1982, in the United Kingdom, and the 12 April in the USA. There are several ways of typing the date, perhaps

12th September, 1982

being the most common, but a growing number of firms are now discarding the use of st, nd, rd and th after the number of the day, and

12 September 1982

is becoming the acceptable way to write the date in a letter. The best place for the date is on the right-hand side of the page, where it can be quickly seen by a filing clerk searching through the file.

Mailing Instructions

The name and address of the addressee must appear at the top of the letter, as explained in the section about letterheadings. As this internal address is used in the preparation of the envelope it is usual to include two other items, the **mailing instructions** and the **attention line**. They thus become part of the inside address and are incorporated on the envelope. As regards mailing instructions, many letters are sent by special mail services—for example, air mail, registered post, recorded delivery, express, etc. It is usual for these instructions to be typed above the internal address, in block capitals. Because the envelope is usually prepared from the internal address, the mailing instruction can then be typed on to the envelope, or if a rubber stamp is available the instruction can be stamped boldly on the envelope. Besides drawing attention to the special instructions when the envelope is being prepared, the inclusion of the mailing instruction on the letter in this way assists subsequent enquiries about the non-arrival of a letter by pinpointing the method of dispatch.

Attention Lines

Where a letter is addressed to a particular individual within a firm it is more expeditiously handled when mail is sorted in the addressee's mail room. The address would therefore start with the individual's name. Where this is prevented by an instruction in the addressee's letterhead requiring all letters to be addressed to the firm, it is customary to mark the letter and the envelope 'Attention of ....'. This attention line should be underscored, and may be adapted to direct the letter to a particular department. Typical attention lines would be

> Attention of Mr David Lane
> Attention of J. Senior, Esq., Sales Manager
> CONFIDENTIAL: Attention of the Personnel Officer

Although a firm may reserve the right to open all mail such a letter would almost certainly be put unread into the mail tray of the person required to attend to it, while the confidential letter would probably not be opened.

The Internal Address

The internal address serves the two purposes of (*a*) naming in the letter itself the other party to the correspondence, and (*b*) providing a guide to the secretary in the preparation of the envelope. If the internal address is correct then the envelope prepared from it will be correct too. Individuals are addressed by their correct titles. The reference books mentioned in the Suggested Further Reading to this chapter will solve all the problems which arise in addressing individuals and firms.

The Salutation and the Complimentary Close

The salutation is the greeting at the start of the letter, and the complimentary close is the closing remark before the signature. These two parts of the letter are related in that the degree of familiarity or formality shown in the salutation will be conformed with in the complimentary close.

Subject Headings

A subject heading is used whenever it will expedite the addressee's handling of the letter. It is usual to insert the subject heading directly after the salutation. The subject heading assists in the distribution of mail when it is opened in the addressee's mail room, but it is also a constant reminder to busy executives of the content of a particular letter when searching through a file of correspondence.

The Body of the Letter

The secretary will transcribe what the executive has dictated, using the style of display which is appropriate (see Figs. 6.1 (*a*), (*b*), (*c*) and (*d*)).

MADE SIMPLE BOOKS
Publisher: Robert Postema
WILLIAM HEINEMANN LTD
10 Upper Grosvenor Street: London W1X 9PA
Telephone: 01-493 4141 Telex: 895 4961 Telegrams: Sunlocks London W1

17th September 19..

Our ref. JB/OJ
Your Ref. SSLO 31 August 19..

AIR MAIL

Gulf Textbooks Ltd
Bahrain Island
Arabian Gulf

<u>Attention of Secondary Schools Liaison Officer</u>

Dear Sirs

MADE SIMPLE TEXTBOOKS

Thank you for your enquiry about textbooks suitable for senior
classes. There are a number of titles which are appropriate.

In the Business Studies field the titles which are most popular
include Book-keeping, Commerce, Office Practice, Economics, Law
and Practical Typewriting.

In Languages, English, French, Italian, Spanish, Russian and
Latin are strongly demanded.

Other titles which may interest you are Childcare, Acting and
Stagecraft, Dressmaking, Photography and Woodwork.

I note that you do not sell Science books so I have not listed
these titles.

We shall be delighted to supply books to you on favourable
terms, as shown in the price list attached.

Yours faithfully

J. Broughton
Sales Executive

Enclosure 1
    Chairman: Charles Pick
   Publishing Director: Nigel Hollis Literary Director: Roland Gant
   Sales Director: T.R. Manderson Financial Director: Michael House, A.C.C.A.
 Directors: Judith Elliott, Christopher Forster, Peter Ireland, John St.John, W. Roger Smith, N.M. Viney

Although every reasonable care is taken of manuscripts while in our hands we can accept no responsibility for any loss or damage thereto.
Registered Office as above   Company No: 185152

Fig. 6.1 (*a*). A letter in fully-blocked style.

MADE SIMPLE BOOKS
Publisher: Robert Postema
WILLIAM HEINEMANN LTD
10 Upper Grosvenor Street: London W1X 9PA
Telephone: 01-493 4141 Telex: 895 4961 Telegrams: Sunlocks London W1

FIRST CLASS MAIL   Our reference JB/OJ
                                     Your reference PDC/ts

Robbins & Caulder Ltd
Ross Villa
LITTLEWICH
Norfolk
NR8 4EV   17 September 19..

Attention of Purchasing Officer

Dear Sirs

Availability of Made Simple Series

Thank you for your enquiry about the availability of MADE SIMPLE
titles. We shall be delighted to make supplies of these books
available.

The great merit of MADE SIMPLES from the retailer's point of view
is that the range of titles available offers a comprehensive coverage
of most subjects being studied at home. The goodwill of one title
carries over to other titles in related subjects, the customer
returning again and again to the familiar orange-yellow-black format.

I enclose for your information a current price list showing the
discounts available, and an order form.

Yours faithfully

J. Broughton
Sales Executive

Enc. 2

Chairman: Charles Pick
Publishing Director: Nigel Hollis Literary Director: Roland Gant
Sales Director: T.R. Manderson Financial Director: Michael House, A.C.C.A.
Directors: Judith Elliott, Christopher Forster, Peter Ireland, John St. John, W. Roger Smith, N.M. Viney
Although every reasonable care is taken of manuscripts while in our hands we can accept no responsibility for any loss or damage thereto.
Registered Office as above   Company No: 105152

Fig. 6.1 (*b*). A letter in modified fully-blocked style.

MADE SIMPLE BOOKS
Publisher: Robert Postema
WILLIAM HEINEMANN LTD
10 Upper Grosvenor Street: London W1X 9PA
Telephone: 01-493 4141 Telex: 895 4961 Telegrams: Sunlocks London W1

R. Mason, Esq., B.Sc.(Econ.),   17th September, 19..
   Department of Business Studies,
      Riverview Technical College,
         RIVERVIEW, Essex.
           ES1.3WL

Dear Sir,

<u>Made Simple Textbooks</u>

    Thank you for your enquiry about the business studies titles in the
Made Simple Series.

    The range of titles is very wide, but they may be divided roughly
into intermediate level textbooks and degree level textbooks. In the
first group our most successful titles are

               Book-keeping Made Simple
               Office Practice Made Simple
               Economics Made Simple
               Commerce Made Simple
               Law Made Simple

In the second group our leading titles are

               Business Economics Made Simple
               Applied Economics Made Simple
               Management Made Simple
               Transport and Distribution Made Simple
               Financial Management Made Simple
               Computer Programming Made Simple
               Cost and Management Accounting Made Simple

    I enclose a leaflet listing all the titles in the series since
some books on the fringes of business studies may also be of interest
to you.

               Yours faithfully,

               J. Broughton,
               Sales Executive.

Fig. 6.1 (*c*). A letter in indented style.

⊔   **herman miller   international collection**

Bath, 16 December 19

R Brown Esq
15 Riverside
Brookdale
Cambridge
CB3 1PT

Dear Mr Brown

Thank you for your note requesting information about
the "action office" system.

I enclose brochures describing and illustrating this
approach to office planning and look forward to hearing
from you if you would like any further information.

Yours sincerely

Ann Jones
Marketing Co-ordinator
fcl

enclosure

Herman Miller   Registered Office   Planning and Sales Office   Directors
Limited   Lower Bristol Road   2 Goodge Street   S.H.Snoey (Chairman)
                   Bath BA2 3ER England   London W1P 1FF   F.R.Appleton (Managing)
                   Telephone:0225 27331   Telephone:01 580 8964   D.E.Williams
                   Cable:HERMILLER   R.J.Wood
                   Telex:44809 MILLER BATH   R.B.Silvester A.C.A.
                   registered no 1097772 in England

Fig. 6.1 (*d*). A letter using a house style.

(Courtesy of Herman Miller Ltd)

The Signature

After the complimentary close it is usual to leave sufficient space (five
single lines) for a handwritten signature followed by the typewritten name of
the person who has signed the letter, and his official position. Some companies
like to have the name of the company included in the subscription. It often

happens that an executive asks his secretary to sign a letter p.p. (per pro) himself. The actual meaning of per pro is '*per procurationem*', which means 'by the action of' and implies that the person signing has the authority to sign. Strictly speaking this authority can only be conferred by a power of attorney, which most secretaries do not have, and it is better to avoid the use of the term. The following styles of signature might therefore be appropriate:

Yours sincerely,

T. Brown,
General Manager.

Yours sincerely,
THE FARM EQUIPMENT CO. LTD,

T. Brown,
General Manager,

Yours sincerely,

Rosemary Squires,
Secretary to Thomas Brown,
General Manager.

Enclosures

It is usual to put details of the enclosures at the end of the letter. These are generally placed at the left-hand margin of the page, and may include the number of enclosures, thus: Enclosures 4. Alternatively, this may be abbreviated to Encs. 4. It is possible that the enclosures will be enumerated to prevent any misunderstanding, so that the entry reads:

Enclosures: 1) price list
2) catalogue
3) order form
4) reply-paid gummed label

It is the responsibility of the person actually dispatching mail to ensure that the envelope is 'stuffed' with all the items it should contain—that is, the letter itself and the correct number of enclosures.

Distribution

It often happens that a letter is intended to go to a number of people, either because they are all equally interested (the members of a committee, for example) or because they must be kept informed of the contents of the letter. Usually the distribution list comes at the end of the letter, thus:

Distribution: Head of Department – Engineering
Head of Department – Sales
Head of Department – Production
Chief Accountant
Managing Director
Chairman

Where the distribution is limited to one or two people only, the abbreviation c.c. (carbon copy) would be used; for example, c.c. Mr Charles Smith. The addressee then knows that Mr Charles Smith has been acquainted with the contents.

Sometimes it is desirable to pass a copy to some other party without the addressee being aware of the fact. Thus if it was felt advisable to pass a copy to the legal department without letting the addressee know, a request to send a carbon copy to the legal department might be marked NOO—not on original. The top copy of the letter is removed before this is typed on to the second copy. Seeing the NOO sign the legal department knows that, for the time being anyway, the addressee is not aware that legal action is being considered against him.

Continuation Sheets

Letters on headed notepaper are continued on to sheets of plain bond paper. The word 'cont'd. . .' leads on to the next page where the page number, addressee's name, and date are typed at the top to assist in identifying a loose page, should it become separated from the body of the letter. This can be typed right across the top of the continuation page, thus:

Mr Thomas Cross   –2–   23 December, 19 . .

Transcribing the Notes

The secretary will now type the letter as quickly and as accurately as possible, using the **house style** if one is laid down (see Fig. 6.1 (*d*)) or a style similar to Fig. 6.1 (*a*), (*b*) or (*c*).

Fig. 6.1 (*a*) shows a letter in **fully-blocked** style. With this style each line of typing starts at the left-hand margin, the point to which the carriage or the typing element returns. With the **modified style** shown in Fig. 6.1 (*b*) the references and the dates are typed on the right-hand side for rapid reference by filing clerks; the rest of the typescript is in fully-blocked style, with open punctuation. 'Open' punctuation means that all punctuation marks are omitted in the internal address, and can be omitted also in the salutation and conclusion. This gives a very open, uninhibited appearance to the letter. Fig. 6.1 (*c*) shows a letter in **indented style**. In this example the internal address is also indented, but it is quite acceptable to block this.

The experienced secretary will have learned during her training all the very precise details regarding correct layout and spacing of letters, but she will more often than not find that in actual practice she has to conform with her executive's preferences or the company's house style. Many executives have their own whims for at least parts of letters, be it with the complimentary close or the actual display of the letter itself. She may find it difficult to 'unlearn' all that she has been taught, but must remember that she should adapt herself to her new situation. She may even be able to point out tactfully the correct theoretical procedures to her executive, who may be impressed by the sound knowledge of her skills and thus accept her points of view. The main thing to remember is that the letter represents the company and should be neat and accurate, as well as being nice to look at.

As each letter is completed from the shorthand notebook the secretary puts a line through the dictated record, which should not spoil it in any way but makes it clear that the letter has been transcribed. It is important to keep shorthand notebooks for several months at least in case the original notes are called for. If the covers are marked with the range of dates of the contents—say, 5 May 19. .–12 July 19. .—and kept in order with an elastic band around them it will be fairly easy to find a particular letter when required.

Correcting the Letter

Before the letter is removed from the machine it should be read through to discover any **literals**—errors in the typing. These errors should then be corrected as invisibly as possible, using one of the products available on the market. Some firms produce their products in a range of colours to suit coloured letterheads, thus making it possible to correct invisibly even on coloured paper. Secretaries who use a coloured letterheading may find it helpful to approach the supplier to find out which typing correction product is most suitable for their range of coloured papers.

Typing the Envelope

The transcriber should now type the envelope, using the internal address on the letter as a guide. This will contain all the necessary information, the mailing instructions, the 'attention' line if any, and the address itself, including the post code. Single line spacing is usual for foolscap and commercial size envelopes, whereas double line spacing is better for larger envelopes. The top line of the address should never be higher than the middle of the envelope, thus leaving ample room for the Post Office to frank it. Two examples of typed envelopes are given in Fig. 6.2; one shows the address typed in fully-blocked style and the other in indented style.

Presenting the Letters for Signature

When typed, the envelope should be placed over the top of the letter, and any enclosures should be obtained, arranged in order and clipped on to the letter itself. The letter, together with any copies intended for other people, should be placed in a special folder marked 'For Signature'. If the carbon copies are to go to people outside the building, or if their content is confidential, a separate envelope should be typed for each carbon copy.

Company policy sometimes dictates when letters are presented for signature. The earlier in the day that a letter can be dispatched the better, since it will ease pressure in the mailing department and be more expeditiously handled by the Post Office. At the very latest letters should be presented one hour before closing time, to ensure that they are signed, sealed, stamped and dispatched before the office closes for the day. The signed letters should be checked to ensure that they have indeed been signed; that the correct envelopes are attached, since it is not unknown for them to become muddled during the signing process; that the address is complete, the mailing instruction correct, the contents comply with the enclosure list and that any item to be sent under separate cover is dispatched correctly. The letters should then be sealed and passed to the post department for mailing. The carbon copies should be filed away appropriately and the desk cleared ready for a new start next morning.

```
R Brown Esq
15 Riverside
Brookdale
CAMBRIDGE
CB3 1QT
```

```
R. Mason, Esq., B.Sc.(Econ.),
   Department of Business Studies,
      Riverview Technical College,
         RIVERVIEW,
            Essex.
```

Fig. 6.2. Envelopes in (*a*) fully-blocked, and (*b*) indented styles.

Summary

1. Transcription is the conversion of dictated material into finished correspondence ready for signature. It requires complete mastery of the typewriter and of shorthand, correct use of English, an understanding of the firm's policy and its house style, and adequate provision of facilities, letterhead, etc.

2. The layout of a business letter in the 1980s tends more and more to be a fully-blocked style, modified to move the date and the references over to the right-hand side of the page. The secretary must understand the principles behind each part of the letter, from the letterhead at the top to the distribution list at the bottom.

3. Transcription consists in collecting any non-dictated details which are to be put into the letter, typing the letter as dictated in correct style and

incorporating the details collected, proof-reading it and correcting errors where necessary and submitting it for signature.

Suggested Further Reading

Secretarial Typing, D. M. Sharp and H. M. Crozier, McGraw-Hill, 1975.
Standard Handbook for Secretaries, L. Hutchinson, McGraw-Hill, 1973.
Titles and Forms of Address, A Guide to their Correct Use, A. & C. Black, 1972.

7

BUSINESS CORRESPONDENCE—TYPEWRITING AND WORD PROCESSING

Recent Developments in Typewriting

During the last decade the electric typewriter has come to exert a powerful influence in the office, where it is largely replacing the manual machine. Even in the portable range there are electric machines which embody many of the features of bigger machines. The great advantage of electric machines is the reduced effort to operate them, for the merest touch on a key completes the circuit to type the character. There is no need to pound a keyboard all day as with manual machines. Considerable savings are also achieved because of the **repeat actions** on certain vital keys—the dot, dash and underlining keys, for example. Repeat action backspacing and space-bar operation also save time and effort. Some features of the electric, and the even newer electronic, typewriters are illustrated in Fig. 7.1.

The second major development in the last decade has been the emergence of really successful single element typewriters. The IBM Selectric 'golfball' typewriter did away with the noisy and space-consuming carriage movement of earlier machines, the **typing element** travelling instead from side to side. absence of type-bars eliminates jamming, and the top speed of the machine is raised. Other refinements introduced in this and similar machines are cartridge ribbons which snap in and out in a few seconds, a larger range of repeat action keys, line finders and end-of-page indicators. The most sophisticated machines incorporate error correction through a **correctable film ribbon**, **stroke storage** to ensure that characters are typed in the sequence in which keys are depressed and **automatic impression control** to ensure even impressions on the paper. Some typical machines are illustrated in Plate 8.

The next development was the introduction of the automatic typewriter. Typical of such machines is the Friden Flexowriter. The Flexowriter is a typewriter which has two accessories attached: a paper-tape punch and a paper-tape reader. It can punch out paper tape at the same time as it types a letter or document. This paper tape can then be filed in a tape storage file, for use as an input tape when the same letter is required again. When inserted into the tape reader the input tape will instruct the machine so that it types the document automatically, error-free, at 145 words per minute. The machine will stop automatically at places where the secretary needs to type in information of interest to the particular addressee only. Then it will, unattended, complete the rest of the document, automatically adjusting the line endings as necessary.

The machine never makes a mistake, mis-spells or overtypes, and can skip a paragraph if required. It enables letters which appear to be personally typed to be prepared automatically at speeds three times as fast as the average typist.

With the increasing sophistication of electronic technology, however, the early seventies took a new hard look at the stenographic requirements of modern offices. A new term—**word processing**—began to creep into the vocabulary. It establishes a link between the ordinary communication medium of offices—words—and the ability of electronic equipment to process input material and make decisions about it. As a result 'word processing' has contributed new cost-saving techniques to the secretarial range of activities.

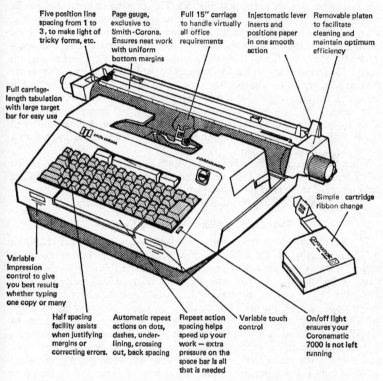

Five position line spacing from 1 to 3, to make light of tricky forms, etc.

Page gauge, exclusive to Smith-Corona. Ensures neat work with uniform bottom margins

Full 15" carriage to handle virtually all office requirements

Injectomatic lever inserts and positions paper in one smooth action

Removable platen to facilitate cleaning and maintain optimum efficiency

Full carriage-length tabulation with large target bar for easy use

Simple cartridge ribbon change

Variable impression control to give you best results whether typing one copy or many

Half spacing facility assists when justifying margins or correcting errors.

Automatic repeat actions on dots, dashes, underlining, crossing out, back spacing

Repeat action spacing helps speed up your work — extra pressure on the space bar is all that is needed

Variable touch control

On/off light ensures your Coronamatic 7000 is not left running

Fig. 7.1. The Coronomatic cartridge ribbon electric typewriter.
(Courtesy of SCM (United Kingdom) Ltd)

What is Word Processing?

Word processing is a system of typing correspondence and reports with an automatic typewriter similar to a conventional electrical typewriter but capable of processing material fed into it in a variety of ways. The machine records automatically all keyboard operations, so that a letter or report typed by a typist will be automatically stored in some sort of memory. This may be a reusable magnetic card or magnetic tape cassette. Although instructions are stored on a magnetic carrier, the actual line as it is being typed is temporarily held in a buffer memory before transfer to card or cassette, and this feature permits extremely rapid and positive correction of conscious errors (those that are noticed almost as soon as they are made) by backspacing and over-typing. At any future time this recall card or tape can be put into the machine and the letter retyped—at speeds of about 200 words per minute.

Suppose a letter or report has been typed, and 12 errors have been made in it. In addition, the executive has decided to delete one paragraph and re-place it with a new paragraph twice as long. The report need not be re-typed in full. All that is needed is for the recall system to be fed into the machine and instructed to stop at the first mistake. This is possible because it can be controlled to progress a paragraph at a time, or a line at a time, a word at a time or even character by character. When the first mistake is reached the typist overtypes the error—which alters the recall material. Even if it changes the length of the line the machine will process the whole of the next paragraph until it has found room for the extra words or used up the spaces left because the amended phrase was shorter than the original. The machine can distinguish between a carriage return that is **mandatory** (it must be obeyed) and one that is **optional.** Thus if the typist typed a subheading it will be reproduced in the recall typing, but if the machine comes to the end of an ordinary line and has an extra word to insert, it will put it in provided it has the room, before it obeys the carriage return sign.

When the corrections have been made, and the additions incorporated, the entire letter or report can then be reproduced in full at top speed and does not even need to be read for errors—since none can occur.

Clearly word processing has much to offer the top secretary.

Introducing a Word-Processing System

The justification for introducing a word-processing system lies chiefly in the low productivity of the ordinary secretary, faced with the boring repetitive-ness of much typing work. For example, many letters follow a standard pat-tern, dealing again and again with the same query. Many items like price lists have to be up-dated continually (especially in inflationary times). The re-typing of such documents is boring and even a good secretary becomes dis-gruntled. Lengthy and difficult reports may have to be re-typed because of spelling or punctuation errors. Poor typists frequently make several attempts at a letter, discarding expensive letterheading in the process. The word processing firms claim that—over a working day—the average secretary achieves only 8 words per minute no matter how high her speeds. One firm which doubted this evidence held a systematic enquiry into its stenographic output only to find that it was achieving a mere $6\frac{1}{2}$ words per minute on average. Clearly there is a great need to improve this level of performance. How is it to be done?

It is useless to try to introduce a word-processing system simply by purchas-ing a single sophisticated machine. What is needed is a full work-survey of typing requirements and output. It is often necessary to change the office organisation to extract the maximum advantage from the equipment. Such a survey requires the secretarial output to be classified under various headings: letters, reports, invoices, etc. This classification may reveal that a large pro-portion of letters are repetitive in character and can be catalogued into a number of standard paragraphs. Special treatment of such letters can be arranged.

Another result of the survey is the separation of typewriting activities from non-typing activities. This can result in a change to greater specialisation—the secretary who enjoys producing impeccable correspondence taking a larger share of this work and handing over some of her non-typing work to an administrative secretary who prefers the administrative aspects.

Usually the survey will reveal that some residue of work does not lend itself to the word-processing format and will be left to be done on the ordinary typewriter.

The resulting **workflow system** and the general reorganisation give very valuable savings in time and effort. This does not necessarily mean that staff have to lose their jobs. Usually there is an element of casual labour—temporaries, etc.—which can be phased out to achieve the necessary staff cuts. The increased efficiency means that salaries may actually improve, but the greatest savings for management arise from reductions in non-wage staff costs, such as floor space, car park space, canteen provisions, etc. This kind of increase in efficiency is of great importance to the nation itself, and has a great part to play in the general economy, quite apart from the benefits to the individual firm.

The introduction of a word-processing system inevitably leads to some alterations and adjustments. New jobs may be created and others may disappear. There is a period of acclimatisation during which output may actually fall. This is soon passed and once staff realise the new opportunities that exist in an office relieved of the tiresome typing of repetitive material they are only too happy to use the new equipment, and productivity soars.

Word Processing Applications

The applications of word processing are many, and a few lines about the more important aspects will assist the top secretary in evaluating their usefulness to her own situation.

1. Standard Form Letters

The preparation of standard form letters to deal with particular situations is a well-known technique. Word processing extends this idea to include the writing of standard form letters which fit any routine situation. This is achieved by using **standard paragraphs** rather than standard letters. A **search-and-find facility** in the equipment enables the typewriter to search out paragraphs in the correct sequence and type them. Heinz, the food suppliers, have developed a package of 70 standard paragraphs which enable ledger clerks to write appropriate letters on a wide variety of topics simply by specifying the numbers of the paragraphs required. Formerly they specified one standard letter out of a variety of letters available, which the typist then typed. Now the word-processing machine is supplied with the variable details (the name and address, etc.) and coded with the numbers of the required paragraphs. The machine searches for them in correct sequence and types them out. A letter which used to take 10 minutes is completed in from two to three, and executive time in checking is saved because the result is guaranteed accurate. The letter also gains in effect by its personalised appearance—there is no sign that it is in fact a standard letter; it appears to have been prepared as an individual letter. This has had favourable effects on cash flow when letters about overdue accounts are dispatched.

2. Repetitive Typewriting

Many documents contain standard paragraphs in which appear small variable details. Examples are contracts of employment, conveyances, tenders for contracts, insurance policies, conditions of carriage, etc. The documents concerned are often lengthy and are invariably similar in nature, with a relatively small amount of variable information incorporated into a standard body text making the significant difference between one document and the next. Because of their importance such documents can rarely be typed by junior staff; they need to be accurate in every detail. The word-processing system uses two tapes, one with the variable data, the other with the standard data. The searching facility enables the typewriter to switch from the variable data to the correct point in the standard letter, and then back again for the next variable detail.

3. Revision Typing

Many texts are subject to revision and amendment before being produced in a final form. The classic example is the report, invariably prepared as a rough draft, hacked around and tidied up, passed to other people for comment and suggestions, revised, redrafted and resubmitted. Every intermediate stage may require partial or complete retyping before progressing to the next. Many documents will be of wholly original text, others may lend themselves to profitable combination with standard paragraph techniques.

Further instances that come under the heading of revision typing include engineering documentation, policy and procedures manuals, maintenance manuals, directories of all sorts, inventory listing and so on. Some personnel documents—such as job descriptions—are revised and updated from time to time.

All such revision typing lends itself very easily to word processing. The original draft can be amended as explained earlier, so as to correct the odd mistake and incorporate amendments and re-phrasing. Then the correct version can be typed out at very high speeds.

4. Graphics

Many reprographic departments produce typed text which becomes the master for photographic or electrostatic copying processes. The word-processing typewriter is not only suitable for this type of work because, like some electric typewriters, it has a facility to change type-faces, but it can also be used to try out different lengths of text line without re-typing, by using the facility for adjusting line lengths and margins.

5. High-Volume Pool Typing

In typing pools work quality is lower than typing by the personal secretary, and the need for a rapid correction facility is greater. The provision of a word-processing typewriter provides this facility, but of course the greatest use of this type of machine in the typing pool is its use for 'standard paragraph' letters. Even so, the variable matter for each letter, i.e. the internal address, date, etc., will be greatly improved by the rapid correction facility and enable less well qualified staff to produce good-quality work.

The Equipment Available

There are nearly twenty types of word-processing equipment on the market, according to the *Business Equipment Guide*, which offers a comprehensive picture of the range of performance available. Some of the details which are of interest are given below.

Input Media. The input media are of four chief types: punched tape, magnetic tape, magnetic card and edge-punched card. One system has an input of typed documents read by an optical page reader.

Printing Heads. The printing heads are of three types: the traditional typebar machine, the interchangeable golf-ball unit, while the Rank Xerox 800 prints by means of interchangeable light-weight print wheels. Machines with interchangeable units can switch from ten-pitch typestyles to twelve-pitch typestyles, giving both Pica and Elite to suit typing needs.

Correction Features. Many word-processing systems offer a correction feature which lifts characters off the paper, and out of the memory, when the back space key is pressed. The secretary then types in the correct version.

Ribbon Changing. Ribbons are usually of the cartridge variety, and can be changed easily and cleanly.

Line Length Adjustment. This is automatic, so that text can be added and deleted during revision without concern for spacing.

Tabulation. Tabs are stored electronically and can be cleared in one operation. Decimal tabulation also ensures that numbers are printed correctly with the decimal values correctly aligned.

Automatic Centring. Headings can be automatically centred without calculations, even over columns, so that time and trouble are saved.

Automatic Underscoring. By keying in a code the secretary can ensure that words to be underscored are automatically underlined, in both the original and the replay versions.

Master Preparation. In most cases the master preparation is by an integral unit and not by separate equipment. The typist operating the machine is at the same instant preparing the master, and any corrections she makes by backspacing and overtyping will correct the master at once.

Speed. All machines play back at speeds in excess of 100 words per minute; most of them exceed 150 words per minute. The fastest of all at present is the Rank Xerox 800 which types at 350 w.p.m. because it eliminates carriage return, typing forwards on one line and backwards on the next line.

A typical word-processor is shown in Plate 9 (*a*). It shows the one-line thin window display which enables the operator to check for accuracy and a full-page display exactly as it will be printed. The significant feature of the Rank Xerox 800 is the printer, which operates, as explained above, at about twice the speed of other machines. The detailed diagram of the Xerox 800 typewriter keyboard (see Fig. 7.2) shows clearly the difference between character keys and 'function' keys. In all these word-processing systems the typist is using basically the machine she knows—the electric typewriter—but with additional keys for the new functions.

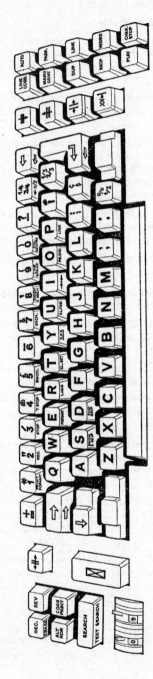

Fig. 7.2. The keyboard of a word-processing typewriter.

(Courtesy of Rank Xerox Ltd)

Notes:

Stroke Storage Keyboard—(N Key Roll over)—All strokes are captured and no matter how fast the typist types.

Electronic—When key is depressed impulse sent to console, then to typing head.

Manual—Depression of the key causes actual movement of the head without the message first being sent to the console.

Quasi-Electronic—Partially mechanic and electronic.

Backspace Error Correct—Permits typist to eliminate errors by back-spacing and typing over them.

Line Erase—Operator can erase an entire line of copy by depression of a single key.

Auto Justification—The typed document has perfectly straight right and left hand margins—extra spaces are added between words to achieve this.

Auto Centring—This allows the user to instruct the machine during rough draft preparation to centre a line of typing on the page.

Auto Decimal Alignment—This relates to the ability of the machine to line up columnary material with a straight right edge—allows operator to prepare a rough draft and machine aligns the tab work at a decimal point or right column edge.

Memory Backspace—The machine remembers the size of the letter printed (when using proportional spacing) and allows for this when overtyping a new letter.

operator needs to locate a document quickly. Some machines search in either direction.

Two Media Capability—This refers to the ability to use either two cards or tapes at the same time and thus make substantial editing changes or draw from both when composing a document, e.g. names and addresses on one card and letter text on another—combined when playing back.

Controlled Transfer—Permits the user to transfer data from one tape to another without printing out and to control the process so that an editing location within a document can be reached quickly.

Full Revision Control—This relates to the amount of time it takes to produce a final copy and is limited on machines without 2 media capability as editing can mean re-typing a considerable part of the document.

Tab Memory—Permits indented paragraphs to be amended and revised. It remembers to tabulate (x) number of times after a carriage return code.

Multi Paragraph Tab Control—Where 'tab memory' only relates to a single indented paragraph; this feature permits editing in a format where two or more blocks of copy are required on the same line (columnar copy layout). If an editing change is made in the second copy block the machine must remember to re-position line endings and positions only in that block.

Automatic Tab and Margin Setting—Margins and tabs are recorded on the media and need not be recorded elsewhere, thus eliminating necessity to set tabs and margins before a document is played out.

Page Control—Machine can control the number of lines of copy typed out on a page and ensures even top and bottom margins without operator control.

Variable Pitch—Operator can select number of characters to the inch or proportional spacing.

Proportional Spacing—Each alphabetical and numeric character has a different amount of space allocated to it.

Buffers vary in size, depending on the machine.

Margin Control—Permits the user to edit documents by adding or deleting copy while not having to be concerned about re-locating line endings. The system terminates the line at the most appropriate position based on line length selected by the operator.

Margin Zone Control—The area at the extreme right of the line where spaces or hyphens are converted to carrier returns. The wider the zone, the more ragged the finished copy; the smaller the zone, the 'tighter' the copy.

Auto File Listing/Auto Log—This permits the user to automatically print out the names of each file on a given tape with the reference mark position and the margin and tab data.

Text String Search—This applies to tape where the machine will search a document for the first few unique letters of a paragraph or line.

Track Seek—This applies to card where the machine will search a card to a specific coded track.

Full File Erase—Operator can effectively erase an entire cassette or card ready for re-use.

Auto Carriage Return—Operator can continue typing without pushing the carriage key. The machine will automatically carriage and re-member the characters and order in which they are to be printed at the beginning of the new line.

Language Feature—Different languages available on interchangeable typing fonts.

Column Centring—Enables operator to centre headings over columns instead of setting tabs.

Buzz Test—If there is a suspected fault on the machine, the operator presses the code button, all lights go on and a buzzer sounds if the machine is not faulty.

Reverse Playback—Text is recorded normally but machine plays back left to right, *then* right to left.

Single Double and 1½ Line Spacing—Recorded on media so that the machine changes line spacing automatically.

Summary

1. Recent developments in the typewriting field include the development of the electric typewriter, the automatic typewriter and sophisticated electronic word-processing machines.

2. Word processing is a system of typing perfectly correct letters and reports by automatic electric typewriter, which is capable of making decisions according to pre-coded instructions about line length, margins, etc. Insertions or deletions can be automatically taken into account.

3. Its chief applications are the preparation of standard letters from pre-coded standard paragraphs, the elimination of tiresome re-typing, the progressive revision of reports, price lists, etc., and its uses in graphic layouts.

4. The introduction of a word-processing machine calls for a detailed analysis of stenographic requirements to get the best out of the system.

Suggested Further Reading

Business Equipment Guide, BED Business Journals Ltd, published annually.

8

TELEPHONE TECHNIQUES

The Secretary and the Telephone

Technical advances have completely changed the rôle of the secretary as far as communication by telephone is concerned. Not all these changes have been advantageous from the executive secretary's point of view. Formerly, for example, she could ask the telephonist to get her a number and carry on with other work until she was put through. Today she is more likely to have to dial the number herself, with all the waste of time this involves if the line is engaged, or the long-distance lines are busy. She must keep her own set of telephone numbers, look up her own area codes for STD, wait while the telephonist at the other end locates the individual her executive wishes to contact, etc. All these petty activities use up valuable time. It is important to reduce this waste of time as much as possible by having the best possible facilities. Some of these facilities can be arranged within her own office, others require large company layouts, involving decisions at the highest level. Not all executives are even aware of the availability of the latest devices, so that a secretary who knows about these matters may be helpful in raising the whole question of the adequacy of the telephone equipment available. It is the chief purpose of this chapter to describe the equipment available. Before doing so we need a word about the importance of a good telephone technique to the secretary.

The telephone is the most direct and personal link firms have with their customers and business contacts today. It is possible to lift a receiver, dial a number halfway round the world, and within seconds be speaking to the very individual we desire to contact. Compare this with the difficulties in meeting in any other way—the long flights, the crowded airports, the need to book hotels, the expense, the fatigue. The telephone link is our best, most immediate link. Then we must not waste it. Smile into the mouthpiece, and say a cheerful 'Good morning'. The person the other end is hoping to do business with you. It is possible, by using the telephone correctly, to convey an impression of cheerful efficiency, self-confidence and good manners. Every telephone call is an opportunity to enhance your company's reputation. It can also destroy utterly the formerly favourable attitude of an important client. Within your own firm it can cement departmental solidarity or it can lead to distrust and interdepartmental strife.

The following points will be helpful in developing a good telephone technique:

(a) *Use a pleasant, clear speaking voice at all times.* Never speak aggressively, or in a bad-tempered way. The caller may be important, and you may do incalculable harm by upsetting him. Don't have two voices—a nice voice and a telephone voice.

(b) *Announce your firm's name, or your department's name, and your own*

71

name, immediately you answer the call. 'Sales Department—Whitehead speaking—can I help you?' is an excellent start to any conversation. It may bring it to an end at once, because the caller, realising he has the wrong number, rings off at once. This saves your time and his money, and thus pleases both parties.

(c) *Whatever the situation, help it forward constructively.* Nothing is worse to a caller than to connect with someone who is totally negative in his approach. Contrast the following exchanges:

(i) 'Is Mr Brown there?'
   'No.'
   'Do you know if he will be in today?'
   'Afraid not.'

(ii) 'Is Mr Brown there?'
   'I'm sorry, no. He's at the Board Meeting. Mr Larch, his assistant, is here. Would you like to speak to him?'
   'Yes, that would be very helpful.'

The caller's reaction to the first is one of total frustration. What kind of dull individual do they employ at this firm anyway? The second exchange, by contrast, has proceeded speedily and informatively to a constructive solution of the difficulty.

(d) These days it is often necessary to answer more than one telephone at a time. It is important to develop the right technique. If you are already holding one conversation and another telephone rings, wait until your first caller finishes a sentence and then say, 'Would you excuse me for a few seconds, another telephone is ringing.' You can then answer the second telephone, and either give it priority treatment or ask the caller to wait as you must conclude a call which has already started. **Give priority to outside calls,** since you can always ring back internally without incurring public network charges. The chief rule in handling more than one telephone is to keep cool and polite all the time. Your callers know that you cannot deal with more than one at a time. If a person is calling from a call-box he must be given priority or he may run out of money. Even a managing director will not mind being called back if you have such a caller on the other line. He is a servant of the company too.

(e) The economics of telephone usage have changed enormously in the last year or so. **Subscriber Trunk Dialling** (or STD) calls make it possible to dial almost anywhere and very cheaply indeed so long as what you have to say can be said in a few seconds. If it is going to take minutes the cost will be considerable. A five-minute call over 56 kilometres will cost about £1. This soon builds up an enormous telephone bill. For this reason it is a good idea not to offer to ring back, unless the person who has called you is important. If he holds on it is up to him to pay the bill. If he prefers to ring again later you can help him by giving a firm time. 'I'll tell Mr Smith you will ring him promptly at 2.30, if that is convenient. He should certainly be available then.' Then make sure Mr Smith knows that the call is coming.

Never indulge in long-winded courtesies over the telephone. They are ruled out by the increased prices. A bright 'good morning' and then come to the point. If you are calling long-distance, make this clear at once:

'Good morning, Mr Senior. General Electronics here. I'm calling long distance so I mustn't speak too long. We want to arrange the appointment for Mr Johnson on Thursday. What time can you see him please?'

If you try saying that passage in a polite business-like voice you will find it takes about six seconds. You still have four seconds left of the first ten seconds you are allowed for the basic unit charge.

The Secretary's Telephonic Requirements

To be really efficient you must be properly equipped. A full list of the available equipment is too long for this book, and much of the more elementary equipment is explained in the simpler companion volume *Office Practice Made Simple*. The top secretary should see that she has the following aids. The major ones are described in detail later in this chapter.

(*a*) Her local directory or directories.

(*b*) Her local STD code booklet.

(*c*) If out of London it is very useful to order the London directories, since so many firms and government departments have head offices there. The cost is very small indeed.

(*d*) Some sort of index of telephone numbers, where she can record the numbers she uses more regularly. In Plate 1 there is a **Shannostrip flipover unit** on the secretary's desk. Other firms make wall-mounted strip index units, but the one shown is compact, efficient and can be kept absolutely up to date and in perfect order by typing out the necessary strip every time a number changes or a new business contact is made.

(*e*) A **loudspeaking telephone** leaves the hands free to sort through correspondence or make notes (see page 78).

(*f*) An **automatic call maker** is a real time-saver. It records the number you want to dial, either on a tape or a punched card. Each time you need to dial that number you either turn to it on the dial, or slip the correct card into the machine. It will dial the number automatically (see page 78). If the line is engaged, you can end the call and then use the machine to dial again, until you do get through.

(*g*) An **ITT Terryphone** is a major system which finds anyone in a building in five seconds. It is the best way to locate anyone absent from his post (see page 80).

(*h*) The best machine of all perhaps is a **telephone-answering machine with play-back facilities** (see page 79). This records every aspect of a conversation and can be played back at any time. Imagine a situation where your executive is wanted urgently by an important customer. You explain that your executive is out, but as you are recording the conversation perhaps he would like to tell you all about the matter and you will play it back to your executive when he rings in, or returns. The executive hears the whole conversation, what you said and what the customer said. What is more, instead of stopping work to tell him about it, you can get on with your work while he listens to the caller.

(*i*) Other telephonic devices include the **telenote** (see page 37 and Plate 5), the **facsimile copier** (see page 82), which copies documents to anywhere in the world in four minutes, and the **Telex** (see page 82).

The Secretary and Switchboards

The secretary may be provided with a variety of equipment, ranging from a simple extension telephone to a private automatic branch exchange (PABX). She must make herself familiar with the equipment used in the firm, and get to know how it is switched over at nights. Inevitably there comes a time when she is working late, or at weekends, when she may need to use the telephone, or to ensure that she can be reached by those who know she is working in the building. The chief types of equipment are as follows:

1. A Main Telephone, with one or two extensions

This is a very simple Post Office system, as illustrated in Fig. 8.1 and Plate 11.

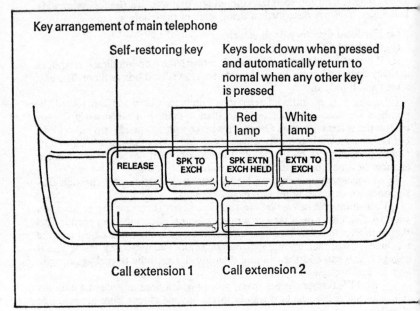

Fig. 8.1. A main telephone with two extensions.

(Courtesy of The Post Office)

Notes:

(i) Pressing down the SPK TO EXCH key connects the telephone to the exchange line, either to receive a call coming in or to make a call.

(ii) If the call is for someone on an extension the secretary presses the SPK EXTN EXCH HELD key. This holds the exchange call while the secretary announces it to the correct extension, which she has called by one of the Call Extension buttons. A red lamp comes on while this is happening, to show that the exchange line is being held.

(iii) The exchange line is put through to the extension by pressing the EXTN TO EXCH key, and a white light comes on to show that an extension is using the exchange line.

(iv) The release button restores any key that has been depressed to its original position, thus disconnecting the extensions or the exchange line.

2. Keymaster (1 × 5) or (2 × 10) Installations

These systems provide intercommunication and conference facilities between either 5 or 10 extensions, and enable calls to be made or received over one or two exchange lines. They represent a further development of the system illustrated in Fig. 8.1, but of course extra buttons are required to connect up to 5 or 10 extensions. These economical arrangements are suitable for small factories, offices, schools, etc. The 2 × 10 telephone is illustrated in Plate 11.

3. Cordless Private Manual Branch Exchanges (PMBX 4 × 18)

There are several sizes of cordless switchboard to link extensions to lines. The larger sizes are called private manual branch exchanges, or PMBX for short. The 4 × 18 PMBX is illustrated in Fig. 8.2 and Plate 11.

4. Private Automatic Branch Exchanges (PABX)

Private automatic branch exchanges are highly sophisticated pieces of equipment which provide both internal and external telephone networks. They have a wide range of facilities available, including operator dialling; trunk call barring to prevent low level staff making calls other than local calls; trunk offering—which allows the operator to offer an outside call to an extension which is busy with an internal call; hold for enquiry facilities, etc. An illustration and full description is provided in *Office Practice Made Simple*, pages 71–75.

5. Direct Speech

In the majority of organisations more than 70 per cent of all telephone calls are internal. What is not generally appreciated is that present systems are very often inefficient, causing unnecessary frustration and needless waste of many thousands of pounds. Many firms, for example, use PABX systems which supply both internal and external networks. Unless the system of 'trunk offering' is available, the PABX system cannot contact an extension which is busy on an internal call, resulting in a high proportion of costly return calls. The PABX system requires that a telephone extension is given to all members of staff requiring to make internal or external calls. These are expensive to rent from the Post Office Corporation. They can be dispensed with in all cases where staff only make internal calls if a 'direct speech' system —such as the ITT 511 intercom system shown in Plate 12—is installed.

'Direct speech' installations are very simple to operate. The control stations are compact instruments with push button dialling. They are roughly the same size as normal telephone sets and can, for convenience, be placed alongside a conventional telephone. There is also a small instrument which utilises a minimum of desk space and can be hand-held for discreet listening. The user merely pushes the buttons for the required number and at once receives an alerting tone to indicate connection has been made and that he can speak. At the receiving end a brief alerting tone warns that a call is coming. This is followed by the caller's voice. Conversation can then commence as if they were both in the same room. Because there is no need for a handset—one talks straight into the instrument—both people may walk about their offices talking from any point in the room; they can go to filing cabinets, fetch papers, or take notes without either of them touching their instruments. It is

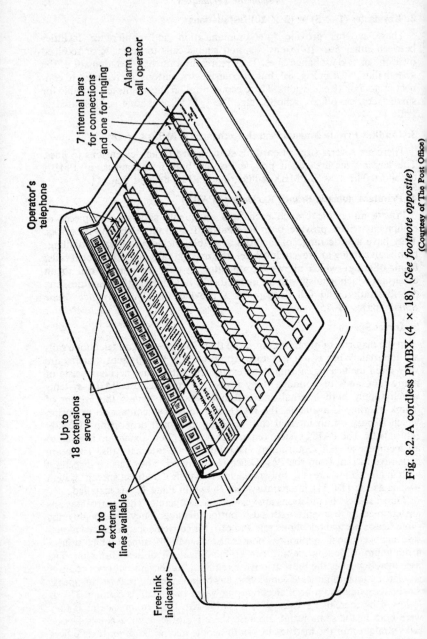

7 internal bars for connections and one for ringing

Alarm to call operator

Operator's telephone

Up to 18 extensions served

Up to 4 external lines available

Free-link indicators

Fig. 8.2. A cordless PMBX (4 × 18). (See footnote opposite)

(Courtesy of The Post Office)

simplicity of operation that has gained ITT 511 Direct Speech systems the reference of 'hands-free'. Since the speech is heard by everyone in the room, often from a wall-mounted speaker, personal gossip is reduced, and the average length of a call is cut from $2\frac{1}{2}$ minutes on a hand-held telephone to less than 40 seconds.

The separation of internal calls from external calls means that incoming external calls can be put through to the required person at once as he will not be engaged on an internal call, obviating the need to call back at the firm's expense. This in itself can effect considerable savings. One call back per day for each of the extensions on a 100-extension exchange could amount to £10,000 per annum avoidable costs.

Since the secretary is the one who needs to stop working to answer the telephone she has the most to gain by persuading her 'boss' to install 'direct speech'. If seven out of ten calls are internal calls she must obtain very real benefits, both in time and effort saved, from the system.

Other Sophisticated Telephonic Aids

Switchboard installations of one type or another are essential to the office. We must have some station at which calls can be received and directed through to the correct individual. Equally we must be able to filter calls, to prevent top executives being bothered by trivial matters. In general, switchboard choice is made at the highest level bearing in mind the consultant advice of the Post Office Corporation or one of the authorised manufacturers. The secretary can play little part in such decisions. By contrast, she can exercise considerable influence over the equipment actually used by herself. For the junior secretary this may amount to no more than a choice of the colour of the instrument she uses. For the senior secretary in a top post of responsibility it should mean that she can demand more sophisticated apparatus, which will improve her efficiency. The cost of equipment today is much less than the

---

Notes to Fig. 8.2:

(i) The four lines of keys illustrated in the diagram are used to make connections between exchange lines and extensions, or between two extensions. In the normal central position all keys are disconnected. If they are pushed up they connect to a bar above the key inside the body of the unit, and if they are pushed down they connect similarly to a bar below the key. Since there are four rows, there must be eight bars. One of these is used up as a ringing bar—the keys in the bottom row, when pressed down, ring the extension required. The other seven bars can be used to connect two keys together. Thus external line 1 and extension 1 can be connected by pushing both keys up. They will then be connected along the bar and the callers are able to speak to one another.

(ii) Since seven bars are available seven calls or interconnections can be arranged.

(iii) The term PMBX (Private Manual Branch Exchange) is appropriate since the operator manually connects up those requiring telephone or intercom services.

(iv) Any extension telephone, if it has a dial, can dial out calls by asking the operator for a line.

(v) A line of 'free link' lamps tells the operator the next link which is free.

annual cost of an employee's wage or salary. Therefore an employer will listen more attentively to an application for efficient equipment, even if it is expensive. The chief aids have already been mentioned (see page 73) but a more detailed description of them is given below.

1. Loudspeaking Telephones

There are several types of loudspeaking telephone, but perhaps the best is the one illustrated in Plate 13. There are many business occasions when it is convenient to answer the telephone and have the hands free—particularly if you are taking notes, locating file references, booking orders or reserving tickets, or just continuing your ordinary work while the caller outlines his ideas. Altering visual planning displays in accordance with the caller's point of view on such matters as rotas, duty rosters, etc., is another example.

The instruments generally consist of three units, which may be embodied into a single piece of equipment. The system requires a telephone containing a loudspeaker, an amplifier which boosts incoming speech, and a control unit comprising a microphone, dial and pilot lamp. Post Office loudspeaking telephones are quite inexpensive to hire. The charges are negligible compared with the advantages conferred. In the instrument shown in Plate 13 the loudspeaker is on the left and the microphone on the right. For conference use a small extension microphone and loudspeaker unit can be plugged in to enable any member of the group to join in the discussion and contribute information, or a point of view.

2. The Key Callmaker

A key callmaker is designed to call outside lines which are constantly being required. It has a desk unit control panel on which 32 key calls can be recorded (see Fig. 8.3). Numbers no longer required can be deleted and new ones substituted. Once a number has been stored in the wall unit connected to the control panel it will automatically dial that number every time the button is pressed. A 'cancel' button concludes any call instantly. No dialling noises are heard, but a small loudspeaker enables the progress of the call to be followed. When the call is answered the handset is lifted and the call proceeds like a normal telephone call.

The illustrations produced of key callmakers tend to show executives using them. Since the secretary is more likely to make routine calls there is a strong case for arguing that they are more economic when used by the secretary, except in firms such as those on the London 'Money Market', where it is customary for executives to make their own calls so as to save seconds in the difficult business of balancing the financial books.

3. Tape and Card Callmakers

These pieces of equipment are similar to the key callmaker in that they will dial out any call that has been recorded on the tape or punched into the card. The former has a capacity of about 400 calls, far more than the key callmaker described above. The card callmaker has infinite capacity. Calls are stored by plugging in a portable dial set, or by using a special punch.

4. Telephone Answering Sets

An answering set may be a very simple machine which merely answers the telephone and gives the caller a 20-second message. This is enough to say where the secretary is, or where she can be contacted, or what extension to ring to obtain the person who is covering her work while she is absent. Other machines give longer messages, up to two minutes. They are used extensively to give such information as weather forecasts or details of arrangements made in emergency situations. Other machines ask a caller to leave a message, and tell him when to begin dictating it.

The best types of machine, like the Autophone illustrated in Plate 14 (*a*),

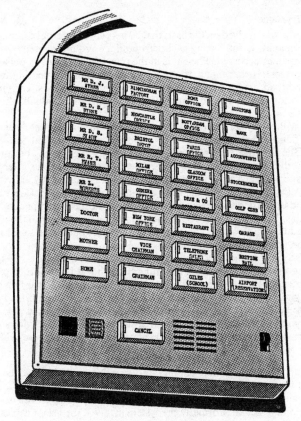

Fig. 8.3. A key callmaker.

(Courtesy of The Post Office)

by Shipton Telstor Ltd, serve a dual purpose for the secretary. In her absence the Autophone stays on duty, answering the telephone, giving callers information and taking messages. When she gets back she switches it to record every call she receives, or just those concerning her 'boss'. When he rings in to see what is happening, all or parts of the calls can be played over to him. He gets the information straight from the caller's mouth. Contrast this with what happens when he rings in to a secretary with no Autophone.

She reads from her notepad the calls she has received, some of them accurately reported, some not. He hears items he does not understand, queries them with her, and perhaps finds she cannot remember the conversation. All such problems are lifted from the shoulders of the secretary who has an Autophone. She simply says 'I'll play it over to you' and gets on with her work while he listens in. This facility can be hired for less than £2 per week, which is negligible compared with the secretary's salary. Why employ an expensive secretary and then underequip her?

5. The Terryphone

Terryphone was evolved on the basis that 80 per cent of internal communication in companies is the asking of brief questions requiring brief answers. Where companies become inefficient is in the time lost by their key personnel, such as top secretaries, ringing around various extensions or waiting for the operator to broadcast for people, just to ask these brief questions. Terryphone offers five-second location and communication between individuals wherever they may be on the premises.

The Terryphone system incorporates a locator button in the hand-set and a voice reproducer. Let us say that the secretary wishes to find the works manager. She lifts the Terryphone hand-set, presses the locator button and speaks into the mouthpiece: 'Works manager please, Terryphone.' Her voice is heard over every Terryphone in the system simultaneously, also from detached voice reproducers in the large and noisy areas. The works manager, wherever he is, hears his name and simply lifts the nearest Terryphone hand-set. He is then having a private conversation over the hand-set with the person who called him—in this case, the secretary. The amount of time saved in the average company is quite dramatic.

Of course the installation of a Terryphone system is a major project, and one that a secretary cannot implement for herself, but it is the sort of project which raises efficiency so dramatically that it is worthwhile suggesting when the opportunity arises—for example, at staff conferences. Some firms have a Suggestion Box which enables anyone to raise such matters at any time. Terryphone, an ITT company, offers a free survey and design service so that the system can be suggested and investigated without expensive survey charges.

Telecommunication

In Chapter 4 the telecommunication side of communication was deliberately postponed until this chapter. The speed of telecommunications sets it apart as the instantaneous means of communication, travelling seven times round the world in one second. Formerly the system involved the use of cables. The term 'telegram' was reserved for inland messages, and 'cablegram' was used for overseas messages. Today, aerial satellite systems have developed to the point where they compete seriously with cable facilities and no doubt will replace them eventually. A full account of telecommunications, as indicated diagrammatically in Fig. 4.1, requires us to consider seven major fields. These are:

  (*a*) The public telephone network
  (*b*) Internal telephones
  (*c*) Terryphone and similar devices
  (*d*) Telegrams and cables

(*e*) Telex
(*f*) Facsimile copying
(*g*) Datel services

The first three of these have already been described. We will now consider the others.

Telegrams and Cables

Today the vast majority of telegrams and cables are relayed through to the final destination by telephone, the actual telegram or cablegram being sent on next day as confirmation. Where the final destination has no telephone number the message is delivered by special messenger.

When is it desirable to send a telegram or cablegram? The answer includes the following cases:

(*a*) Where we wish to communicate quickly with someone who is not on the telephone.

(*b*) Where we wish to communicate with someone who is travelling but whose stopping places are known.

(*c*) Where the message consists largely of statistical or other data which would be tiresome to dictate over the telephone but must be transmitted more quickly than by letter post.

(*d*) Where the telephone charges greatly exceed the cable charges or calls are subject to interruption and delay.

(*e*) Where the time-lag between countries makes it difficult to contact the overseas client in his normal working hours. The Telex system (see below) is a great advantage in this situation.

Full details about telegrams and cablegrams are to be found in the current edition of the *Post Office Guide*. Those living abroad should refer to the similar publication by their own Post Office organisation. The chief points are:

1. Inland telegrams may be sent to places in Great Britain, Northern Ireland, the Isle of Man and the Channel Islands. There is a higher charge for telegrams to the Republic of Ireland. Telegrams tendered on Sundays and certain other holidays are subject to a surcharge.

2. Greetings telegrams sent on attractive decorative forms are available at a small extra charge. They may also be given in for deferred delivery, in other words, given in early, for delivery on a certain day.

3. Telegraphic money orders are still acceptable although ordinary money orders have been discontinued. These orders enable money to be telegraphed in emergencies to recipients who are in difficulties.

4. A cheap telegram called an 'Overnight' telegram can be sent to be delivered with the first postal delivery of the following day.

5. For a small annual fee firms can register telegraphic addresses, such as Toothbrush, Nottingham—the telegraphic address of Boots the Chemists.

6. Words are counted for charging as follows. Words in the name, the address, the message and the signature all count as words. Hyphenated words in everyday use count as one word, but words deliberately put together will count as separate words, however they are disguised. Figures with letters are counted as two words. Thus 117A would be charged as two words, except

where it is a house number in an address. For fuller details the *Post Office Guide* must be consulted.

7. International telegrams may be sent to any country abroad, to passengers or crew on ships and aircraft, and photographs and documents may be transmitted in facsimile form if required. Full details of the form and cost of these services can be found in the External Telecommunications sections of the *Post Office Guide*.

Wording the Telegram

It is important to keep a telegram brief, yet at the same time make yourself clear. It is usual to phone the telegram through, so that there is no written copy of the telegram except what the secretary herself records. It is therefore sound policy to type out the name, address, message and signature before dialling the code for telegrams. This will ensure that the best wording has been selected; that the message is clear and that the operator is not delayed while we think of the best wording. The copy then can be preserved as a file copy, and with a note of the charge calculated by the telephone operator. In certain cases we may need to pass a copy to the switchboard operator, and to the Costing Department if they are likely to need to charge the client for the cost incurred.

Telex

The Telex system is a teleprinter service which operates from one subscriber to another by creating a direct link into his office. A dialling unit and a Telex directory (see Plate 14) enable the subscriber to dial directly, or in some cases via the International Telex Exchange, to the teleprinter machine in the office he is cálling. The distant teleprinter immediately sends its **'answer back' code.** This tells the caller that he is correctly connected to the subscriber. The caller then sends his own code, and follows it with the message. He then sends his own code and receives back the 'answer back' code. This confirms that the full message was received and no breakdown occurred during the transmission. Pressing a button marked CLEAR now disconnects the two teleprinters. The service operates 24 hours a day, whether or not the teleprinter is manned, so that the first duty of the day is to distribute to those who need them any overnight messages which have come in.

The Telex service provides instantaneous typewritten communication to Telex subscribers around the world. The same 'copy' is produced at each end of the transmission. It is ideal for the transmission of factual material, information, instructions, orders, etc. It is also relatively inexpensive.

Telegrams may be directed on to the Telex machines of any subscriber by firms and individuals who are not themselves Telex subscribers. Similarly a Telex subscriber may send telegrams to non-Telex business contacts by using certain Post Office points which are prepared to handle international telegrams.

A modern Telex machine is illustrated in Plate 14 (*b*).

Facsimile Copying

The term facsimile copying in business refers to a system of reproducing documents by transmitting them electronically over a distance. The process is equally effective over short ranges of 100 miles or so and long-range around the world. It is an improvement on the Telex in that a Telex message is transmitted by an operator, who may make a slip in transmission, but the facsimile copier sends exactly what is on the paper. If the document, tabulation or whatever it is has been checked for accuracy then that same set of correct data will be received at the far end. It will also transmit charts, line diagrams, maps, etc.

The document is transmitted by breaking up the image into thousands of tiny dots which are picked up by an optical scanning device in the copier. These dots are transmitted as electrical signals to a similar machine at the distant end. There the procedure is reversed and the signals received are recorded again as visible dots. The result is an exact facsimile (perfect copy) of the original. The scanning process takes 3–4 minutes, depending on the size of the document.

The system is very advantageous, provided its use is strictly controlled. It is relatively cheap to hire the copiers, about £20 to £100 a month depending upon size, but it is the hidden costs of telephone line time that are expensive. If the copier is used to transmit trivial memos, or items which are non-urgent and therefore adequately transmitted by post, it will prove uneconomic. Its virtues are the instantaneous transmission of documentary evidence, to arrange distribution of perishable commodities or permit the collection of air cargoes from depots. In personnel matters, where industrial action can be avoided if top management gives a written undertaking on some point, the facsimile copier permits the necessary written evidence to be given to shop stewards or works committees within minutes of the Board giving its consent. Such a message, delivered even by special messenger, would perhaps take hours to deliver and involve considerable transport costs.

Control is best achieved by metering the use of the line to check the duration of each transmission and requiring a log to be kept of the transmissions made. This enables the use of the copier to be monitored, to test whether it is in accordance with the guidelines laid down by management.

Datel Services

These are services provided by the Post Office which permit the transmission of data electronically over the telephone and telegraph network. The data are transmitted in 'bits' (binary digits) at speeds up to 48,000 bits per second. A bit is simply an electrical on–off position, where a meaning can be attached to either on or off. A computer can be made aware of these values, and since it can appreciate a very large number of them in a second and they can be transmitted instantaneously over the Post Office networks it is possible to link anyone in the nation to a computer through the digital data networks.

Summary

1. Recent technological changes have made a great difference to the way the telephone is used in business. As a result the secretary must adapt her own system of work. She must develop a good telephone technique; speak clearly and pleasantly; help callers constructively and avoid unnecessary chatter.

2. The secretary must be properly equipped, if necessary suggesting major changes if management is not aware of the new aids available. In particular she must have directories and STD code books and a strip index unit for telephone numbers. A loudspeaking telephone, an automatic callmaker and a

telephone-answering machine with playback facilities are excellent aids for the busy secretary.

3. Switchboard facilities range from simple circuits built into a telephone itself, enabling it to connect with various extensions, to private branch exchanges which may be manual (PMBX) or automatic (PABX). Direct speech internal telephone networks switch callers through to any destination, where a wall loudspeaker and microphone unit enables the caller to be heard and answered by those present. Similarly, a Terryphone enables every corner of a building to be reached simultaneously to page people absent from their usual work places, giving 5-second communication with anyone in the building.

4. Telecommunication by telegrams, cablegrams, Telex or Datel services give instantaneous transmission of messages and data worldwide, while facsimile copiers enable documents and photographs to be transmitted in about 4 minutes anywhere in the world.

Suggested Further Reading

Local Telephone Directory (including green and yellow pages).
STD local Telephone Dialling Codes booklet.
London telephone directories if your firm is out of London.

9

ROUTINE SECRETARIAL DUTIES—MAIL INWARDS AND OUTWARDS

Mail Inwards Procedures

A full account of the routine activity of handling incoming mail is given in a companion volume, *Office Practice Made Simple*. Here it is only proposed to reiterate briefly the main points about the process, so that the top secretary knows what to look for and can play her part in organising a satisfactory system for dealing with incoming mail.

The general principle is that incoming mail must be opened and distributed early in the day, and later collections must be dealt with immediately on arrival. Wherever possible, mail should be attended to and answered at once. Where this is not possible because certain processes have to be gone through first, these processes should be initiated straight away. The second principle is that mail should be opened only by responsible and trustworthy staff. If lower-level staff are used they should be closely supervised and carefully inducted into correct procedures. A third principle is that it is for the very top level of management to decide policy on the matter of correspondence. If top management specifies that all correspondence is to be addressed to a particular individual, so that he reads and knows about all the firm's affairs, it virtually means that he and his secretary will be bound to do the initial opening and distribution. In larger firms this would be impracticable.

Collecting Incoming Mail

Postal services are no longer delivered seven times a day, as they were in Queen Victoria's time, and to ensure convenient arrival of incoming mail, many firms use the private bag service. This permits them to collect mail in an appropriate bag for safe custody, at times convenient to themselves. Usually the messenger collects the mail early in the day. The charge for this service is £40 per annum at present, £20 for the private box into which the mail is sorted and £20 for the private bag. The collected mail is brought into the mail room or registry and opened by staff who have come in early for that purpose. Other firms may have their mail delivered by the postman in the normal way, but perhaps a sack of mail will be delivered at the early morning delivery, to be sorted and opened by staff specially appointed for this duty.

Letter Bombs

Before opening incoming mail it is necessary to scrutinise it for possible letter bombs. Regrettably we live in violent times, when instruments of danger are all too readily available to the political activist, the extremist, the criminal and the mentally unstable. The executive secretary is in the front line of such engagements, for it is precisely the top executive who is usually selected as a target. In the light of their experience in this field the Metropolitan Police of

London have issued advice to office staff concerned. The advice is printed in the form of a hang-up card which reads:

Bombs in the Post—Be Alert

Look for the unusual:

Shape	Wrapping	Writing
Size	Grease Marks	Spelling
Thickness	Signs of wires or batteries	Wrong name, title or address
Sealing	Postmark	Unsolicited mail

If you are suspicious:

DON'T
1. Don't try to open it.
2. Don't press, squeeze or prod it.
3. Don't put it in sand or water.
4. Don't put it in a container.
5. Don't let anyone else do any of these.

DO
1. Keep calm.
2. Look for sender's name on back.
3. Check with the sender.
4. Check with the addressee.

STILL THINK YOU'VE GOT ONE?
* Leave it where found.
* Evacuate the room.
* Lock the door and keep the key.
* Send for the Security Officer.
* Phone the police—Dial 999.

This advice is self-explanatory and covers the points which have come to the attention of the Metropolitan Police after dealing with several hundred cases in the last few years.

Opening Incoming Mail

The procedure is as follows:

(*a*) Mail is faced—that is, all envelopes are turned the same way round. In this process any mis-sorted mail is usually discovered and appropriate action taken. It would be courteous to deliver it by hand if it was for a firm close by—otherwise it is returned to the postman.

(*b*) Personal and confidential mail is now removed from the pack, and date-stamped on the envelope. Some date stamps also record the time of arrival, which in some types of business is important (Fig. 9.1). The date-stamped envelopes are then placed unopened in the trays of the individual to whom they are addressed.

(*c*) In some offices, particularly Government offices or those where a 'security' aspect is important, movements of confidential and 'top secret' mail would be controlled by a registry where the movement would be recorded. Such classified mail is placed in plain envelopes addressed to the person concerned, and may be delivered by registry staff or collected by secretaries at appropriate times.

(*d*) Mail may be opened by a paper knife or by a mail opening machine such as the one illustrated in Fig. 9.2. Such machines cut off the tiniest sliver of paper from the edge of the envelope, only a thousandth or so of an inch thick. This opens the envelope without damaging the contents.

The contents should now be removed by suitably experienced staff and

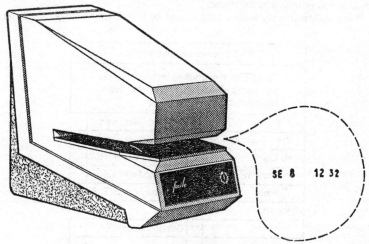

Fig. 9.1. A 'Facile' time stamp for mail inwards.

(Courtesy of Warwick Time Stamp Co. Ltd)

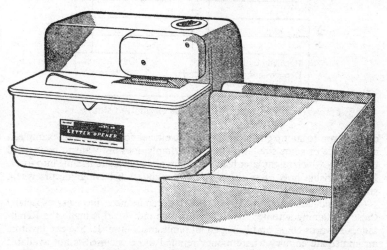

Fig. 9.2. A mail-opening machine.

(Courtesy of Roneo Neopost Ltd)

their contents appraised. The addressee's name should be checked, since letters are often enclosed in the wrong envelopes. If incorrect, it is courteous to dispatch a letter to the addressee, and ask if he has received your letter in error. In most cases letters will merely be routed to particular departments by placing them in the departmental tray. It is wise to check that any enclosures are in fact enclosed. If not the envelope should be checked, and even attached. The best way to check that envelopes are empty is to hold them up to a desk light. Each letter should be date-stamped or time-stamped before passing it on to the appropriate department.

When date-stamping letters, care should be taken not to deface the letter

Mail Inwards Circulation Slip			
Please read the attached correspondence and then pass to next individual ticked or deal with as indicated			
J. T. Ross	✓	Pass to Sales Dept.	
R. K. Beeston		Pass to Advt. Dept.	
M. Light		Pass to Buying Dept.	
R. Peabody	✓	Signify Approval	
T. Jones		Comment to J. T. R.	
Others:		File	
		Other Action:	
Received by Mail Inwards Department and Circulated on date shown		Date Stamp here	

Fig. 9.3. A mail-inwards circulation slip.

content, nor to stamp enclosures which are official documents. For example, a conveyance or some similar document certainly does not want to be marked in any way which might later lead to queries about the date it came into force. It is surprising how often this type of thoughtless behaviour occurs where staff are not properly trained.

(*e*) Particular care should be taken of remittances inwards, especially those containing actual cash. It is best if one individual is made the Remittances Inwards clerk, and is passed all remittances inwards. She can institute an immediate enquiry where money reputed to be enclosed is not available or incomplete. She often records the remittances in a Remittances Inwards book and passes them over to the cashier in return for a signature.

(*f*) With some letters a 'distribution' stamp or a 'circulation slip' is used to ensure that all the persons who ought to see a particular piece of correspondence do in fact see it. A typical circulation slip is shown in Fig. 9.3.

Incoming Mail and the Filing System

A wide variety of procedures is used to deal with mail once it has been opened. If filing is centralised, the problem is at what point to relate the letter to the filing system. If letters are sent to the filing department before being dealt with by the appropriate official long delays may occur if some files are out and letters are kept back until the file is available. If letters are sent to the officials at once, and they then call for a file if it is necessary, there is less likelihood of delay. At least the official will be aware of the matter pending and can chase up the file if it is urgent. On many routine matters the official can deal with them without consulting the file and simply pass over the letter for filing once it has been dealt with and he has put the necessary file marks on it.

Internal Mail

Many offices have sufficient internal movement of mail, memos, etc., to merit a special organisation. This messenger or 'postman' service should be organised at set times. The postman usually delivers to the departmental

Internal Circulation					
Deliver to	Date	From	Deliver to	Date	From
J. Jones A/cs	27.1.77	A. A. K.			

Fig. 9.4. A printed envelope for use in internal mail systems.

secretary, or some recognised internal post-clerk, at the same time collecting 'out' mail for other departments. He will leaf through this, deliver what he can as he completes his circuit and sort the balance ready for his next delivery round. He will also pass ordinary post to the mail outwards department for stamping and dispatch.

It is usual to save envelopes in such internal systems by using ungummed envelopes which can be reused several times. Large envelopes, with printed spaces for directions, can be used repeatedly and are very economical, while at the same time giving ample protection to the contents. Such an 'internal distribution' envelope is illustrated in Fig. 9.4. It would be printed on both sides and thus have a very long life.

A Mail Inwards Register

Mail inwards registers are rarely kept these days in ordinary commercial offices. They are, however, important in certain offices where some types of correspondence deserve to be registered. For example, solicitors may record

Date	Sender's Name	Type of Mail — Tick			Destination — or Signature of Recipient
		Registered	Recorded Delivery	1st Class	
27.7..	M. Roberts & Co.	✓			L. G. Lake.
28.7...	Reynolds Ltd.		✓		Contracts Dept.

Fig. 9.5. A mail-inwards register.

the safe arrival of documents such as conveyances, summonses, etc. Publishers may record manuscripts received, contracts signed, etc. In government departments certain correspondence would be particularly important and would be handled by a special registry which would record its arrival and distribution.

Many letters are registered, or come by recorded delivery. For these letters a signature must be given to the postman or to the counter clerk if mail is collected by private box or bag. It is important to sign for each letter separately. Clearly these letters have then to be routed through the internal organisation and should be entered on a mail inwards register and signed for by the recipient. A mail inwards register might therefore be ruled as shown in Fig. 9.5.

The Top Secretary and Mail Inwards

The secretary may find herself doing any or all of the activities described above. In the small firm she will often have total responsibility for mail inwards. In larger organisations she will at most operate a departmental mail room or post department, but will liaise with some central mail department or registry.

For the average executive secretary her chief mail inwards preoccupation will be with the mail for her own executive. The first point here is that letters delivered by hand during the course of the day, telegrams and Telex messages and express or Railex letters should be taken in at once. They may require instant attention and if dealt with at once cannot be overlooked.

Morning mail should be sorted as already described and personal and confidential mail left unopened. The mail should then be arranged so that these letters are on the top with the opened letters arranged below in rough order of importance. If the contents of a letter lead you to suspect that the file will be needed, or at least the copy of the previous letter in the correspondence, clip the new letter to the previous letter, or to the whole file, and the executive will not need to call for it. You can also indicate which letters in the file actually refer by clipping a thin strip of paper to each one and letting it protrude above the top of the file. You can even label it with a helpful note, such as 'Contract here' or 'Original complaint here'. The total mail inwards may then be put into a file cover—or, if necessary, a 'mail inwards' tray on his desk.

A secretary should read her own executive's mail thoroughly except where it is specifically marked 'confidential'. Even then some executives may prefer that such mail is opened and read first by the secretary who inevitably must learn the contents in the course of her work. The point is that a secretary can only deal effectively with callers and telephone messages if she is thoroughly knowledgeable about her executive's affairs. She can then give the proper priority to enquiries on major topics and intercept minor matters to be dealt with in more routine ways or at times when the executive is not under pressure.

The most routine items of the mail inwards may not need to be shown to the executive at all. These will be matters that the secretary can deal with herself, while he is reading the mail. It is also useful to deal right away with anything that has come in which may be needed for reference later—such matters as changes of address, or changes of telephone numbers should be recorded at once. Supplements to the *Post Office Guide* should be incorporated in the Guide as time allows. New catalogues and price lists should be filed in appropriate places and obsolete numbers discarded into the wastepaper-basket. Certain items like changes of address may be of interest to other departments or individuals. Everyone can recall occasions when some large organisation, although notified of a change of address, continues to send letters from some part of its organisation to the old address. This can only mean that the original recipient of the 'Change of Address' notice failed to think through the implications for her firm of the message received. Having changed the address in her own records the secretary should attach a circulation slip to the notice and circulate it to all departments likely to need the new address.

Mail Outwards Procedures

Once again the most routine activities of a post department are fully described in *Office Practice Made Simple*. The secretary must make herself familiar with the established procedures in the firm, particularly as to the times of collection from departments, so that she can help the general efficiency of the office by getting as much post as possible cleared early in the day. It is quite certain that mail posted early in the day is cleared and sorted more easily and reaches its destination sooner.

Mailing instructions shown on the internal address should be clearly typed on the envelope and the secretary should see that staff under her are trained in this important routine. When letters are typed they should be presented for signature as soon as a convenient moment arrives, and placed in the departmental collection tray, after checking that they are correct in every detail.

In some offices the post department or registry is used as a place where envelopes can be typed and stuffed before dispatch. If this is the case great care must be taken to ensure that envelopes, letters and enclosures do agree. It is useful not to seal the envelopes until a particular batch has been completed. If nothing loose is left it would appear that all is well and the batch can be sealed and stamped or franked.

Postage Books

In some offices the registry keeps a record of all outgoing mail. In others only particular items are recorded, such as remittances outwards, legal documents, certificates awarded by colleges and training departments, passports, etc. Ruled postage books and posting lists for registered letters, recorded delivery letters and parcels are useful in keeping track of items dispatched. Posting lists also save time in busy Post Offices.

Franking Machines

Franking machines are a simple, hygienic and economical way to deal with large quantities of post. They will record the postage directly on to a letter, or for parcels and packets they will dispense and damp a gummed label which records the postage paid. A personal reference or advertisement can be incorporated into the design, which renders the franking less attractive to staff trying to misuse the firm's postal system.

The system is based upon a pre-setting of the meter by an official based at specified Post Offices in a given locality. The postage charge is paid in advance, usually by cheque, and the amount (say £100) is recorded on the meter. The machine is then sealed. Any value of postage can be set on fingertip selectors. Two registers record (a) the cumulative total of postage used and (b) the balance left on the machine as successive frankings are deducted from the original £100. Letters can then be posted in batches without any need for 'cancelling' at the Post Office, and consequently are sorted more rapidly. A weekly return enables the Post Office to control the use of these machines. They can now be re-set electronically by computer, over the telephone.

Post Office Guide

This important publication appears annually, but supplements are issued as and when necessary free of charge to all purchasers of the Guide. The customer completes a postcard issued with the Guide when it is purchased. Supplements then arrive through the post. The supplements are printed on alternate pages, so that they can be cut up and pasted into the Guide. In this way all out-of-date information is covered up by the new correct information. It requires a certain amount of paste work, but the result is a Guide which is always correct.

The Guide contains more than 600 pages of detailed information, and is essential to any post department, while every secretary should also have her own copy for reference purposes.

Datapost

The Datapost service is a country-wide and world-wide postal service offering a regular, completely secure, door-to-door service. The service is supplied and charged on an individual-contract basis for the movement of documents, letters, computer output, paper-tape data, blood specimens, industrial samples, etc. Packages are handled by Post Office staff throughout the journey over established and well proven networks of air, rail or road services, ensuring both maximum reliability and maximum security. The service operates anywhere in the United Kingdom, and also to France, Belgium, Holland, Japan, the USA and Brazil. For example, packages collected at 2 p.m. can be delivered in São Paulo, Brazil, by breakfast time next morning.

The Petty Cash Book

The postal clerk sometimes acts as a petty cashier. The word 'petty' means small, and the function of the petty cashier is to save the chief cashier's time by disbursing such small items as fares for the office messengers, parking meter coinage for chauffeurs, etc. The petty cash book is kept on a system called the 'Imprest System'. This permits the cashier to check the petty cashier's expenditure in a very simple way, and limits her total outlay at any time to a fixed sum—say £20—which is called the 'imprest'.

Fig. 9.6 and the caption notes explain how to keep the petty cash book, and are worth careful study. They are reproduced here from *Office Practice Made Simple*.

The Top Secretary and Mail Outwards

Every top secretary has to prepare correspondence for mailing, frequently late in the day to meet emergency situations. It is vital to her that she can rely upon staff in the post department to give her letters attention however late they are received. She is most likely to receive this kind of treatment if she herself is courteous and helpful at all times, and ensures that both she and her department keep to the rules in all normal matters. Thus she should ensure that as much mail as possible is signed and sent down for processing early in the day, so that the post department can get ahead with the majority of their work. If she knows that vital letters cannot be ready until the last moment, a quick telephone call to the post department supervisor will make it clear that this is so, and enable her to arrange to dispatch the letters.

Where a secretary controls mail outwards for a number of executives it is important to lay down clear guidelines about mail deadlines for posting. Everyone does have the last-minute letter on occasions and a secretary should always accommodate the member of staff with a genuinely urgent letter. The provision of two trays, one for the bulk of correspondence and the other for very urgent mail will usually be sufficient. The mail will be sent down to the post department at regular intervals throughout the day. After the final deadline non-urgent mail will wait until next day, and only the 'urgent' tray will be cleared. An executive who short-circuits the system by treating all his

Dr.	Date	Details	P.C.V.	Total	Postage	Fares	Cleaning	Sundry Expenses	Stationery	Folio	Ledger A/cs	Cr.
20·00	19.. Mar. 25	To Imprest	C.B. 9									
	25	By Stamps	1	1·50	1·50							
	26	" Postage	2	0·65	0·65							
	26	" Cleaning	3	0·45			0·45					
	27	" Sundries	4	0·32				0·32				
	27	" Fares	5	1·45		1·45						
0·30	28	To Telephone Call	L. 3									
	28	By R. Jones	7	1·34						L. 19	1·34	
	29	" Cleaning	8	0·65			0·65					
	29	" Sundries	9	0·40				0·40				
	29	" Travelling	10	1·65		1·65						
	30	" Envelopes	11	0·45					0·45			
	30	" Office Equipment	12	1·65						L. 15	1·65	
	30	" Sundries	13	0·15				0·15				
	31	" Totals	—	10·66	2·15	3·10	1·10	0·87	0·45		2·99	
	31	" Balance	c/d	9·64								
20·30				20·30	L. 5	L. 11	L. 27	L. 36	L. 49			2·99
9·64	Apr. 1	To Balance	B/d									
10·36	1	" Restored Imprest	C.B. 11									

Fig. 9.6. The petty cash book. (*See footnote opposite*)

late mail as urgent will be told of the difficulties he is making and asked to change his attitude. If necessary, he will have to be reported to an appropriate authority who can reprimand him about abuse of the system.

In her general supervisory rôle the executive secretary should ensure that all mail dispatched reaches an appropriately high standard. Her own correspondence will of course be impeccable. Where she notices lower standards from junior staff, mis-spellings and poor layout, she should not hesitate to raise the matter in order to improve the general tone of communications outwards.

It is general practice that a personal secretary has a small supply of stamps and possibly a letter scale for her own use to enable her to stamp and post mail which is prepared late in the day. This adds flexibility to the postal system, since it leaves her free to finish letters after normal hours without troubling the post department. She should keep a notebook of letters dispatched in this way, and present it when seeking a further supply of stamps.

Notes to Fig. 9.6:

The following points will explain the operation of the Petty Cash imprest system, shown in Fig. 9.6 opposite.

(i) The page is divided into two parts, debit and credit, but the 'centre' of the book is offset towards the extreme left of the page. This gives only a very small amount of debit side, while the credit side is expanded to make room for a series of analysis columns. The debit side is for receipts; the credit side for payments.

(ii) The details are written on the credit side, since there is no 'Details' column on the debit side.

(iii) The chief source of cash received is the cashier, who provides the original imprest, but other small sums may be received from staff, for telephone calls, etc. All receipts are debited.

(iv) On the credit side, money spent is first entered into the total column, but is then extended out into one of the analysis columns. This enables the total postage, fares, etc., to be collected together. A special column at the end is used to extend out any items which cannot be mixed with other items; for example, the payment to R. Jones can only be posted eventually to R. Jones' account.

(v) At the end of the week, or when the imprest is nearly all used, the petty cashier rules off the page in such a way as to total the 'Total' column, and the analysis columns. These are then cross-totalled to ensure accuracy. The balance is found; the book is closed off and the balance is brought down.

(vi) The cashier then checks the petty cashier's work and restores the imprest by providing enough cash to raise the balance to the original imprest figure.

(vii) The book is now posted to the ledger accounts, using the totals of the analysis columns and the individual special items in the end column. Folio numbers are entered as shown.

(viii) The petty cash vouchers, which authorise the payments made, are arranged in order, numbered and the PCV numbers are entered in the column provided. The petty cashier is now ready for a further week's business.

(ix) In some stationer's shops it is possible to buy petty cash paper which is ruled with a 'details' column on the debit side as well as the credit side. This makes little difference to the records, but enables the details of debit items to appear on the debit side.

Summary

1. Mail inwards should be collected early from the Post Office, sorted and opened by responsible staff and distributed in time for the arrival of the general body of staff at the start of the working day.

2. A register of important incoming mail, registered letters, recorded delivery letters, telegrams, etc., should be maintained.

3. The executive secretary should open her 'boss's' non-confidential mail, find files which are likely to be required, and arrange the mail in order of probable importance. She should then deal with routine items while the executive is reading the mail.

4. Mail outwards procedures should be thoroughly understood by the secretary, who should ensure that her executive or her department cooperates fully and observes the rules laid down.

Suggested Further Reading

London Post Offices and Streets, Post Office Corporation, latest edition.
Office Practice Made Simple, G. Whitehead, Heinemann, most recent edition.
Post Office Guide, Post Office Corporation, published annually.
Post Offices in the United Kingdom, Post Office Corporation, latest edition.

10

ROUTINE SECRETARIAL DUTIES—FILING AND RECORD-KEEPING

The Executive Secretary and the Filing System

The filing system has been described as the 'memory' of the office, where information can be stored until it is required. When this moment arrives it should theoretically be possible to return to the filing system and retrieve within seconds the body of information stored there. It can then be used as a basis from which to resume the activity concerned, in the light of the information and experience stored in the file. In the process the file will be updated, and when the new surge of activity is completed the file will again return—in its up-dated form—to the memory bank in the filing system.

In practice filing presents many problems of storage, access, retrieval, follow-up, re-storage and space. Any filing system has an inertia which keeps it in existence even when it has become outdated and inefficient because the labour of changing a system and the expense involved are enormous. It is probably true to say today that management attitudes are due for a change in this respect, since inflation has altered the relative costs in office work. Personnel costs are now so high that the payroll may take as much as 75 per cent of all costs, while office equipment rarely exceeds more than 5 per cent. It follows that today to change to a new system of office equipment and achieve more efficient use of staff in the process, may save on payroll costs more than the costs of the new equipment. Since investment allowances (the amount of a new investment which may be written off against taxation) are also very high at present a great proportion of the cost of a new installation may be written off against profits. This also makes it easier at present to change to a new system. The executive secretary may have an opportunity to point out these facts, and should not hesitate to do so if the filing layout used in her department is particularly antiquated and inefficient.

Whichever system of filing is used, management must review its effectiveness from time to time and if necessary spend money to sustain and improve the system. Sound management in this respect can only be achieved if it is based on reports from those using the system at grass-roots level. The executive secretary probably not only uses the system herself but controls filing clerks doing the majority of the work. She is therefore soundly placed to hear complaints about the system by those actually servicing it, and grumbles from executives held up by some delay in the tracing of a file. This should enable her to pinpoint weaknesses in the system. For example, failure to trace a file may be due to a lack of adequate in-house training of staff in the correct procedure. Someone may have gone to the system and taken a file without putting an 'out-marker' to indicate where the file has gone. A regular series of half-day or whole-day courses may be desirable to remind staff of the essential points, or a seminar on the filing system may be introduced as part of the induction programme for new staff.

In bringing the attention of such matters to the appropriate authority it is better to put in a written report than just to make an oral complaint. Try to work within the system rather than against it—raise the matter with the persons chiefly concerned wherever possible and give them the opportunity to meet the complaint in the normal process of ensuring the efficiency of their department.

A filing system must serve the office staff, not vice-versa. Thus where the perfection of the system itself becomes of greater importance than the use the staff are able to make of it, there must be something wrong with the system. Just as one finds librarians who will not lend anyone a book, and archivists who will not let even genuine students into their archives, one finds filing supervisors who will not let anyone borrow a file. So long as a file is borrowed in a proper way, and its whereabouts known, the file is not lost and the system is serving the office. Executives and their secretaries who habitually abuse a system by failing to return files when they are not being used, or failing to advise filing staff when they need to extend a deadline, deserve to be called to account. Staff who *do* abide by the rules must be able to obtain files easily and quickly.

Departmental Filing *v.* Centralisation of Files

One matter that is often debated is the relative value of departmental filing as opposed to centralised filing. With departmental filing each department looks after its own filing, the work either being performed as an extra chore by the departmental secretary or by an assistant typist/filing clerk who is directly supervised by the departmental secretary. The system is therefore small, localised, direct and constantly available during normal working hours. Centralised systems on the other hand are large, impersonal, indirect, and access can only be obtained to a file by going through a procedure for requesting it. Their advantage is that the large scale of the system makes it worthwhile to buy specialist equipment and employ specialist staff. Some systems, such as microfilm filing, are clearly more appropriate to a centralised system. The acid test of any system is whether the advantages outweigh the disadvantages.

The secretary should keep up to date with equipment and methods. The best way is to ensure that her department receives one of the 'free-distribution' monthlies which are mentioned in the Suggested Further Reading at the end of this chapter—*Business Equipment Digest*, for example. On receiving this publication she should read it through in a quiet interval, starring items which appear to be appropriate to the needs of her own section. She should then attach a circulation slip to the front cover, naming those executives who might like to have their attention drawn to particular points. Thus a line might read:

Mr Jones. You may find p. 34, No. 19, of interest!

It is best if the secretary puts her own name on the last line of the circulation slip so that the magazine returns to her eventually.

Whether the filing system is a centralised one or a departmental one, the executive secretary will almost invariably find that she has a few files of her own to keep in her office. It may be that her executive does a lot of confidential or private work which he does not want the rest of the staff to read; it may be that she finds it more convenient to keep some copies of correspondence more readily to hand. She will inevitably acquire various papers which have no place in a centralised or departmental system, but to which she needs to refer from time to time. Having read about all the various systems and files available, she should choose that most suitable for her purpose—perhaps just a small locking cabinet with suspended vertical files for her boss's confidential correspondence. She may like to keep a lever arch file labelled 'Daily Copies' in which to file an extra copy (perhaps in a distinctive colour copy-paper) of every letter or memo that she types. These would be filed in date order and copies would perhaps be destroyed after, say, six months. This particular system is invaluable if one has a forgetful boss, a boss who takes home file copies and mislays them, or a firm which, despite constant complaints and requests, still operates a bad filing system.

Every firm will have its rules and methods concerning filing, as indeed every other aspect of its business, but it is up to the secretary to make the system work for her. She will often have to have her own set of filing rules to maintain the efficiency of her own department, but of course these should work in with the firm's rules and not interfere with them. If her boss constantly takes out files without telling anybody, or misfiles pieces of correspondence, then his secretary must devise a system of her own to combat this. Top executives display human failings like everyone else; at times they can be irksome and infuriating when they break all the rules they themselves have laid down. It is therefore essential for the secretary to bend the rules (without appearing to deviate from them) to keep things moving efficiently. It is this sort of talent which makes a secretary into a top secretary. Whatever system she develops to circumvent the waywardness of the executive she serves, she will eventually win his respect and cooperation. If she can provide almost immediately any document or copy he requests, then he will be impressed by her efficiency, and will gradually mend his own ways to conform with her (clearly superior) methods.

Basic Principles of Filing

The basic principles of filing have been fully described in a companion volume, *Office Practice Made Simple*, and it is assumed that the executive secretary is already familiar with them. The whole subject of filing embraces many aspects and countless systems. A brief review here is included only to remind the executive secretary of the variety of the work. The filing system used in any office is a study in its own right, and every secretary on appointment to a firm must become thoroughly familiar with it.

The broad classifications are two: alphabetical filing and numerical filing. Alphabetical filing is generally based on the names of the firms or companies dealt with (name filing). We can also file by subjects in alphabetical order (subject filing) and by geographical area (geographic filing). Numerical filing has many advantages, especially for very large systems. Alphabetical filing only has 26 divisions to correspond with the 26 letters of the alphabet, but the number of divisions is infinitely large with a numerical system. However, a numerical system has to be associated with a card index or some other index which is in alphabetical order so that the file number can be readily discovered. A particular type of numerical system is the Dewey decimal system used for libraries.

Finally, and outside the two broad classifications of alphabetical and numerical, we have chronological filing. This is useful in certain circumstances —for example, where the secretary keeps an extra copy of all the letters she types on a distinctive coloured paper and simply preserves this file in date order. Chronological order is also the order used in every type of filing system for the *internal* contents of any folder, the latest copies being placed on top of the file as it is opened. A few words about each of these systems is given below for revision purposes.

Name Filing

Since much of the business we do is with other firms, sole traders, partnerships, limited companies or institutions like local authorities and nationalised industries, filing under the name of the firm or institution is the commonest system of filing. Naturally, difficulties arise as to exactly where it is best to file a particular item. The problem is usually resolved by regarding each element in the name as an **indexing unit** and then selecting the most important as the first indexing unit. Thus T. H. Smith has three indexing units, of which Smith is the most important, so that Smith, T. H., would be chosen as the method of filing. With names like Department of Health, the first indexing unit is the one which distinguishes that particular organisation from others: 'Department'—there are many departments; 'Health'—there is only one Department of Health, so it would be filed under 'Health, Department of'. Even so it is usual to put a cross-reference in case of difficulty, so that an index might read:

Department of Health—please see Health, Department of

A few organisations use other methods; for example, in the case of companies registered in the United Kingdom the official filing system at Company House is based upon every letter of the name conferred upon the company by law under its Certificate of Incorporation. Thus A. C. White Ltd. would be found in the A's and not in the W's, and T. R. Jefferson & Company Ltd. would be in the T's and not the J's.

Geographical Filing

In some situations, particularly sales department filing, geographical area is important. In such circumstances, where the filing naturally falls into a system of export areas, or of salesman's territories, geographical filing may be logical and convenient.

Subject Filing

Subject filing is convenient in the work of many executives. For example, an administrative officer has many activities to supervise: buildings, maintenance, insurance, staffing, etc. With insurance, for example, he may need to secure cover for premises, motor vehicles, public liability, life assurance for key personnel, etc. He might therefore use a subject heading, 'Insurance', subdivided under various headings. Similarly, maintenance of buildings could be filed under a general heading 'Maintenance', subdivided into the various properties to be maintained, and further subdivided into aspects such as plumbing, redecorations, alterations, etc.

Numerical Filing

With numerical filing a new correspondence is given a number reference to suit the convenience of the system, rather than the alphabetical order of the name. Thus the filing cabinet bulging with 'Smith's' ceases to be a problem, for a new Mr Smith can be given a numerical reference in an empty drawer, or anywhere there is space for one more file. A full account of this system is given in *Office Practice Made Simple*.

Every secretary must acquaint herself with the filing system in use in her own office and ensure that she conforms with the procedure when, for example, a new client or supplier is entered into the system. A 'miscellaneous file' is used initially for all new business contacts, and only when negotiations harden into a firm relationship is a file opened for that particular individual.

Methods of Filing

There are numerous methods of filing and dozens of filing systems devised by individual manufacturers to take advantage of the different methods. It is impossible to review them all, and only visits to such international exhibitions as the International Business Show (formerly called the Business Efficiency Exhibition) can give a comprehensive view of the range of equipment available. The chief methods may be divided into five groups. They are:

Suspension filing: in which the files are suspended from some sort of framework. This group includes

vertical filing
lateral filing
side-filing
mobile filing
powered filing

Shelf filing: in which the matter to be filed is filed in some sort of container and then placed in order on a system of shelves. This group includes

lever-arch filing
box filing
wallet filing
rotary filing
card indexes

Binder filing: in which the matter to be filed is secured in some sort of binder. This group includes

thong binders
post binders

Visible-index filing: in which the edges of cards and documents are staggered in such a way as to be visible all at the same time, so that the eye can quickly select the item required. This includes

strip-index systems
visible-index card binders
visible-index panels
visible-index cabinets

Specialist filing: in which the matter to be filed is of awkward shape or size, so that conventional filing methods are inappropriate. This includes the filing of such items as

plans, charts and blueprints
microfilms
dictation machine tapes
computer tapes
data processing print-out
punched cards

Each of these methods of filing has its advantages and disadvantages, some of which are referred to in the brief résumés which follow. Since any filing system may require the storage of a variety of items, some sort of flexibility is desirable and many firms specialise in units which incorporate some degree of versatility. An example of this versatility is given in Plate 15, where the Shannon storage unit illustrates shelf filing, lateral filing, roll-out drawers for card index trays, stationery storage, a working surface and microfilm storage and a roll-out frame for suspended files.

Suspension Filing

Suspension filing depends upon the use of files suspended on some sort of framework or rack, which may be viewed either from above (vertical filing) or from the side (lateral filing). Vertical filing requires the use of filing cabinets, with drawers which pull out. Lateral filing requires the use of storage units, with files suspended from racks and visible from the side, rather than from on top as with filing cabinets. A word about each of the systems of suspension filing is advisable at this point.

(*a*) *Filing cabinets for vertical filing:* 2-, 3- and 4-drawer cabinets are available for this most traditional form of filing. The individual units are relatively cheap, and the system can grow with the business by the purchase of further cabinets, so that the system is suitable for many businesses. Adequate supplies of filing aids—files, file covers, index tabs, out-markers, special warning flashes, etc.—should be provided. Meanness with supplies wastes time and involves the business in hidden costs out of all proportion to the cost of an adequate supply of materials.

(*b*) *Side-filing cabinets:* The traditional filing cabinet has the files suspended across the front of the filing drawers, and a drawer has to be pulled right out to find items at the back of the drawer. With side-filing, the files are not suspended across the drawer, but sideways. It is therefore possible to have very wide drawers with hundreds of files on view as the drawer is opened. The filing clerk must turn her body slightly to view the files, which are not directly facing her. A safety device incorporated into the cabinet prevents more than one drawer being opened at once. The index tabs are visible from above—i.e. vertical filing is used.

(*c*) *Lateral filing:* Here covers are suspended in cupboards or storage units using cross rails from which they hang with one short edge facing the filing clerk. The index holders are adjustable to suit their position in the rack, which may be as much as six shelves high. This is more economical of space than cabinets, which are never more than four drawers high. Some units have a pull-out shelf for a working surface, and the unit is more stable than cabinets which have pull-out drawers. Some lateral filing can be seen in the illustration of a Shannon storage unit already referred to (see Plate 15).

(*d*) *Mobile filing:* Where it is desirable to get a very dense concentration of filing into a limited space the system of mobile suspension filing is appropriate. Such a system is mounted on tracks which enable a particular storage unit to be pulled out easily for access to the files suspended in it. After use it is pushed back again into the densely packed array of storage units. Another advantage of this type of filing system is that it can also be made absolutely dust-proof, and this can be particularly advantageous in industrial applications for the storage of such things as fabric samples.

(*e*) *Powered filing:* Powered filing is used to deliver a particular file to a work-station where the filing clerk can service it. These systems are suitable for large-scale organisations with vast numbers of records to maintain. The largest in the world at the time of writing is reputed to be the Halifax Building Society's Conserv-a-trieve system, which can handle four million files. It has more than 50 electronically controlled machines each patrolling a twin-bank of filing containers and capable of bringing any one of them to a filing operator's work station when instructed by the computer.

One automated system, the Sperry-Remington Lektriever, is suitable for quite small offices, and can deliver any nominated file in seven seconds to a work station. It thus offers a means for decentralising some of the massive filing in large organisations, giving each department a convenient point-of-use system. This is illustrated in Plate 4. The saving of fatigue, etc., is enormous with these types of powered systems. Regrettably, the filing clerks do face the problem of putting on weight in their now sedentary occupations.

Shelf Filing

Shelf filing uses containers such as wallets, box files, card index trays, etc., which are arranged like books on a bookshelf. Either the wallet itself, or in some cases the wallet contents only, are removed from the shelves when required—in each case leaving an obvious gap to show that a file is out. An out-marker can be inserted here indicating who has the file. If the shelves are themselves circular platforms, forming a rotatable unit around a central supporting pillar, they can not only store a large number of files in a compact space but can be accessed from three working stations disposed around the free-standing unit. These are called 'rotary' filing systems.

The chief types of shelf filing units are as follows:

(*a*) *Wallet files:* these are wallets of manilla or linen which have sufficient capacity to make a free-standing package on any shelf. They may be gusset files or box files, according to capacity, and usually have plastic tabs and labels which can be specified in two positions to give easy visibility on the shelf.

(*b*) *Lever-arch files and box files:* These are rather similar. The lever-arch system retains documents which have been punched with a two-hole punch. They can be retrieved from the file without disturbing other documents filed above or below them. Box files are used to store papers and pamphlets. They do not have to be punched, but are held in position by a spring-loaded clip.

(*c*) *Card indexes:* These are still widely used in systems where a particular card is not likely to be consulted very frequently. They are easily prepared and maintained, particularly where the individuals to whom the cards refer make out their own cards on applying to join the system—such as where students apply to join a college or to use a library system. Where repeated access is needed a visi-index system may be preferable.

Binder Filing

Binders meet many filing needs. Perhaps the most useful are record books for salesman, sales catalogues, prices lists, service manuals, orders, invoices, stock sheets, costing sheets, etc. The National Loose Leaf Company specialises in making binders to suit customer specifications in a wide variety of mechanisms, spine thicknesses, sizes, colours and with company or house designs to give a 'corporate cover' image. The loose-leaf system is clearly a convenient one, and the variety of mechanisms to meet different working conditions while still preserving the loose-leaf format reflects the ingenuity of the industry. They vary from ordinary two-ring binders of the type familiar to every student to post binders several inches deep capable of freeing any page at any point without disturbing the pages on either side.

(*a*) *Thong binders:* Where only a few pages have to be secured the thong binder is cheap and simple to operate. It consists of a folder, with the back cover reinforced by a strip of thicker cardboard which secures inside it the ends of two thongs. These thongs may be like treasury tags, or may be metal strips. The thongs are passed through the holes punched in the papers to be bound together, and then secured by tying, hooking round a wire spring catch, or in some similar way.

(*b*) *Post binders:* Post binders are suitable for relatively long-term use, where the papers have to be consulted over a period of months or even years. File copies of many standard documents, invoices, delivery notes, cost sheets, student records, etc., are easily stored in this way. The binder covers are usually of very thick cardboard, covered with a bookbinding cloth. The back cover has two smooth steel bolts secured into it and when the cover is laid flat on the desk these bolts stick up to receive documents which have been punched with a two-hole punch. Usually the steel posts (hence the name 'post binders') are about two inches tall, and threaded to receive a broad-headed securing nut once the top cover has been put on. If the pile of documents stored in the file grows too large for the folder, extension rods can be screwed into the posts to give a 3 inch, 4 inch or 6 inch thick pad of documents. Very often such things as student records for a large college can be kept in this way for reference, with all the A's in the first post binder, B's in the second, etc. Some post binders have four posts, two in the front cover and two in the back. This enables the binder to be opened at any point and separated off, without losing the order, so that an extra copy can be filed in its correct place without disturbing the rest.

Visible Index Filing

The visible index system of record keeping is probably the most convenient method of keeping many records such as stock records, accounts for customers, student records, etc. The industry has devised a wide range of applications, which all depend upon staggering the cards or sheets of paper just enough to reveal the edge of the paper which bears the name of the person or firm referred to. Some of these applications can be seen in Plate 16, where the variety of applications shown by one supplier is illustrated. The illustration shows the four applications described below.

(a) *Visible index binders:* The Shannoleaf binder illustrated in Plate 16 (a) is basically a card index system in a book, with the record cards firmly held in position by a specially designed binding action. There is a double locking device which enables sheets to be removed or inserted without disturbing the sequence. A standard range of cards is available and specialised record cards can also be provided. Each record card has an immediately visible edge; there is a range of signals for providing instant record control.

Plate 16 (b) shows a Shannovue visible index card system. This system of visible records is easy to refer to and control. It is basically a card index system, with the cards housed in panels, books or cabinets according to the capacity required. The cards have visible edges for easy reference; edge signals in a choice of colours provide instant record control. The cards can also be slipped into pockets. The Shannovue panel and Shannovue book are ideal for desk top use. The Shannovue cabinets are particularly suitable for systems of over 1,000 records. The book shown in Plate 16 (b) is ideal for constant desk top reference; it holds up to 100 cards and measures 15 × 9 inches when closed.

(b) *Visible index cabinets:* This illustration (Plate 16 (c)) shows the visible index system for several thousand customers, housed in cabinets each holding over 1,000 records. Each panel can be removed individually if required. This is a feature which is sometimes useful—for example, each tray might contain the records of the customers of one particular salesman, or the mark records of students in a particular class. The tray could then be taken to a meeting to discuss the sales record, or the class achievements, without disturbing the main system.

(c) *Visible strip index:* Shannostrip is a system of one-line visible records. The strips containing brief salient information are mounted in frames; the frames can be housed in different units, depending on the amount of information to be recorded and where the unit is to be used. These units are the small portable flipover unit, the desk unit, the revolving stand and the wall unit. Shannostrip is simple and fast to use and easy to up-date. It is thus ideal for use as an index to more complex records in all kinds of administrative functions, notably for telephone numbers or for the index to a numerical filing system. Illustrated in Plate 16 (d) is the Shannostrip desk unit which is ideal for desk or table use.

Specialist Filing (including Microfilm Filing)

Many items which one would not think of normally as being part of a filing system do in fact have to be filed in some logical system. The dentist has the impressions of his patients' mouths taken when fitting false teeth, and the printer has the blocks for artwork from books. Modern data processing has led to a completely new range of accessories for filing print-out and paper tape. A few of these items are described below.

(*a*) *Plans, charts, blueprints and artwork:* These are stored in large horizontal or vertical plan cabinets. The vertical kind are useful in permitting the examination of individual charts without removal from the cabinet. The horizontal cabinets have a large working surface which permit trays to be lifted out and placed on top so that individual items may be selected and examined.

(*b*) *Microfilm filing:* For many years microfilming has been limited to the filing of inactive records, such as archive material. More recently it has begun to revolutionise the filing of active information in such fields as client files for insurance companies, building societies, finance companies and solicitors, and accounting records in wholesale trade.

The great economy achieved by microfilming is in the space required to store original documents. Many of these pieces of paper are of different size, so that files have to be large enough to accommodate the paper sizes likely to arrive in any firm from external suppliers, customers, etc. With microfilming every document is reduced to the same size, giving a convenient uniformity. After a brief retention period for verification to ensure that the documents have been correctly photographed, the original documents may be destroyed. Thus foolscap or even brief-sized documents are reduced on the film to a size such that 60 document images appear on a single micro-jacket measuring 6×4 inches, and this can be increased in some systems to 500 documents per 6×4 inch microfiche. In one system recently installed 50,000 files holding 6,000,000 documents and previously occupying 3,000 sq. ft. of floorspace, were accommodated in 450 sq. ft. of floorspace, including all the microfilm equipment, and this included spare capacity for double the number of files to permit expansion over a 10-year period.

The illustration given in Fig. 10.1 will enable the reader to follow the description of microfilm filing which follows.

The essential sequences in a microfilm filing system are as follows. First, for the input:

Film
Process
Verify (and destroy original)
Insert into jacket
File the jacket

In the filming process the documents are photographed in the correct order, and the film is then processed (i.e. developed) to give a roll of film. This roll of film is then viewed through a roll film reader to verify that all the photographs are clear and no essential data have been cut off by bad placing. When this comparison of the photographs with the original documents is completed, the original documents may be destroyed. Of course certain documents, such as the title deeds to houses, would not be destroyed, but virtually all correspondence is disposed of. The roll of film is now cut up in a machine called a **reader filler** into strips which can be 'filled' into a 6×4 inch micro-jacket file. This file is now a complete record of the correspondence with the client. At the start only a few images may appear on the file—they will be added to as the correspondence continues. With 60 images per file and 100 micro-jackets to an inch of drawer space an enormous filing system can be accommodated in a small room, and some security systems are actually operated in a strongroom or vault.

The output process has three alternative systems. These are:

System 1
Retrieve jacket
Read in a filemaster reader

This is appropriate where the file is to be read in the filing area itself, and does not have to be sent to anyone in another part of the building.

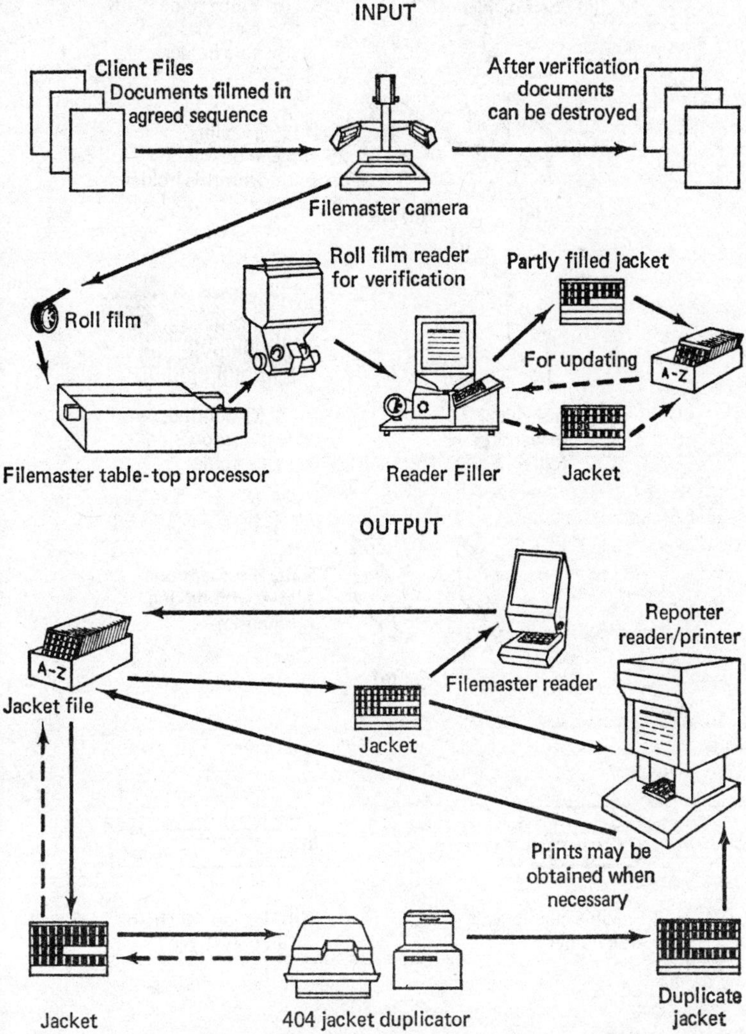

INPUT

OUTPUT

Fig. 10.1. A typical microfilm filing system for client files.

(Courtesy of Bell & Howell Ltd)

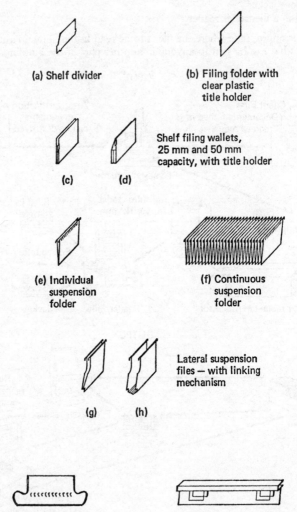

(a) Shelf divider

(b) Filing folder with clear plastic title holder

(c)   (d) Shelf filing wallets, 25 mm and 50 mm capacity, with title holder

(e) Individual suspension folder

(f) Continuous suspension folder

(g)   (h) Lateral suspension files — with linking mechanism

(i) Flexible clear plastic title holder

(j) Flat top title holder in polystyrene

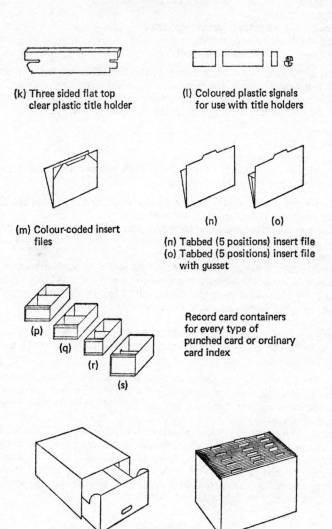

(k) Three sided flat top
clear plastic title holder

(l) Coloured plastic signals
for use with title holders

(m) Colour-coded insert
files

(n)   (o)

(n) Tabbed (5 positions) insert file
(o) Tabbed (5 positions) insert file
with gusset

(p) (q) (r) (s)

Record card containers
for every type of
punched card or ordinary
card index

(t) Archival storage unit in.
heavy-duty cardboard

(u) A desk-top filing unit
and work organiser

Fig. 10.2. A complete range of filing aids.

(Courtesy of The Shannon Ltd)

System 2
Retrieve jacket
Make a duplicate (in a jacket duplicator)
Send duplicate to person requiring it
He reads the duplicate on a reader

This system enables a perfect copy of the file to be sent out without the original file moving from the filing system. No 'out-markers' required here, a file is never out, and two or three people can have duplicate copies of the same file at the same time. After use the duplicate is destroyed.

System 3
Retrieve jacket
Select image required
Reproduce a 'hard copy'—a dry electrostatic print—on a reader-printer
Send this copy to the person requiring it

Clearly this is only used where the person requiring a copy does not have a reader; perhaps a client or other external party.

Where documents have to go to courts, judges usually want to see a 'hard copy' but it is wise to take the filemaster and a reader so that the actual film can be produced in evidence if necessary.

Despite the number of pieces of equipment needed to equip executives with filemaster readers, the savings in space, effort and even sickness (everyone hates dusty files of old correspondence, full of last year's germs) promise to make microfilm filing more and more popular as we move into an era of increasing technology in office work. In particular computer output micro-filming has a great future, since computer printout is large and heavy, whereas 208 pages can be microfilmed on a single fiche and be sent through the post in an ordinary letter.

(c) *Data processing*: As computer printout is becoming more widely used in companies, the need for its housing and efficient retrieval has increased. Manufacturers such as Twinlock have introduced comprehensive ranges of binders and housing units specifically designed to provide the most efficient method of housing and retrieval of printout, whether burst or unburst. These include data binders, data trolley units, desk reference racks, data storage frames, data storage cabinets and computer tape racks. Specialist firms like Shannon Limited produce a full range of data storage equipment, including binders, suspension filing, archival storage, punched card storage, paper tape racks, cupboards, trolleys, tabs and labels.

Filing Aids

No filing system can possibly be efficient unless a proper range of filing aids is available and adequate stocks are held. Decisions have to be made about the system to be adopted, and a measure of uniformity is desirable. Staff should then be told what aids are available in the range selected and adequate supplies ordered to ensure that the system operates effectively. The business equipment field is highly competitive and a good deal of advertising pressure is exerted on executives and secretaries to get them to order 'new' items of equipment. This tendency should be resisted or it results in a proliferation of many unrelated items each of which must be ordered in small quantities without taking advantage of quantity discounts. It is better to stick to a major supplier and only authorise one individual to place orders for supplies in sufficient quantities for all departments.

It is impossible to illustrate in a book of this size every type of filing aid available even from a single manufacturer, but Fig. 10.2 shows a typical selection offered by one of the major suppliers.

Summary

1. Filing is the memory system of the office. It is a storehouse of information which can be retrieved, used, up-dated and re-stored ready for the next occasion. Money must be spent to sustain and improve the system and its effectiveness must be reappraised periodically.

2. A good secretary will keep herself up to date on filing methods by subscribing to one of the monthly business equipment magazines and circulating new developments to interested executives.

3. The chief methods of filing are alphabetical filing and numerical filing. We also meet geographical filing and subject filing, while the Dewey decimal index system is used for libraries.

4. The commonest methods of filing, which are described in this chapter, are suspension filing, shelf filing, binder filing, visible index filing and microfilm filing. There are several other specialist systems for such items as data processing and punched cards.

5. Whichever system is adopted, an adequate supply of filing aids, folders, tabs, colour signals, etc., is essential for an effective filing system.

Suggested Further Reading

Business Equipment Digest, BED Business Journals Ltd, monthly.
Business Systems and Equipment, Maclean Hunter, monthly.
Office Practice Made Simple, G. Whitehead, Heinemann, most recent edition.

11

ROUTINE SECRETARIAL DUTIES—REPROGRAPHY

The Executive Secretary and Reprography

Reprography is the art of reproducing copies of documents, bulletins and reports so that everyone who needs to have a copy can be supplied. It is part of the communication network which is so essential to modern business organisations. Without reliable copying facilities the large-scale enterprises of today are unmanageable. Not only must successive echelons of management be advised of developments, but our increasingly democratic industrial and commercial structure requires everyone to be informed. No one is more aggrieved than the manager who did not receive his copy of a bulletin which has already reached his subordinates; and no one more gratified than the new member of staff who finds proof positive that his arrival has been noticed in his inclusion in the circulation list for relevant documents.

The executive secretary is largely responsible for reproducing top-level reports and documents, and for maintaining and servicing distribution lists in the communications field. She also tends to be the one who supervises more routine bulletins and orders of the day. It follows that a good system of reprographics is a matter of great importance to the executive secretary, who is also concerned about the availability at all times of staff with the necessary skills in operating the machinery selected.

In some large-scale organisations, such as busy local government offices, college offices, etc., the centralisation of reprographic facilities is a recent trend. The advantages are, of course, that the whole reprographic process can be subjected to a rigorous examination and equipment of the right type to meet the needs of the organisation can be purchased. A central organisation which is large enough to command a budget of its own may be able to afford with ease expensive machines which could not be purchased departmentally. Since top-quality typing is clearly preferable in such a large central department, and since the whole tone of the organisation may be affected by the quality of the output achieved, it is essential to have a person in charge who can produce impeccable work, displayed sensitively. It follows that the person appointed to this type of work should have first-class practical knowledge of typewriting and display work. The post requires a good working relationship with the executive secretaries who will largely be responsible for feeding work through to her, and she must be able to understand their requirements and know how to implement their ideas.

Where reprography is organised on a departmental basis, the supervision of a competent executive secretary is essential to ensure that the output achieved is of a high quality, tastefully displayed and reproduced economically by the most appropriate method.

Basic Principles in Reprography

In order to build up and maintain a reprographic system which is suitable for the needs of any organisation, certain basic questions must be answered. They may be mutually irreconcilable, so that a perfect system cannot be achieved, and a compromise must be arrived at. It is as well to embody the discussions that take place and the conclusions arrived at in a definitive report which can be referred to on future occasions. In reprographics there is always the chance that someone who needs a particular form of copying will be permitted to waste money on his pet equipment unless restrained by reference to an agreed procedure. Modifications to the system should only be allowed as a result of a full reappraisal which takes account of changed needs within the firm.

The questions to be answered are as follows:

(*a*) What types of communication material need to be circulated in this organisation?

(*b*) What is the range of quality desirable? Some copies may need to be of good quality because they are to be circulated to important business contacts, customers, etc. Others may be perfectly adequate if they are on poor-quality paper.

(*c*) To what extent is speed a factor in our reprographic needs? For example, a lecturer who decides he needs 30 copies of a wiring diagram for a lecture in 15 minutes' time cannot wait while a cumbersome bureaucratic process is followed. Of course it can be argued that everyone who needs copying or duplicating should be expected to think ahead so that the bureaucratic process devised is not an encumbrance. This argument overlooks the point that if man's genius in the reprographics field is such that instantaneous copies are possible, why not make the service available? To do so will improve the lecturer's lessons; to fail to do so is a waste of the talents of the reprographic design engineer.

(*d*) What is the range of print runs envisaged? Some reprographic systems are only economic if runs are fairly long. If we want chiefly to do one-off copies it is essential to pick a system that is economic in this respect.

(*e*) To what extent is accessibility a requirement? Some machines can be worked by anyone who can press a button, so that any member of staff can run off his own copies provided he has access. Other systems require either a specialist operator, or a typed master, or perhaps both.

(*f*) To what extent is colour a requirement? Colour can often be helpful; it may sometimes be positively advantageous. For other purposes it may be unnecessary, and it certainly restricts the choice of a reprographic system if colour is important.

(*g*) To what extent is it worthwhile preserving the master document?

(*h*) Is interchangeability of masters desirable; in other words, should we produce and preserve a master which can then be used to make a master for an alternative system? Proposals to be put before a small committee may later be submitted to a whole conference, and the documents run off on some cheaper long-run system.

(*i*) Finally, we need to know the characteristics of each system of reprographics; the advantages and disadvantages and the costs involved.

Answering the questions listed above enables us to match the reprographic needs of the firm with the systems required to satisfy them. It is a question of deciding the best buy, but some overlapping is inevitable and indeed a variety of back-up facilities may be positively desirable. More than one firm faced with power cuts which have immobilised its machinery has turned in times of energy crisis to hand-operated machines.

Systems of Copying and Duplicating

The term 'reprography' covers all aspects of copying and duplicating, which has been a business preoccupation for over a century. There are many systems in use and developments are made each year. It is impossible to cover all aspects, and a full coverage of basic techniques is given in the companion volume *Office Practice Made Simple*. A comparative chart from that book is reproduced in Fig. 11.1 to assist those readers who do not have the elementary book.

The field of copying and duplicating may be described under nine main headings. These are:

(*a*) Simultaneous copying, using carbon paper or some other method
(*b*) Stencil duplicating
(*c*) Spirit duplicating
(*d*) Photocopying
(*e*) Heat transfer copying
(*f*) Dual spectrum copying
(*g*) Dyeline copying
(*h*) Electrostatic copying and duplicating (plain-paper copying)
(*i*) Offset litho duplicating

In general, the term 'copying' refers to the production of a single copy, or a small number of copies, while the term 'duplicating' refers to the production of a large number of copies.

Simultaneous Copying

Most of these methods of copying are so much a part of our everyday lives that little description is required. They depend upon the immediate production of the required number of copies, as when the typist assembles her package of letterhead, carbons and flimsies. For repetitive activities like invoices and export documentation the package is often already made up with 'snap-apart' sets of documents interleaved with the required number of sheets of one-off carbon. These may be snapped apart when required in a single action to leave the set of completed documents free for distribution. Some sets are made up in 'continuous stationery' form, with special devices to permit the insertion of carbons, and to remove them before the completed documents are torn from the pack. Other sets are made up with appropriate patches of one-off carbon spotted on to the back of the document where it is desired that transfer to the copy below should occur. This is an economical use of copying material, and also permits the preparation of some documents with information on them which others in the pack do not have. For example, in an invoice pack the advice note will clearly need the details of the goods supplied, whereas the delivery note will not. The van driver may be tempted to pilfer the goods if he knows they are desirable, or his documents may be seen by undesirable characters in roadside cafés. By leaving out the carbon at this point on the back of the document above the delivery note the delivery note will not say what goods are being carried.

A major development in the simultaneous copy field was the development of NCR paper (no carbon required). The essential feature of this process is the coating of the document in encapsulated chemical droplets. When these droplets are broken by the pressure of a pen or the typewriter keys, the chemicals are released and mix with those of the page opposite to become visible, reproducing the shape of the writing impressed on the original. A variety of systems has been developed in the years since NCR paper originally appeared, and a variety of prepared documents is now available in this type of snap-apart set.

Stencil Duplicating

The original stencil duplicating was developed by David Gestetner in the last century. The essential feature of stencil duplicating is that the stencil is pierced through with the lettering, etc., which is required to be reproduced and ink is then forced through these holes to reproduce the copies. Improvements in stencil manufacture have adapted the system so that David Gestetner's original toothed wheel is no longer essential, though it may still be used. The keys of the typewriter will cut a modern stencil easily. Electronic stencil cutting, which uses an electric eye to scan a pasted-up master copy and reproduce dark spots on the master as holes in the stencil, means that virtually any illustration or text can be reproduced. This gives the system great versatility. Stencil manufacturers will even supply stencils pre-cut with a company letterhead, which is useful if duplicating matter has to be sent out on letterheading. The ordinary stencil comprises the perforated heading (which is used to secure the stencil to the duplicator when copies are run off), the stencil and backing sheet. This pack is inserted into the typewriter and typed normally with the typewriter keys set at the 'Stencil' position. Errors are corrected with a special correcting fluid which is painted on to the wrongly typed character or word and the correct text is typed over the dried fluid. It is always worthwhile checking a stencil carefully, to ensure that it is absolutely correct and contains all the required information. It is laborious to correct thousands of copies which were printed too hastily.

Stencils are run off on hand or electric rotary duplicators. Such a duplicator has a drum covered with a soft cloth, and as this rotates the cloth becomes evenly saturated with ink which has been inserted inside the drum. The stencil is fastened round this drum by means of the perforated heading, and the ink is squeezed through the typed matter on to the special absorbent duplicating paper which is fed into the machine. More then 6,000 good copies can be printed from one stencil. The stencils can be removed from the duplicator, stored and used again as required. It pays to keep them hanging in a stencil storage cabinet, specially fitted for this purpose.

The chief problem with stencil duplication is that a stencil has to be cut one way or the other. Electronic stencil cutting is efficient, and special heat-sensitive stencils can be cut in a heat transfer machine (see below). There are, however, many situations where the stencil must be typed; a really fast accurate typist is invaluable in a reprographics department, and renders the ink-stencil duplicator a 'best buy' for any office. Illustrations of typical machines appear in *Office Practice Made Simple*.

Spirit Duplicating

Spirit duplicating systems are very efficient indeed, and where a large number of very cheap copies is called for they can hardly be bettered. For example, in the classroom they permit copies to be produced at little more than the cost of the paper, and the masters can be filed away and used again and again up to their life limit of about 300 copies. In the hands of inexperienced staff they can be messy, and the operator needs to be fully briefed about the machine and to have it serviced regularly. The smallest machines are so cheap that it would pay any teacher, for example, to buy her own machine and keep it for her own personal use. The small charge for regular servicing is well repaid by the trouble-free operation that results, while the filed masters which accumulate as the years go by permit well-organised lessons at the drop of a hat on every subject in the syllabus.

By contrast, at the other end of the price range, spirit duplicators can be extremely sophisticated, with **automatic line selection** features which permit the preparation of such items as job cards for production departments.

Masters are easily prepared by hand, or in the typewriter. The special master paper has china clay incorporated in the reverse side to give a smooth brilliant-white surface. When struck by the typewriter keys this reverse side picks up a reverse image of the words typed in thick hectograph carbon, from a hecto master sheet placed behind it. Errors are corrected by scraping off the incorrect letter or word from the master with a special blade; a small piece of new carbon is inserted behind it and the correct letter retyped (the carbon sheet can only be used once). When the master is prepared it is fixed to the drum of the spirit duplicator and the text is transferred to the paper by special spirit instead of ink as with stencil duplicating. The copy paper must be dampened with spirit before it is in contact with the master, and thus dissolves the dye. When the cylinder is rotated the copy paper becomes moist. This spirit dries almost immediately so that the final copy is dry. A range of seven colours is available, all of which can be used on the same master, so that this system is most appropriate for duplicating such items as wiring diagrams where colour coding is helpful.

Illustrations of typical spirit duplicators may be found in the companion volume, *Office Practice Made Simple*.

Photocopying, Heat Transfer, Dual Spectrum and Dyeline Copying

All these systems are similar in that they will copy an original exactly as it appears provided the conditions for their particular operation are fulfilled. **Photocopying** is a photographic process which depends upon the use of lighting to make the copy. Inevitably the copy that results is wet, or at least damp, and this feature led to a demand for dry copiers.

Heat transfer copying works on the infra-red band of waves which produce heat, and is only sensitive to inks which have a carbon content. It will not 'see' vegetable dyes such as are used in ordinary ballpoint pens. This can be a great inconvenience in these days when ballpoint pens are ubiquitous. A typed document that has been corrected with a ballpoint pen cannot be copied with its alterations in a heat transfer machine, unless the ballpoint pen is one of the special 'photographic' pens which are filled with ink which has a carbon base.

The **dual spectrum machine** operates in both the light spectrum and the infra-red heat spectrum to overcome the difficulty of the heat transfer machine. Its negative copy is exposed to light from the original which is to be copied, and 'sees' what is on it whether it is in carbon or vegetable dye. The negative is then processed through the heat unit with a positive paper which becomes the dry copy.

Dyeline or **diazo copying** uses the ultra-violet spectrum. It is a very early system which is widely used. The translucent master allows ultra-violet light to pass through it except where print or other material obstructs the light. The diazo paper is coated with diazo salts which are bleached by the ultra-violet light and only the unbleached material where the light was obstructed is developed by the developer, to give a perfect copy.

Illustrations of all these machines are given in *Office Practice Made Simple*, and some of them are to be found in most offices. They are convenient for copying, but as each copy has to be dealt with individually they are too time-consuming and costly where a number of copies is required.

Electrostatic Copying and Duplicating

It is generally acknowledged that dry copies are eminently desirable; that the copying machine should be able to 'see' everything on the original and not be selective; that individual handling to produce multiple copies is tedious and time-wasting; that instant access is advantageous; that unskilled push-button operation is helpful and that long runs must work out cheaper per copy than short runs. Electrostatic copying on the most sophisticated machines is the answer to everyone's copying and duplicating problems. Whether one copy is required or 500, the machine will supply them at the press of a button. The original electrostatic copier was marketed by Xerox, and took its name from the Greek word for 'dry'. Xerography is the art of giving dry copies, and the name Xerox has become synonymous with dry-copying. However, the name is of course a trade mark, and other manufacturers of similar machines now use the term 'plain paper' copiers. Others use coated papers in a semi-dry electrostatic process.

A sophisticated Xerox machine is ideal for single copies and for long runs. It produces dry, clear copies at a speed of one every half second; it can be used in connection with a collator which will assemble successive documents ready for stapling or binding and it is completely foolproof provided certain basic activities like the insertion of paper supplies are understood. It will cope with any weight of paper, even if it is mixed in the pack of paper. It will feed in up to 50 originals one at a time, printing as many as are required of each, and without interrupting the flow. It will reduce the size of an original in any one of three specified reduction ratios.

Of course, like all sophisticated products it does break down, and consequently is usually best leased from the manufacturer, with a built-in service contract. The more essential the machine the greater the loss when it is out of action, and this type of machine can become a vital tool in many firms. For this reason a good technician on call is essential.

Staff have to be trained to get the best use out of such a machine. A rather inexperienced member of staff who is trying to decide exactly what she wants to copy and is holding up five or six people who want one second each on the machine and can then get away about their business must be discouraged

Aspects considered	Carbon Copies	No Carbon Required (NCR)	Dyeline Copying	Ink Stencil Duplication	Spirit Duplication	Dual-transfer Photocopying	Offset-litho duplicating	Electrostatic and plain-paper copiers
1 Materials required by the process.	Carbon paper. Flimsy copy paper.	Prepared sets of specially coated documents.	Paper coated with diazo salts and sensitive to ultraviolet light. Translucent originals.	Stencils with wax or plastic surface. Absorbent run-off paper. Black or coloured inks.	Spirit master paper. Hecto carbon paper. Run-off paper. Spirit.	Intermediate paper. Copy paper.	Greasy ink. Water. Paper, metal or photographic plates.	Run-off paper. Ink powder or toner.
2 Quantity produced.	Up to 4 copies. Up to 20 with electric typewriter.	Up to 4 copies.	Any number—but cheapest from 1-15 copies.	Thousands if necessary. It is economical over 20 copies.	Up to 300 copies. Less for some colours.	Single copies or runs of up to 25 on automatic models.	Paper plates up to 2000 copies. Very long runs on metal and photographic plates.	Very long runs possible.
3 How operated.	Typewritten or handwritten.	Typewritten or handwritten.	Electrically operated.	Hand or electrical models available.	Hand or electrical models available.	Electrically operated.	Electrically operated.	Electrically operated.
4 Suitable for reproducing								
(a) Black typewritten.	(a) Yes	(a) Yes	(a) Yes	(a) Yes	(a) Yes	(a) Yes	(a) Yes	(a) Yes
(b) Coloured typewritten.	(b) —	(b) —	(b) Yes	(b) Yes	(b) Yes	(b) —	(b) Yes	(b) —
(c) Handwritten.	(c) Yes	(c) Yes	(c) Yes	(c) Yes—but less satisfactory.	(c) Yes	(c) Yes	(c) —	(c) Yes
(d) Drawing.	(d) Yes	(d) —	(d) Yes	(d) Yes	(d) Yes	(d) Yes	(d) Yes	(d) Yes
(e) From photographs.	(e) —	(e) —	(e) —	(e) Yes	(e) —	(e) Yes	(e) Yes	(e) Yes
(f) On both sides of paper.	(f) —	(f) —	(f) —	(f) Yes	(f) If thicker run-off paper used.	(f) —	(f) Yes	(f) Yes but not all machines on the market.
5 Applications:								
(a) Small circulations.	(a) Yes	(a) Yes	(a) Yes	(a) —	(a) —	(a) Yes	(a) —	(a) Yes
(b) Medium circulations.	(b) Yes	(b) —	(b) —	(b) Yes	(b) Yes	(b) Yes	(b) Yes	(b) Yes
(c) Large circulations.	(c) —	(c) —	(c) —	(c) Yes	(c) Up to 300.	(c) —	(c) Yes	(c) Yes
(d) Documentation.	(d) Yes	(d) Yes	(d) Yes	(d) —	(d) Yes	(d) —	(d) Yes	(d) Yes
(e) Reports.	(e) Yes	(e) Yes	(e) Yes	(e) Yes	(e) Yes	(e) —	(e) Yes	(e) Yes
(f) Advertising.	(f) —	(f) —	(f) —	(f) Yes	(f) Yes	(f) —	(f) Yes	(f) Yes
(g) Educational.	(g) —	(g) School reports.	(g) —	(g) Yes	(g) Yes	(g) Makes transparencies.	(g) Yes	(g) Yes

(b) Costs per copy.	needed. (b) Low.	(b) Fairly low.	great. (b) Cheap ½p.	great. (b) Falls to cost of run-off paper only, therefore cheap.	great. (b) Falls to cost of run-off paper only, therefore cheap.	great. (b) Every copy costs the same, i.e. expensive for long runs.	expensive. (b) Costs per copy fall almost to cost of run-off paper, therefore cheap.	expensive to hire. (b) Usage meter—cheaper for long runs.
7 Maintenance requirements.	None.	None.	Regular servicing advisable. Some machines need venting.	Regular servicing advisable (reasonable charges).	Regular servicing advisable (reasonable charges).	Occasional servicing advisable.	Regular servicing advisable.	Sophisticated machinery must be maintained regularly—but service free to hirers.
8 Advantages.	I. Simultaneous copies. II. Cheap. III. No special skill needed.	I. Simultaneous copies. II. No carbon required. III. No skill required—public can use them easily.	I. Instant copies. II. Cheap for low runs. III. Good copy quality. IV. Adaptable for certain work. V. Only 1 original prepared. Easy to correct. VI. Economical of labour in business systems work (i.e. monthly statements).	I. Cheap. II. Simple. All typists can cut skins. III. Writing and drawing can be added to typed stencils. IV. Electronic stencil cutting very effective. V. Very long runs possible. VI. Colour possible. VII. Simple storage. VIII. Heat master very quick.	I. Cheap. II. Simple. III. Colour very effective. IV. Drawing simple. V. Storage simple for masters. VI. Ideal for aligned documentation.	I. Copies all colours. II. No skills required. III. Dry copies. IV. Makes overhead projector transparencies. V. No errors.	I. Very long runs. II. Cheap copies. III. Wide variety of uses. IV. Very high-quality work possible.	I. Very quick II. Very simple to operate. III. Facsimile copies. IV. Overlays available for aligned documentation.
9 Disadvantages.	I. Not easy to correct. II. Only a few copies possible. III. Carbons do dry out in long-term storage. IV. Quality of copies falls away.	I. More expensive than ordinary forms. II. Every copy costs the same. III. Cannot be altered. IV. Can be spoiled easily and wasted.	I. Fairly expensive machine. II. Every copy costs the same. III. Ammonia machines need a vent to atmosphere.	I. A little bit messy with cheaper model machines. II. Uneconomic below 10 copies.	I. No good for very long runs. II. Masters can be spoiled by inexperienced operator. IV. Fluid inflammable, needs careful storage.	I. Too expensive for very long runs. II. Individual hand feeding on cheaper machines.	I. Not convenient or cheap for small runs.	I. Expensive. II. Skilled servicing required.

Fig. 11.1. A comparison chart for reprographic methods.

from dithering in public. She must step aside and let the machine be used, if its leasing charge is to be recovered in raised efficiency.

One particularly clever adaptation of Xerography is the Rank Xerox **Automatic Overlay Device.** Executive secretaries working in export departments should draw the attention of their departmental heads to this system, which can prepare five ranges of export documents automatically on ordinary plain paper. The process is controlled from a pegboard panel in the Xerox copier which controls an overlay web to position the framework of the required form over the copy paper. Only those parts of a master copy which actually need to appear on a particular form are reproduced. Instead of having stocks of invoices, bills of lading, consignment notes, etc., the documents are prepared as required in only one second, from the same pack of plain copy paper. The saving in inventory costs is obvious, and the machine cannot make any copying errors from one form to another as often happens when forms are typed manually.

Other Plain-paper Copiers

Since the original dry copiers were invented developments from the xerographic process using the electrostatic system now use a liquid toner instead of dry powder. The result is that the copies are slightly damp, but dry very quickly, and the image does not need to be fused by heat onto the paper. There is consequently no warm-up period for the machine, and the technical problems associated with the presence of dry, fine powder are eliminated. Plate 10 shows a Nashua Copycat machine of this type, which produces excellent, fast copies from a compact machine which has no bulky heaters, and stands on an ordinary desk or table.

The explosion in plain paper copying recently demonstrates that industry is prepared to pay for the convenience it gives in copying and duplicating. Some of the newer firms are selling machines rather than leasing them, but it is still true to say that adequate servicing in breakdowns is a major requirement. The firm leasing a machine to a customer has a built-in reason for sending round the mechanic when anything goes wrong. A full explanation of how electrostatic copiers work is given in *Office Practice Made Simple*.

Offset Litho Duplicating

Offset litho copying is a system of reprographics based upon lithography, which uses the principle that oil and water do not mix. A greasy ink image is offset on to a rubber blanket and then offset again on to the copy paper. The first offset on to the rubber blanket gives a reverse image, which is then offset on to the copy to give a correct image. The result is a highly efficient duplicating process which gives clear copies and very cheap long runs. Masters can be prepared very easily with an electrostatic platemaker, and the machines accept a wide range of papers.

The system is excellent where matter has to be distributed looking immaculate. Ordinary typed reports appear to have been printed, and a letter which has to be circulated to many people also looks as though it has been printed and not just photocopied or duplicated. This gives a very professional look to circulated matter. Any erasures to the orginal master do not show on the copies.

Collators

A collator is a device which puts sheets together in correct sequence so that they are ready to be stapled or bound. It is a tedious business laying out pages of a report so that they can be checked and bound before distribution. Most duplicator systems have a collation accessory which eases the work considerably, and leaves each set of pages conveniently accessible for stapling or binding in the types of equipment illustrated in Plate 4.

Conclusion about Reprography

The chart reproduced in Fig. 11.1 from *Office Practice Made Simple* includes a detailed comparison of most of the reprographic systems available today.

A useful booklet mentioned in the Suggested Further Reading, the *Guide through the Copying Maze*, gives some impression of the relative costs of the various methods and the advantages and disadvantages of each.

Summary

1. Copying and duplicating is an important aspect of the executive secretary's work, although her rôle will normally be supervisory. Adequate reprographic facilities are essential to modern large-scale organisations.

2. An adequate system of reprographics should be provided as a result of a detailed appraisal of the needs of the office concerned; not by the haphazard accumulation of devices purchased to meet the whim of favoured executives. A list of basic questions which should be asked in the course of such an appraisal may be found in this chapter.

3. The chief systems of copying are carbon copying, NCR copying, photocopying, heat transfer, dual spectrum copying and dyeline copying.

4. The chief methods of duplicating are ink stencil duplicating, spirit duplicating and offset litho duplicating. Electrostatic copiers are also able to achieve long production runs at very great speed, and therefore serve a dual purpose. Full details of these copying and duplicating systems are given in the companion volume, *Office Practice Made Simple*.

Suggested Further Reading

Business Equipment Digest, BED Business Journals Ltd, monthly.
Business Systems and Equipment, Maclean Hunter, monthly.
Export Documentation, Rank Xerox, current A.O.D. brochures.
Guide Through the Copying Maze, A. E. Phillips, SCM United Kingdom, 1976.
Office Practice Made Simple, G. M. Whitehead, Heinemann, most recent edition.

EXECUTIVE SECRETARIAL DUTIES—DIARIES, APPOINTMENTS AND RECEPTION DUTIES

The Efficient Secretary

The modern tendency is for the executive secretary to play an increasingly important part as a member of the management team. She is a communications centre for the effective coordination of her department's work and its inter-relation with the work of the rest of the organisation. She sets free her executive by assuming many routine duties, but still remains the hub of the department, around which everything else revolves. The routine work is a subordinate activity performed incidentally while she mans her post. This is not a life of dull routine, but one where enormous job-satisfaction can be achieved, with great possibilities for self-development and advancement.

The opportunities offered the executive secretary, in the new climate of management require her to organise her time effectively so that she is able to assume the many burdens thrust upon her. She may need to delegate these to subordinates, so that she may find herself controlling a small staff of secretaries and clerical assistants. However she operates she is bound to plan her own activities and those of others within the limitations and constraints imposed by the executive's needs. Other constraints may be imposed by the general framework of the organisation which employs her, the programme it is pursuing and the deadlines laid down. These constraints will also be varied by developments that arise as a result of outside influences, so that the best-laid schemes of the secretary may yet 'gang aft agley'.

In the context of business efficiency the secretary's ability to control her executive's diary is of primary importance. She must supervise his appointments and assist them to proceed speedily to a fruitful conclusion by ensuring that he is supplied with everything he needs to make sound decisions. The other activities of the day must be fitted in around the appointments so that each day's programme will be planned to allow the time necessary to receive visitors, settle them down before the appointment, pick up the threads of other work while the interview proceeds and generally fit the many tasks of the day into the time available. It is most important not to over-organise the executive. His secretary should liaise with him to find out his policy regarding appointments: does he want to see everyone who wants to see him, or does he prefer to choose who sees him personally, perhaps requesting other senior staff to take over some appointments? The secretary who fills her boss's diary with appointments, thus precluding him from getting on with his other work, will not be popular.

Diaries

A secretary invariably has three diaries to contend with; her own, the executive's desk diary and his pocket diary in which the wretched man is sure to make appointments without consulting her. Some tactful arrangement must be made to ensure that he coordinates the arrangements he has made personally with the arrangements she has made on his behalf. The executive will usually have a desk diary, perhaps a prestigious one like the *Economist* diary; and his pocket diary will be similarly a purchased product. Diaries can be purchased already printed relevant to a company's business; for example, there are special Lloyd's diaries for insurance personnel, and education diaries

DATE	SPECIAL EVENTS (if any)			
	MR. ARBUTHNOT			SELF
TIME	Visitor's Name	Place	Purpose	Notes
9.00				
9.15				
9.30				
9.45				
10.00				
10.15				
10.30				
10.45				
11.00				
11.15				
11.30				
11.45				
12.00				
12.15				
12.30				
12.45				
LUNCH				
2.00				
2.15				
2.30				
2.45				
3.00				
3.15				
3.30				
3.45				
4.00				
4.15				
4.30				
4.45				
EVENING APPOINTMENTS				

Fig. 12.1. A 'daily diary' ruling.

for schools and colleges, which are printed to embrace scholastic sessions from September to August rather than January to December. These specialised diaries contain many useful facts and figures and the secretary may find them extremely useful.

The secretary may find it more convenient to use a 'home-made' product consisting of a ring binder with a distinctive cover in which she has inserted prepared sheets which have been run off in the reprographics section. Such a diary can be ruled to give more pertinent information than an ordinary desk diary, and may be prepared in advance on a monthly or quarterly basis. Fig. 12.1 illustrates a typical ruling but is freely adaptable to meet the secretary's personal needs. Once a basic design has been decided on and drawn up, copies can be taken and dates inserted. Such a diary rolls forward endlessly. A few blank pages at the back can be used to start up the necessary page if someone wishes to make an appointment months ahead, and this page will then get fitted into the system as the weeks roll by. Obsolete pages can be filed away until needed to recall details of an earlier engagement, etc.

The advantages of such a ruling are that it gives a panoramic view of the day, which is easily completed when arrangements are made, and pinpoints events and the reason for the arrangement. If single-sided pages are used the reverse side of the previous page is a blank sheet facing the daily diary on which other details can be noted down. This may include detailed arrangements to be made, or routine chores to be performed on that particular day.

Rules for keeping a diary include:

(a) Write clearly, and ensure that all essential information is recorded. This is particularly important as regards forward appointments. It is no good making an appointment for, say, five weeks' time and just inserting a name in the diary. By the time the appointment comes round, no one can remember the visitor's status or his reason for requesting the interview.

(b) Print names of visitors, and always obtain first names or initials in case letters have to be written.

(c) Take telephone numbers wherever possible in case arrangements have to be changed.

(d) It is not unknown for hoax callers to make appointments for important people just to be a nuisance. If in doubt ring back and ask for the details of the appointment to be confirmed.

(e) Where the appointment is a social or business function note the exact time, i.e. 19.30 for 20.00 hrs, and details of dress to be worn. Keep a file for such functions and file invitation cards, agenda, etc., in date order. If the social functions involve the executive's wife it is essential to liaise with her fully over the arrangements. If she is herself an executive it is better to liaise with her secretary or personal assistant.

(f) Enter all relevant information as soon as you get to hear about it. If the boss has to go to Birmingham on the 20th you will need to keep other appointments clear of that date, and if you fail to enter the appointment and start booking in people there will be a lot of rearrangements to make. The space for Special Events in Fig. 12.1 enables you to pinpoint such events.

(g) In booking arrangements the general pattern of the day's work has to be borne in mind. Avoid appointments early in the day if you usually take dictation at that time. Leave short periods where you can, so that your executive can read letters and sign them in time to catch the internal postal collections. Try to follow an important appointment with less important ones, so that if the VIP interview exceeds its allotted time those waiting will appreciate the situation. If an important executive insists on being booked in at an awkward time at least warn him that he may be delayed. He probably has some important reading to do and will bring it with him.

(*h*) Often appointments are made for meetings in other buildings such as annexes. Many an executive has had his driving licence endorsed for speeding whilst trying to reach impossible destinations in the time limit set for him by his secretary. It is not enough to allow the travelling time between the two places. A previous interview may run over by a few minutes and he is immediately under pressure. It is better to allow at least double the time. Then he has time to get there safely, read his notes and relax for a few minutes. It is also advisable to warn the previous interviewee that a time limit has to be adhered to because of the executive's busy programme. The long-winded visitor will then know that if he drags out the interview he will find you very uncooperative next time he wants to get in for a quick word with your boss.

(*i*) When appointments are made by telephone the secretary should always confirm them the same day in writing, repeating the entry in her diary. If two copies are made of this letter one can be entered in the file of appointments for action on the day arranged. The other can be used to advise the executive so that he knows what has been arranged and can consider whether any preliminary activity needs to take place. This could be part of the discussion next day when the secretary takes dictation, and any work necessary can be undertaken in good time. A smooth daily timetable is only possible if the preliminary work is done well in advance. A secretary who is constantly put under pressure by the procrastination of her executive must get him to see how unfair and unnecessary this is.

(*j*) Finally, at convenient times in the day the secretary should compare her own diary with that of her executive and bring both up to date. A daily check on the executive to discover whether he has made any entries in his pocket diary is also advisable.

'Busy Person' Indexes

Many firms produce 'Strip Index' systems which can be adapted to many uses. One of the best uses of this type of strip index is the 'busy person' index which can be of service to both the executive and his secretary.

The essential of a strip index system is a band of strips which can be fed into a typewriter or even into a data-processing system so that items to be remembered can be typed on to a strip. Each strip can then be separated, and fixed in its correct alphabetical position by means of the little tabs built into its shape. These clip around the strips in the 'busy person' folder. The Kalamazoo model illustrated is an Executive Reminder Index, which is marketed in two sizes, one with four pages and the other with six. It is small enough to be carried around in a briefcase, and can be divided into sections such as weekly, monthly and quarterly lists for jobs to be done at regular intervals. A 'personal' page reminds him about birthdays and similar occasions, while the other pages may be reserved for major events, like the annual conference of sales executives. Jobs to be performed at intervals can be ticked up as they are executed.

The secretary can keep her own copy of the Executive Index by simply typing two strips each time there is an addition to the Index, and can check it at regular intervals. If items to be attended to are worked into the ordinary diary as they become due according to the index, time can be allocated to perform the work and the occasion should never arise when the executive is caught napping.

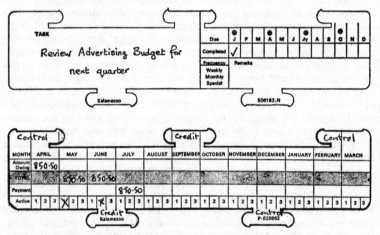

Fig. 12.2. Strips from an executive reminder index.

(Courtesy of Kalamazoo Ltd)

Follow-up Systems

Similar reminder indexes in book form can be used as part of a general follow-up system. This consists of an index having 31 pages for the days of the month, and 12 pages for the months of the year. An item to be followed up or received on a particular day of the month can be recorded on a strip and filed on the page allocated to that day. Items to be reviewed at rarer intervals are filed in the monthly section. As each month comes round the strips filed in that monthly section are removed and allocated to appropriate days in the daily section. If there is no particular date allotted to the activity it will be fitted in to keep the work load as even as possible throughout the month. The whole system is easy to operate, and a quick glance at the next day's list ensures that time is allotted to every task. Once a task has been performed the strip is removed and re-inserted in the index at the appropriate time for the next review. It will then become 'live' again in due course.

Such systems are adaptable to such needs as the follow-up of overdue accounts. One of the strips in Fig. 12.2 is ruled with monthly columns and indicates each month which of three letters is to be sent to the debtor. Letter No. 1 requests payment. Letter No. 2 threatens to cut off supplies if payment is not received. Letter No. 3 notifies the debtor that further orders will not be honoured and that the debt has been passed to a debt collection agency. Kalamazoo claim that the greatest advantage of such a system is that the debtor knows that a proper follow-up system exists. Failure to pay in answer to such a request is never overlooked, and final action is swift and sure. Nearly always the debtor pays up to the supplier who has an adequate system, knowing that slow payers are not tolerated by this company. He will turn instead to take advantage of someone whose system is slipshod and unmethodical.

Year Planners and Visual Planners

There is a huge range of year planners on the market these days. Some are wall charts; others are desk charts; while most diaries include a 'Year at a Glance' feature too. Even the modern style of pocket diary, which is a piece of paper folded into twelve monthly sections, pulls out to give a complete view of the year, six months on one side and six months on the other. The advantage of the year planner of course is the long-range view it gives to the executive and his secretary. While the wall is an obvious place to put such charts, it has to be stated that constantly jumping up to write on walls is a nuisance, and ballpoint pens have to be held at an awkward angle. Spirit pens are better but use up more space. For this reason there is much to be said for a desk chart, which the secretary can keep up to date as notification of events arrives and deadlines for various matters approach. By suitable 'early mentions' she can remind her executive on the year planner that he has to make arrangements for events still some days or even weeks away.

Some institutions, such as schools, colleges and universities, have very complex planning requirements. To fit classes into rooms with lecturers who can teach the appropriate ranges of subjects can be a tiresome and difficult business. Similarly, in the production field machines and computers have to be kept busy with appropriate work loads. In both the industrial and commercial fields visual planning charts are available in great variety to meet all the secretary's needs. There are self-adhesive systems, magnetic systems and chart channel systems which display the vital facts in an 'at-a-glance' visual pattern. Although such systems require preparatory work in the preparation of labels and colour flashes, they repay this effort in their ability to save time at moments when quick adjustments have to be made to arrangements. Usually the preparatory work itself can become a time-filler activity which can be picked up at appropriate spare moments in the period before planning begins, and the actual planning sessions then proceed fairly rapidly with no tedious interruptions to write out the necessary labels.

A celebrated name in this field is Sasco Ltd, a name derived from their original product, self-adhesive signs. The range of Sasco products today is very great, and the Sasco planning catalogue, available from their Bromley offices, is well worth requesting at times when a review is being held of the adequacy of visual planning arrangements.

The Working Day

The executive secretary must plan her working day so as to fit in her many duties around the arrangements she has to make for the executive she serves. There will inevitably be heavy days and light days, reflecting perhaps the activities taking place, his presence in, or absence from, the office, etc. Certain times of the day are routine, and will follow largely the same pattern. Other periods will depend entirely upon the appointments made, the meetings arranged and the functions being held. Each day must be 'thought through' the day before, and certain important days must be anticipated weeks, or even months, before. A typical day might therefore have at least some of the following arrangements.

The Start of the Day

(*a*) Arrive punctually, or even before time.

(*b*) Unlock desk and files (except confidential files). Switch on any equipment, especially if there is a warming-up period. Check telephone and greet telephonist.

(*c*) Check executive's room for warmth, ventilation, lighting, etc. Prepare desk. Check that clock is right. Change desk calendar to current date, open diary to correct page, check that pens and pencils are in working order.

(*d*) Harmonise diaries, remembering to check when he comes in whether he has made any separate arrangements in his pocket diary which you should know about.

(*e*) Collect mail, open and sort. Re-route misdirected mail. Read the mail carefully and secure to it any enclosures, relevant previous correspondence or even the whole file. Analyse it appropriately in order of urgency, some for action, some for the pending tray, some to be read and digested, some to be dealt with by yourself.

(*f*) Review list of priorities for the day (prepared yesterday) and use the time interval until his arrival to consolidate any arrangements. Check waiting room, chat area and any other facilities for visitors which are part of your responsibility.

(*g*) When executive has gone through the mail give out such work as you can delegate to others, with instructions and time limits if necessary. Make a note of these on your pad and follow them up as the day proceeds. Deal with your own share of the work as expeditiously as possible bearing in mind the other matters to be attended to, such as the arrival of visitors or staff who have made appointments.

Receiving Visitors

Visitors must be received warmly, for first impressions are often the most enduring. It helps to circulate a daily list of expected visitors to any porters' lodges or reception areas so that the visitor can be greeted by name. Manifestly an office must be well organised if even the lowly porter knows that Mr A is due at 11 a.m. for an appointment with Mr Z. By contrast, a visitor may be completely put off by a grumbling receptionist who mutters that 'They never tell me anything'. For security reasons it may be desirable to have visitors conducted to the various offices, and it is certainly a courteous thing to do with important visitors. It may even be desirable to go down and collect them, particularly if the building is a vast one.

Visitors may have travelled some distance by train, or have driven a long way to reach your office. They may feel dishevelled and uncomfortable, or be weighted down with coats, umbrellas and a briefcase. They will therefore appreciate being relieved of such encumbrances and being given a chance to wash their hands and straighten their ties in a cloakroom before meeting the person with whom they have arranged an appointment. If time allows, a cup of coffee should be provided. An executive secretary who organises for herself one of the coffee percolators available today which makes proper coffee and keeps it hot indefinitely will certainly create a favourable impression and be remembered by all who visit her. If a waiting room is available or the interview is to take place in a 'chat area' where the visitor can wait until the executive is free, it is helpful to provide a selection of recent magazines. The *Economist* is a suitable periodical for businessmen, who will also usually be interested in past copies of the house magazine if your firm produces one. There is a wide selection of glossy magazines available for other visitors, and two or three recent copies should be provided.

So far as possible you should anticipate difficulties and forewarn the visitor of any alterations in the plans made. For example, if the visitor has to be kept waiting a word or two of explanation and an assurance that he is not forgotten will be appreciated. An important engagement following his own appointment may be disrupted if he overstays his allotted period. It is well to caution him on this point if he is quite clearly the less important of the two, and he will be prepared for a sudden termination of the discussion if necessary.

Part of the reception of a visitor includes some exchange of small conversation. Poise for such occasions can only be acquired by experience, but it is very helpful if the hostess takes a genuine interest in her visitor and listens with intelligence and interest. This does not take many minutes from the working day, and may indeed relax the daily round considerably. It is always interesting to hear about other firms or other parts of the country, and the visitor who engages in this type of conversation unwinds a little and will probably meet your executive to discuss the real subject matter of his visit in a friendly, conciliatory manner. A useful topic to raise at this point is his situation at the end of the interview. Has he a train to catch? Does he know the bus route he needs to reach the station? Is he familiar with the roads to bring him to the motorway?

Introducing People

Part of the reception of visitors involves introducing people to one another. The rules for this are very simple but it is easy to get muddled. Men are introduced to women, juniors are introduced to seniors and everyone is introduced to VIP's. To make an introduction say the name of the person to whom the other is being introduced first, and then say 'may I introduce Mr So and So'. Then say the name of the more important person for the benefit of the less important person. So we might have situations like

'Sir John, may I introduce Joan Beamish, our accounts supervisor—Sir John Percival.'

'Miss Jones, may I introduce Mr Ian Parsons, our sales manager—Brenda Jones.'

'Mr Smith, may I introduce Peter Dorling, who is applying for the "creative graphics" post—Mr John Smith.'

When an individual arrives to join a group, the chairman of the meeting will say:

'Oh. Here is Brenda Fortescue.' He then indicates the ladies in the group first, saying their names and official positions, and then the gentlemen. It is usual to say 'How do you do', to which the reply is 'How do you do'. If the group is standing and small it is usual to shake hands; with a large group a gesture of greeting and 'How do you do' is enough.

Before departure a visitor will usually say goodbye to the secretary who received him courteously. It is well to ensure that he has his coat, briefcase, etc., since nothing is more inconvenient than to have to send on items which have been overlooked. A quick check in the waiting room or 'chat area' may enable you to catch him before he departs.

Meetings

Every day brings some sort of meeting for most executives. The subject of meetings is dealt with fully in Chapter 14, but as a part of the working day meetings require the secretary to show her organising ability. An **agenda** will usually be circulated well in advance of a meeting and an executive who arrives without it clearly demonstrates his own incompetence. However, the secretary should always have to hand spare copies of agendae, minutes, etc., for those who do arrive without the relevant documents. Since the items on the agenda include **'Minutes of the previous meeting'** and **'Matters arising'** the executive should also have the minutes available and should have taken the trouble to go through them carefully. For example, if the minutes record that Mr A and his secretary will call a meeting of staff qualified in First Aid to discuss compliance with the Health and Safety at Work Act, someone is sure to ask whether the meeting was held and what decisions were made. If Mr A is prepared for this question and perhaps can table a report on the matter he will meet with general approval. If he has failed to take any action his competence may be called in question.

The secretary should open a file for each meeting and collect in it all the relevant documents. By keeping the file live in her 'follow-up' system she can raise during her secretarial sessions with the executive any matters that need attention. She can agree a date for, and make arrangements about the 'Health and Safety at Work' working party; she will attend and take notes, which she will then draft as a report and circulate after approval in its final agreed form. This is better than tabling the report at the meeting itself. The chairman will probably comment favourably on the efficiency shown.

At the start of the day the files relevant to any meetings taking place that day should be placed on the executive's desk, and the secretary should check that each contains its agenda, minutes, reports for tabling if appropriate, and any other essential documents.

Problem Situations

At almost any time difficulties may arise involving colleagues, business associates and visitors. They range from sudden death to temperamental outbursts from junior staff. The executive secretary will obviously play an important part in dealing with any such situation, and will handle it to the best of her ability with all the tact and personal charm available to her. It is in such situations that the secretary reaps the reward for integrity on previous occasions. If she has proved a staunch colleague and a considerate supervisor in the past she will find plenty of people to turn to for help with any problem that arises. She will perhaps be alerted to trouble before it actually occurs, so that she may assist her executive to circumvent it or at least prepare for it. If not, she will find those above her supporting and helping her in overcoming the difficulty, while those below her will labour mightily to remove any difficulties in her path. The goodwill and cooperation shown on such occasions can be very heartwarming. The professional approach shown by the secretary on countless occasions when others needed help, support or sound advice, and when she put their needs and the firm's needs ahead of her own personal inclinations, is repaid.

External Professional Commitments

It frequently happens that executives get involved in external activities of a professional or civic nature. Many senior executives are made magistrates, or appointed to QUANGOS (Quasi Autonomous National Government Organisations). They often take on posts of responsibility in the trade association of the industry concerned, or become councillors in local government. Most firms approve of such activities, and are even prepared on occasions to 'carry' staff who are busy with work of national or local importance.

A secretary must expect to cooperate with the executive in this type of work, which inevitably has to be fitted in with the rest of his programme so that appointments and meetings do not clash. Such work varies the daily round, enlarges one's circle of acquaintances, and brings social and leisure compensations for the work involved.

The Close of the Day

As the day draws to a close a further sequence of activities must be carried out. They may be listed as follows:

(a) Get the letters completed and signed. Check that all enclosures are correct. Indicate which class of mail they are and ensure that they catch the in-house collections. Remember to alert the post room for any last minute mail, and any very late mail should be posted personally or given to one of the staff to post if you control a small secretariat.

(b) Draw up a list of visitors for the next day and route through to porters' lodges or reception area.

(c) Draw up a typed list of appointments for the next day and put it on the executive's desk. Some bosses like to take this home to think about the forthcoming interviews or meetings. He may prefer to have the actual files to take home too.

(d) Where he has meetings elsewhere the next day, ensure that everything he needs is provided, including travel details if necessary, airline or railway tickets, maps or plans of the town to be visited, etc.

(e) Think through the next day's activities. Prepare any materials, papers, etc., required for the next day's events. Draw up, if necessary, routine orders for those helping with a particular function. If necessary call a quick meeting and go through the chief points.

(f) Check the pending file and move up anything that needs to be progressed next day into an 'action' tray.

(g) Tidy desk, lock files and leave, having ensured all is well for the next day's work.

Summary

1. As part of the management team the executive secretary operates within the constraints imposed by her executive's timetable, appointments and duties.

She relieves him of considerable routine burdens, but has to carry them out while at the same time keeping his programme on the move.

2. The executive's desk diary and the secretary's diary must be harmonised every day, and any private arrangements he makes coordinated as well. The secretary's diary should be kept meticulously, carefully written with full details of visitors, initials, firms they represent, etc. The diary should be filled in accordance with the pattern of the working day, so that dictation periods can be fitted in, etc.

3. 'Busy person' indexes and 'follow-up' indexes are useful aids in keeping track of duties which have to be performed at regular intervals. Year planners and visual planners give a panoramic view of the year's activities, or of the arrangements made in fitting staff into jobs, or salesmen into areas, or machine loading, etc.

4. The working day must be planned with a view to fitting in all the necessary activities within the constraints imposed by the executive's timetable and the general organisation. It is sure to include the reception of visitors and their introduction to people in the office. It will frequently involve one or two meetings. Problem situations will occasionally arise calling for tact and understanding. There will often be extra work involving support for the executive in external professional commitments.

Suggested Further Reading

The Senior Secretary, Rhona Brand, The Industrial Society, 1978.
The Aids to Efficiency devised by Kalamazoo Business Systems, Birmingham are always worth reviewing.
Sasco Planning Charts (brochures from their Bromley offices) are very helpful.

13

EXECUTIVE SECRETARIAL DUTIES—PUBLIC RELATIONS

The Public Relations Department

The Institute of Public Relations defines Public Relations as '*the deliberate, planned and sustained effort to establish and maintain mutual understanding between an organisation and its public*'. PR work requires a great diversity of skills and experience, so that a PR department usually consists of a team of executives and their secretaries, each member contributing his or her particular skills to the work of the department.

The Public Relations department of a firm exists to promote and preserve the image of its company or corporation. It fulfils a number of functions which may be listed as follows:

(*a*) Routine activities of a wide variety to maintain a firm's public image at an acceptable level.

(*b*) Consumer relations activities, which deal with complaints or suggestions from the public.

(*c*) Promotion activities which seek to draw attention to the firm's products or activities.

(*d*) Defensive activities which seek to anticipate adverse public criticism and advise other departments about possible public relations aspects of proposals they are making.

Dealing with these four aspects in turn, the following points are of interest.

Routine Public Relations Activities

Inevitably any large firm is of interest to the general public if only as a facet of the ordinary way of life of our citizens. Everyone is interested in products in common use, the way they are designed and manufactured, the organisation necessary to obtain raw materials, convert them to finished goods and market them around the world. Some of the greatest spectacles today can be seen on a visit to a steelworks, oil refinery, motor vehicle assembly plant, cement works, airport, container port, etc. Each such enterprise is as large as, and more complicated than, the organisation that was necessary to build the pyramids, for example. We must therefore expect to receive requests to visit such plants from school parties, college groups, women's guilds, old age pensioners' societies, etc. Such public relations activities become absolutely routine, and in some organisations are so well organised that specialised arrangements are available at all times without prior booking. Thus the London Stock Exchange has built into its new buildings a viewing hall overlooking the floor of the Exchange. Displays of the work of the Exchange and details of its history are given in display cabinets in the viewing hall, and there is a cinema which any member of the public may visit during prescribed times. The presentation of the work of the Exchange and its importance in the economic affairs of the nation may be studied by all who are interested, while the dealers making bargains on the floor of the House may be observed like busy ants hurrying about their business.

Many young secretaries cut their 'public relations' teeth in the organisation of such events, and it can be very pleasant work for those who enjoy this kind of activity. The essentials of a smooth organisation may be listed as follows:

(*a*) When the original arrangements are made it is helpful to the group organiser if some sort of preliminary handout is sent to him, in sufficient numbers for each member of the group. This gives him an opportunity to explain what the firm is, what it produces, why a visit is worthwhile, etc.

(*b*) Warn Reception that a party is expected and let them know whom to contact when it arrives. If the time has arrived and the party is late, go down to Reception to receive the visitors anyway so as to save time and keep on schedule.

(*c*) Think about the security aspects—coats, hats, handbags, etc. A lockable room is advisable for those who wish to deposit such articles. If security equipment—a crash helmet perhaps—is obligatory in the works, see that supplies are available and instruct the group appropriately. If matches, lighters, etc., have to be handed over ensure that this is done.

(*d*) The great defect of all such visits is the inadequacy of many of the people detailed to show groups round. They often finish up talking to one or two people only. The rest finish up unable to hear or understand what is going on, and may become bored. It is often best to give a fairly detailed briefing in a pleasant lecture room, with well-chosen diagrams of the plant layout and a brief explanation of the functions of each section of the plant. Then when the actual tour begins, the guides should be equipped with a portable public address system which enables all to hear the more limited description that is offered as each part of the plant is reached.

(*e*) The tour should terminate at some reasonable place of refreshment, where the acoustics are not too awful. These days acoustic panels are very cheap and even the works canteen can be rendered acoustically perfect at very small cost. If management realised what benefits are achieved by installing such panelling (more relaxed industrial relations, for example), they would make more effort to improve working conditions in this way. Secretaries forced to try to entertain large groups in acoustic madhouses should exert strong pressure to change the arrangements.

(*f*) At the end of the tour a souvenir, perhaps in the form of a booklet about the plant and its activities, ensures that the members of the group will take away a durable reminder of their visit, and will perhaps turn to using the firm's products or feel favourably inclined towards its activities.

Consumer Relations Activities

Today consumer relations are of enormous importance. Not only is the general competitive atmosphere intense in many large industries, but the legislative atmosphere has changed entirely to favour the consumer. Large firms are deemed to be so powerful that successive governments have passed legislation to protect the consumer on many aspects, such as prices, quality, contractual terms of trade, rates of interest on hire purchase, trade descriptions, etc. It is essential for firms to be careful in the public statements they make about their products, the clauses they insert into their conditions of sale, and their reactions to criticism.

Generally speaking, it is desirable to reply at once to consumer criticisms and suggestions, but with a placatory letter only which promises a full examination of the problem. To reply at once, in a final way, rejecting the criticism or rebutting the allegation may only add fuel to the fire. Consumers know that any large firm has some sort of bureaucratic method of dealing with such matters and a too-rapid final response suggests a total failure to put the bureaucratic process into gear. Such initial responses can be in a standard form, sent off by the public relations department at very little cost, and keep the whole complaint 'pending' while comments are called for from appropriate departments.

On the positive side, consumer relations gives a feedback to production department and design department about a firm's products. Consumer complaints may reveal poor work on the part of established agents handling our products, or may suggest that improvements in warehousing are required. Instructions to retailers may need to be amended in the light of complaints received. More spectacularly, we have all noticed such matters as the calling-in of all vehicles sold to effect modifications in a particular component, etc. For all these reasons the public relations department must ensure that complaints are adequately dealt with, and must expose to top management any tendency by design staff or other personnel to dismiss serious criticisms of the product or the service being supplied. A secretary should keep such complaints 'live' with her executive, so that he takes the necessary action within a reasonable time, and a regular check through the 'pending' file to 'action' any complaints subject to unreasonable delay is very desirable. In this connection telephone enquiries are frequently made about the progress of complaints. It is important that each complaint should be easily traceable so that the consumer is convinced of the sincerity of the complaints department's interest in the matter. A 'pending' item which has been the subject of a telephone enquiry should be 'actioned' next day when the secretary sees her executive at the daily dictation section, to see if it can be finalised. A further placatory letter explaining the difficulty may be desirable if the complaint still cannot be finalised.

Promotional Activities

Certain aspects of the public relations department's work may be described as promotional activities, in that they support functions which are held to draw the attention of the trade, customers generally or even the entire public, to the firm's products. Such events will usually require a good deal of cooperation with the sales department, or perhaps the export department. Many of the activities are similar to those described later (Chapter 15) about the organising of conferences and social functions.

A list of events coming under this general heading must include such matters as exhibitions, displays, trade fairs, British Weeks and British Pavilions, meetings for local businessmen, fashion shows, dinners, luncheons, press conferences, etc. The public relations department can assist in many ways and should generally assume an influential rôle in planning the event. This will ensure that the standard of the event reaches a desirable level; that the budget is adequate to make the event effective; that the programme is properly conceived, planned and carried out; that the right people are invited so that the objectives of the events are achieved, and so on.

In dealing with these matters the public relations department is not just an extension of the sales department. Its task is to highlight the strengths of the firm's organisation, products, etc., and to divert attention from its weaknesses. It will do these things best if other departments, such as design department, production department and above all the management, develop the strengths of the firm and solve the problems in weak areas. No amount of good PR work can overcome fundamental weaknesses in product design, production, distribution or marketing.

The secretary has a crucial part to play in these matters, particularly in relation to the press. It is important to keep in touch with the local and national press, establishing a friendly and helpful relationship. It is important to see that reporters are invited to all public events and are kept in touch with any newsworthy story about the firm's products, export achievements and successes. The secretary should ensure that enquiries by the press and other media are dealt with by staff at a suitable level, so that any statements made are authoritative. A file of press cuttings is invaluable. Public relations departments should receive and comb through two copies of each local paper each week. The cost is not great, and the resulting files are most informative. (Two copies are necessary because stories often appear on opposite sides of the same page.) If copies are cut up and the relevant stories pasted into scrap books they form a permanent record of the impact of the firm on the local papers—and even reflect to some extent the success or failure of the department's work. Two scrap books for each paper, one headed 'Favourable or Neutral Stories' and the other headed 'Adverse Stories' will bring out even more clearly the coverage secured (or merely accorded) by the press.

Defensive Activities

We live in a world where new materials, new products and variations on old products are constantly developed. The costs of development have to be recouped by sales, so there is a constant pressure to market the product as quickly as possible, while the fear that rivals may introduce a similar product also urges early marketing. Consequently, products do go into production before they have been fully investigated—some regrettable tragedies will spring to mind in the medical field alone. A public relations department exists to minimise the dislocations that can be caused by such events. This does not mean a cover-up operation necessarily, though a cover-up may be part of the process of minimising adverse effects. So long as injustice is corrected fully, a cover-up may be legitimate in that even greater harm may result from a loss of public confidence.

The defensive function of the PR department is seen at its best in the routine appraisal of the firm's products, advertising, etc., while these are in a formative stage. For example, a particular form of packaging may have environmental effects never envisaged by the design staff. A change to plastic cups for ice cream from traditional cardboard cartons led one firm into serious difficulties with environmentalists. The plastic cups proved to be almost indestructible and provided a source of permanent litter. Since plastic floats, whereas even waxed paper eventually sinks, a change to plastic cups on ferry boats resulted in pleasure beaches being covered with plastic cups thrown overboard by ferry boat caterers who traditionally disposed of their garbage overboard. If a PR department is automatically consulted on each product, each advertising campaign, each marketing manoeuvre, and comments are invited on likely PR effects, many difficulties will be prevented and many bad ideas stillborn.

The secretary will usually play some part in these activities of appraisal of products. She may even be asked, or may volunteer, to try out a product for a few weeks to report on its practical suitability for the purpose for which it is intended. By collecting in a suitable file a list of points to be borne in mind when appraising products she may provide a useful framework for such appraisals. This can be added to whenever a press report on some other company's difficulties catches her eye. Such matters as the following spring to mind at once:

(i) Does the product work?
(ii) Is it attractively packaged?
(iii) Are the instructions clear, especially to the eventual customer?
(iv) Is the translation into foreign languages adequate? (Here, of course, the secretary must know the language.)
(v) Can it be unwrapped easily, without damaging the article?
(vi) Is the colour chosen satisfactory?
etc., etc.

There are a great many aspects to be considered, and raising them will call forth howls of protest from the production department. Henry Ford once made a famous remark that 'Our customers can have any colour car they like, so long as it is black'. This is the classic response of production department to suggestions that their designs are less than perfect. A 'take it or leave it' attitude these days usually means that the public will leave it. It is part of the defensive rôle of the PR department to envisage any such attitude by the public beforehand, and prevent it by calling for modifications to the prototype product.

Protocol

Protocol is diplomatic etiquette, a term which in its highest meaning is used with regard to international relations. Its more popular meaning refers to any circumstances of business life, where there are right and wrong ways to go about things. Generally speaking, it is best to go about things in generally accepted ways rather than in unorthodox ways. On the other hand, protocol can be a restrictive arrangement which ensures that those in authority keep things that way, and can be a cause of frustration and disharmony. Office protocol operates at all levels and the commonest complaint of superiors to inferiors is 'I do wish you had spoken to me about it first'.

In every organisation there is a chain of command which moves upward and downward from the very highest level to the lowest level. The bigger the organisation the more extended the system of command. A common claim of top management is that the Board Room door is always open, so that in theory every employee has access to the topmost level if he is dissatisfied in any way. A common complaint of ordinary staff is that if they make any such direct attempt they are at once accused of a breach of protocol, and in fact the 'ever open door' is in fact only forced open by a ponderous bureaucratic procedure calling for enormous tenacity on the part of the aggrieved member of staff.

Since the secretary is a part of the bureaucratic process, a filter through which most applications must pass, she can do much to ensure that the process works smoothly. She will be able to route complaints quickly to the right person. She will have contacts with secretaries in other departments who ought to know what is going on and are in a position to take action if they do know. In assisting customers and staff to air their complaints to the correct person in a proper manner at the right level and clearing away obstacles by alerting those concerned, she can do much to ensure that protocol is observed without bureaucratic delay.

There are many aspects of protocol which affect the work of the public relations department. It must be ready to advise on matters of both internal and external protocol, ranging from the correct method of address for letters to the Ambassador of Transylvania down to the rights to air her grievances of the lady who dispenses tea. A range of reference books should be available to look up difficult points (see Chapter 22).

In her personal relations with the 'boss' a secretary may frequently find herself listening to long accounts of important matters which are on the executive's mind. By unburdening himself to her about the problems of the firm the executive is thinking through the problem aloud, seeking the correct solution. It is important to listen attentively, and comment if invited to do so. She must *never* repeat anything said to her, or use the information revealed in any way. It would be an absolute breach of her privileged position to do so, and would destroy the trust which must exist between the secretary and her executive.

Secretaries engaged in public relations work should consider taking up membership of the Institute of Public Relations, which seeks to establish the widest understanding of protocol and professional behaviour in all aspects of PR work.

Summary

1. The Institute of Public Relations has defined public relations as 'a deliberate, planned and sustained effort to establish and maintain mutual understanding between an organisation and its public'.

2. The public relations department is a specialist department charged with general responsibility for representing the firm in its relations with the general public, suppliers, customers and local and national institutions.

3. Many of its activities are routine, such as showing visitors round the works, etc. It also has duties with regard to consumer relations and in the promotional field. It should exert an influence over product design, marketing and advertising so that public relations aspects are fully considered and aesthetic and environmental aspects given due weight.

4. There are many matters of protocol which need to be observed in the day-to-day affairs of a firm. The public relations department will exercise a general supervision of protocol in external matters. In matters of office protocol the secretary is well placed to assist and advise so that in general younger staff will be able to air grievances in a proper manner and secure redress through the normal procedures.

Suggested Further Reading

Planning Special Events, Institute of Public Relations.
Preparation of News Releases and Captions, Institute of Public Relations.
Public Relations as a Career, Institute of Public Relations.
Public Relations Made Simple, F. Jefkins, Heinemann, London, 1982.
Titles and Forms of Address, A. & C. Black; most recent edition.

14

EXECUTIVE SECRETARIAL DUTIES—MEETINGS

The Importance of Meetings

In modern business the meeting is one of the most important parts of procedure. Meetings take place at all levels, from board meetings at the top of the tree to shop floor meetings at lower levels involving even the most junior and lowly members of staff. It must inevitably be so in today's large organisations, where the size of the business prevents many voices from being heard at the decision-taking level, and consequently a chain of briefing meetings and reporting-back sessions is necessary if staff are to be fully informed and able to express their views.

Every meeting must conform to the rules laid down for its conduct, so that some preliminary constitution or body of rules is necessary. In the case of limited companies these detailed rules are called Articles of Association. In the case of many other bodies the term Constitution is used. Such bodies of rules usually permit the setting up of any committee that is deemed to be necessary, and empower the board or other ruling body to lay down such orders as it thinks fit for their conduct, within the general framework of the Articles or Constitution.

The chief types of meeting may be listed as follows:

(a) *Statutory Meetings.* These are meetings required by law to ensure proper communication between the directors of a company and the other interested parties, the shareholders. A Statutory Meeting must be held not earlier than one month or later than three months after a company commences business. The duty of such a meeting is to consider a Statutory Report sent out previously to all members.

(b) *Annual General Meetings.* These are also required by statute, and constitute an annual reappraisal of the affairs of a company.

(c) *Extraordinary General Meetings.* An Extraordinary General Meeting is called when it is demanded by the representatives of 10 per cent of the voting shares. Its purpose is to consider any abnormal matter which appears to those shareholders to give cause for concern.

(d) *Board Meetings.* These are management meetings of the board of the company, with the chairman of the board or his deputy in charge and the directors present.

(e) *Committee Meetings.* A committee is a group (though it is possible to have a committee of one) appointed to carry out a particular function. They may be more or less permanent (a **standing committee**) or appointed for a particular matter only (an **ad hoc committee**). An ad hoc committee would cease to exist when the matter it was formed to deal with had been concluded. Sometimes an ad hoc committee is called a **steering committee**, or a **special committee**. Any committee may appoint a **subcommittee** to act as a working party for any particular matter which needs to be examined. A subcommittee draws its powers from the authority given to it by the main committee, and reports back in due course its findings and recommendations.

(*f*) *Departmental Meetings.* These may be **operational meetings**, such as a meeting of sales area managers, or **briefing meetings** designed to pass information down through the organisation via the head of department to divisional managers, supervisors and foremen.

Any meeting must be well organised as the people taking part are busy and have many other duties to perform. The chairman has the responsibility for controlling the meeting and ensuring that it moves on as expeditiously as possible. He will be able to do this best if he is himself a master of the rules of procedure, and if the arrangements made beforehand are adequate. It is these arrangements which the secretary is most concerned with, and a certain amount of liaison with the chairman in the run-up period to the meeting is essential.

Activities Preliminary to a Meeting

A meeting can only be held if we know the date, the venue and who is to attend.

The **date** is often decided at the very end of the previous meeting, where it appears as almost the final item on the agenda. Where a meeting is to be convened for the first time, as with an ad hoc committee which has just been set up, the date is arranged at a time mutually convenient to the principal officials. Others to be in attendance are then notified of the date and time arranged.

The **venue** is not usually specifically arranged in advance at the previous meetings, though it may be implied that it will be held in the usual place. If it was definitely intended to hold the meeting in a different venue, perhaps at an annexe or plant remote from the present venue, this would probably be mentioned as a forewarning. Such arrangements are often made for policy reasons; to equalise travelling between the staff, for example, or to afford head office personnel the chance to review procedures and renew acquaintances at outlying branches. More usually, since most accommodation has several uses it is necessary to book a room for a meeting and this requires the secretary to make the arrangements. The venue will therefore be notified when the arrangements and agenda are circulated in the run-up period to the meeting.

The list of **staff to attend** a meeting does vary to some extent. People are often co-opted for a particular meeting because they are well informed on a matter raised on the agenda. Where a departmental representative is called for it may not be the same person each time. The head of department will appoint a suitable representative. The minutes of the meeting will include a list of those attending, and may refer to their capacity, e.g. T. Smith (Sales Department).

A secretary will therefore check such preliminary matters with the chairman beforehand. She will book a suitable room in the correct building for the date and time arranged. The next item is the agenda.

The Agenda

An agenda is a list of items to be attended to at a meeting. It will usually follow a traditional pattern, each numbered item being taken in turn unless a resolution be passed to change the order of the proceedings. A typical agenda might follow the pattern given below.

1. Apologies for absence.
2. Minutes of the previous meeting.
3. Matters arising.
4. Health and Safety—new measures.
5. Salary scales—half-yearly review.
6. Personnel—bronze medal award to M. Jones.
7. Closure of No. 1 Plant.
8. Any other business.
9. Date of next meeting.

Items 1–3 and 8–9 will appear on almost every agenda. Items 4–7 are clearly related to the work of this particular committee. Every committee will have its own topics to discuss.

How do such items become part of the agenda? It is the secretary who is drawing up the agenda and she will liaise with all interested parties to ensure that nothing is overlooked. The chairman will have a number of major items which follow on from the earlier meetings. He will also probably know of new items which have come forward in the intervening period. Everyone who is preparing reports for the committee must be asked whether he is ready for his item to be included on the agenda. Sometimes a wide section of the firm has to be allowed to raise matters—for example, in a welfare committee a variety of problems may need to be aired and everyone may wish to make suggestions for the agenda. It is usual in such cases to use the **house journal** to invite agenda items from all interested—giving a deadline. It is also usual to keep a 'meeting folder' in which there is a **schedule of recurring agenda items** to be considered each time an agenda is prepared. This folder can also be used to accumulate agenda reminders as they are raised in the weeks or even months before the meeting is due to take place.

Having collected all such items together the secretary will prepare a rough agenda for consideration by the chairman, preferably listing agenda items in their order of importance. He will amend it as he thinks fit, and when finalised it will be duplicated ready for circulation a few days before the meeting is due to take place.

Minutes of the Previous Meeting

To preserve continuity in the proceedings each meeting generally starts with the reading and signing of the minutes of the previous meeting. This can be a time-consuming business and in an age of reprographic miracles we can save time by circulating the minutes of the previous meeting to all members of the committee. They can then read the minutes beforehand and come to the meeting already familiar with the matters in hand.

The secretary must draw up the minutes and circulate them with the notice of the meeting. Since any delay between a meeting and the writing-up of the minutes may cause difficulty, since it is hard to remember what was said several weeks after the event, always write out the minutes within 24 hours of the meeting being held. Ask the chairman to glance at them in case the emphasis placed upon any particular point is wrong. Then file the minutes ready to be duplicated in a spare moment in the time interval before the next meeting. The original copy will be put into the minute book, as the official record.

It is usual for each minute to be numbered, for easy reference subsequently. For example, if the first meeting of a committee took place on the 9th June, 1983, the minutes would be numbered 1/83, 2/83 and so on. If that committee continued into the next year, the minutes would start again, being numbered 1/84, 2/84, etc.

Other Papers

Besides the minutes of the previous meeting any number of other papers may be circulated or tabled. Thus each item on the agenda may have its own written report. If this is ready in time it is convenient to circulate it to all committee members before the meeting. With long reports this is really essential. A short report may be 'tabled'—in other words, a copy will be placed in each member's place at the actual meeting. This is not very helpful if the report is a long one. The secretary should check that members wishing to circulate reports have written them in plenty of time for duplication and circulation.

Where reports and papers have to be prepared for large committees it is of the greatest assistance to have auto-sorters and collators such as are supplied by firms like Pitney Bowes Ltd. These can be used to collate the pages of individual reports for stapling or binding; they also enable the various items to be made up into packages of documents ready for dispatch. These devices increase efficiency, accuracy and speed. They operate within a very small desk space—hand-collating often needs papers to be spread around several desks—and are well worth considering for their morale-boosting effects alone.

To summarise the activities preliminary to a meeting, they are as follows:

(*a*) Agree the date, time and venue, and book the accommodation.

(*b*) Invite items for the agenda and give a deadline for the submission of reports for duplication.

(*c*) Agree the agenda with the chairman and duplicate copies of it, together with a notice to members giving full details of the date, etc.

(*d*) Duplicate the minutes of the previous meeting, and any other papers necessary.

(*e*) Dispatch the notices, agenda, etc., to reach the members in plenty of time for the meeting.

(*f*) Ascertain whether refreshments are required and make the necessary arrangements with the catering department.

Activities on the Day of the Meeting

The secretary will usually attend the meeting to take the minutes, and will thus have an important part to play in the meeting itself. On the day of the meeting she will perform many routine duties. It is wise to check the availability of the accommodation to ensure that no last-minute change has occurred. Then confirm the catering arrangements and pinpoint a suitable time for the refreshment interval. Check the room itself, the seating, heating and ventilation. Ensure that table space is adequate, that ashtrays, water and glasses are available and that notepaper and pencils are supplied.

It is convenient if name cards are placed on the table, so that everyone gets seated without fuss, and those who do not know everyone in the room can then refer to the various speakers by name during the discussion.

Next supply spare copies of the agenda, minutes and other papers. Have the official attendance book and minute book ready, and also any letters of apology. Write quick notes bearing telephoned messages of apology should any come in. Liaise with the switchboard about telephone arrangements, diverting calls for those attending the meeting to a suitable secretary who will take messages and exercise discretion about the essential nature of any interruption that is proposed by callers.

It may be advisable to call the chairman and ensure his availability. In emergencies a deputy chairman may be appointed by the committee to act in the chairman's absence.

The secretary should then attend the meeting in good time, properly equipped to take minutes. She should select a seat conveniently placed to hear the voices of all present, and close to the door in case she has to summon staff required to attend for a particular item only.

Before the meeting begins it is advisable to attach a notice to the door of the conference room stating that a meeting is in progress. This ensures that there are no interruptions, and also any late arrivals would know they had found the right room. Reception staff and messengers should be alerted to the possibility of late arrivals, and asked to conduct them to the meeting as soon as they arrive.

During the meeting the secretary should supply the chairman with papers as they are required, and thus avoid any difficulties in searching for them. If they are filed in correct order she can produce them without any fuss.

The Conduct of a Meeting

The conduct of a meeting is in the hands of the chairman, who should be a person of recognised status. He must be a master of procedure and should keep readily available a reference book on the conduct of meetings such as is mentioned in the Suggested Further Reading. The secretary will already have consulted the chairman about the agenda and the minutes of the previous meeting so that he starts in the knowledge that the framework of the meeting is already formed in the way he wished. The meeting starts when the chairman calls those assembled to order. He will not usually do so until the appointed time, otherwise a person arriving in time for the meeting might find it had already started. He will not call the meeting to order even at the appointed time if a **quorum** is not present. A quorum is the minimum number required to be present by the rules governing the meeting. As soon as the required number is present he will call the meeting to order.

From that time on the meeting is subject to the rules which have been laid down for it, perhaps in the Articles of Association of the company, or in the Rules Book of the association, society or club. The term **standing orders** refers to this body of rules, as amended by motions passed in a proper manner over the course of the previous years. At any moment a member who feels that the rules are not being followed may raise a **point of order** which must be settled by the chairman at once. He may himself rule a member **out of order** if he persists in speaking of a matter in an improper way, or at an incorrect time. A member may also be 'out of order' if he uses improper language or displays any breach of good manners or good taste. Such occasions illustrate the need for a strong chairman who must listen attentively to everything said and keep the atmosphere friendly and attitudes positive.

During the meeting all remarks should be addressed to the chairman, and not to individuals. This tends to reduce the personal impact of the statements being made, which are addressed to the whole meeting and not to any individual. It also prevents the meeting breaking down into a number of separate discussions, which the secretary would find impossible to minute since they are all taking place at once.

Apologies for absence are usually called for at the start of the meeting. The letter calling the meeting will usually list those attending, and the chairman compares this list with those present. If a member is not present but has sent his apologies, the meeting can proceed. If he is not present the chairman may wait to see if he appears. Lateness or absence without apologies may indicate some emergency reason for absence, or inefficiency and discourtesy.

During the 'apologies for absence' period the secretary will make a list of those present, either by ticking her notice of the meeting which contains the list of those due to attend, or by circulating a suitable sheet of paper ruled to show the names and capacities of those attending. Sometimes an attendance book is circulated or placed on a table near the entrance so that all sign as they enter the room.

The next item on the agenda is 'Minutes of the previous meeting'.

In theory they should be read out to the meeting, but often it is moved that **the minutes be taken as read.** This saves time, but a member who has not read his minutes is placed at a disadvantage. The chairman then asks that the meeting agree to his signing the minutes, as an acceptance that they are a true record of the previous meeting. If someone wishes to object that the minutes are not a true record he should say so before the chairman signs them.

Once the minutes are accepted as a true record the next item is **Matters arising from the minutes.** In many cases there are matters which arise from the minutes of the previous meeting, but they are on the agenda as an agenda item. Such matters arising are dealt with when their turn comes, so that the only items that need concern the meeting at this point are any matters not on the agenda. Often items dealing with the welfare of individuals may have been resolved in the meantime, and a short explanation will inform the committee of the outcome.

The agenda items proper, which form the main purpose of the meeting, are now dealt with in turn. Each item will usually be introduced by someone who caused it to appear on the agenda. He may already have circulated a report or papers relevant to the item, or he may 'table' them at the meeting itself. After this introduction the subject is thrown open for discussion. The chairman must interrupt anyone who wanders from the subject or who is more voluble than valuable. He must ensure that all who wish to do so have the chance to contribute to the discussion and may invite the views of any member who has not yet spoken. He may summarise the discussion at any point and try to reduce the arguments of the various parties to somewhere approaching a consensus. This may lead to one or more **propositions**, which are eventually embodied in a **motion**—a formal proposal which can be voted upon. Once a motion has been proposed and seconded it can be voted upon, but greater clarity can often be achieved if an opportunity is first given to anyone wishing to modify the motion in any way. A **rider** is an addition to the original wording, while an **amendment** is an alteration to it. If a rider or an amendment is proposed and seconded it will be voted on. If carried it will be incorporated in the wording of the motion. If it is not carried the original wording will stand. The final wording will then be voted upon.

Voting may be **unanimous** (everyone in favour). If it is not carried unanimously a motion may be carried **nem con** (*nemine contradicente* — no one contradicting) or it may be carried by a majority. Sometimes a two-thirds or three-quarters majority is required for particular motions under the standing orders. Voting may be allowed by proxies. A **proxy** is a person appointed to use the vote of another person who is unable to attend the meeting.

Once a motion has been carried it is called a **resolution**, and will usually appear in the minutes with its full wording—Resolved: that, etc., etc.

Where a matter is so contentious that a consensus cannot be arrived at, a motion may be passed that it should **lie on the table**. This means that no action will be taken on the matter at present but it will remain a live subject for consideration and may be raised again at a later date by anyone who feels that it should be placed on the agenda for a further meeting.

In the interest of other items, the chairman may **adjourn** the discussion on any particular item until a later date if it appears that a conclusion cannot be reached without more time. He may also adjourn the whole meeting to an agreed future date, or **sine die** (without fixing a future date), if the time available has proved inadequate.

The item **Any other business** gives those who were too late in submitting an item for the agenda an opportunity to raise any matter they feel should have been included. It is also a convenient point to recognise any particularly stalwart work done on behalf of the committee, or to express condolences or other sentiments relating to personal situations of colleagues, members, etc. The chairman will then fix the date for the next meeting and thank members for their attendance, etc.

Taking Minutes

The secretary will usually take down minutes of the meeting in one of three forms. The first is verbatim, where everything is recorded word for word. The second method is to record conclusions only, so that the discussion that took place, the motions proposed and seconded, etc., are not recorded. The third method is to record a concise summary of the discussion and the conclusions arrived at. The secretary should check with the chairman which style of minutes is required. In any case, the minutes should be kept entirely impersonal, and language which tends to colour the notes should be avoided. Thus to record that a 'violent discussion followed' would not be appropriate language.

The exact wording of every resolution passed and the names of the proposer and seconder should be taken down. It is usual to capitalise all names and official positions, such as Chairman, Secretary, Planning Officer, etc. Where a report is referred to it is usual to identify the report by its name, date and (if it has one) reference number.

A typical set of minutes is given in Fig. 14.1.

Secretarial Duties Subsequent to a Meeting

When the meeting is over the secretary should collect any spare documents left behind by members of the committee, any spare stationery, etc. She should then go through the notes she has made and finalise all aspects of the meeting. This includes the preparation of draft minutes for approval by the chairman,

---

Welfare Committee Meeting - XYZ Ltd.

Minutes of a meeting held at 10.30 a.m., Friday, 1st December, 1983 in the Recreation Annexe

Members Present	Mr. R.T. Lucas, Director (Chairman)
	Mr. A. Jones (Welfare Officer)
	Mrs. J. Aylesford (Restaurant Manageress)
	Mr. R. Peterson (Works Representative)
	Miss P. Jamieson (Office Representative)
	Mr. P. Whyte (Secretary, Entertainments Sub-Committee)
	Miss J. Lee (Minuting Secretary)
	Messrs. J. White, P. Tripp, C. Lea and B. Lucas (Departmental Representatives - Sales)

Apologies   All were present on this occasion.

85/83 Minutes of Previous Meeting

The minutes of the meeting held on Friday, 29th September, 1983 were taken as read, adopted and signed by the Chairman.

86/83 Matters Arising

79/83 Mr. Lucas reported that he and Mr. Jones attended the funeral of R. Lamborne who was killed in a machine shop accident. The widow's welfare had been properly cared for.

87/83 Restaurant Report

The accounts of the restaurant for the half year were adopted. Three complaints about restaurant matters had been investigated and the details were explained. All three had been resolved satisfactorily.

88/83 Christmas Activities

Mr. Whyte reported that the Social on Christmas Eve was fully planned and promised to be successful. The Children's Party had been arranged for January 7th and a full programme had been arranged. A grant of £100 was approved.

89/83 Letter of Complaint

A matter raised concerning toilet facilities in the firm's motor transport department was agreed to need thorough investigation.

It was RESOLVED that a sub-committee be formed (Messrs. R.T. Lucas, A. Jones, R. Peterson to serve).

Cont'd/...

2

90/83   Technical Training

      A complaint about inadequate pre-examination study leave
      was received from the Works Representative.

          It was RESOLVED that this matter be raised at Board
          Room level and the Chairman arrange its inclusion in
          the Board Meeting Agenda. Mr. R. Peterson be
          proposed to attend and explain the matter.

91/83   A.O.B.

      There being no other business the meeting adjourned at
      12.50 p.m.

Date of Next Meeting

      Friday, 2nd March, 1984 at 10.30 a.m. in the Recreation Annexe.

                    Chairman: 2nd March, 1984 _____

Fig. 14.1. Minutes of a Welfare Committee Meeting.

and the typing of any correspondence which arises from the discussion at the meeting. The chairman may like to send brief thank-you memos to any non-members who attended particular parts of the discussion to give specialist reports.

The committee file should be up-dated and put into good order for the next meeting. If possible, the minutes should be duplicated in sufficient quantities to meet the likely attendance at the next meeting. If this is not possible at once a 'follow-up' entry in the secretary's system will ensure that they are duplicated in good time. The date of the meeting should be entered in any diaries or year planners affected. Advance notification should also be sent to any regular member who was absent from the meeting that has just concluded. The catering department should be thanked for their help and any chit to cover expenses presented to the chairman for signature.

Summary

1. Meetings are an important aspect of business organisation. The most important are statutory meetings, annual general meetings, extraordinary general meetings, board meetings and committee meetings.

2. Before a meeting is held the secretary has many duties to perform. In particular, she must arrange the date, time and venue in consultation with the chairman, prepare notices to be sent out to all those interested and draw up

the agenda and minutes of the previous meeting for approval by the chairman before circulation.

3. The chairman is in charge of the conduct of a meeting and must be a master of procedure. From the time he calls the meeting to order when a quorum is present to the concluding 'any other business', all remarks will be made through the chairman and the meeting will be conducted in accordance with the Constitution or Articles of Association, or standing orders.

4. The agenda is a list of matters to be discussed at the meeting. It preserves continuity by recalling the previous meeting, the minutes of which are read and approved. It then proceeds to new business, which is dealt with in agenda order. Any resolutions passed are recorded in full for inclusion in the minutes.

5. Subsequent to the meeting the secretary will prepare the minutes of the meeting just concluded, for approval by the chairman. She will also deal with any correspondence arising from the meeting, and file all reports, minutes and copies of correspondence ready for the next meeting.

Suggested Further Reading

Administration in Business Made Simple, R. R. Pitfield, Heinemann, 1982.

The Chairman's Guide and Secretary's Companion, Frank, Shackleton, Ward Lock, most recent edition.

The Law of Meetings, Sir Sebag Shaw, and E. D. Smith, Macdonald & Evans, 1974.

Current Literature on collators and sorters provided by Pitney Bowes Ltd.

15

EXECUTIVE SECRETARIAL DUTIES—CONFERENCES AND FUNCTIONS

The Importance of Conferences and Functions

In recent years the size of businesses has tended to increase. Large-scale organisations tend to be more economic than small ones, since only the very largest firms can make the best use of expensive equipment such as a computer which enables operations to be carried out in the most effective way. As a firm grows in size the internal communications problems grow, and the firm also makes an increased impact on the community around it. These situations call for a variety of seminars, lectures, conferences and public relations functions aimed at promoting an understanding of the aims of the firm, by both the staff and the general public.

In small firms the morale of the establishment is easily maintained by the personal interest of the owner or manager in the staff. He can convey a sense of purpose, and ensure motivation in the course of the ordinary daily round. In large organisations this is much more difficult. It is all too easy for staff to feel that they are mere cogs in the machine, unknown to senior staff and of no significance in the organisation. Meetings of departments, branches and similar groupings enable staff to develop a team spirit; they are able to learn more about the firm and its aims, and business matters can be followed by pleasant social gatherings.

Large-scale firms have a huge market to cater for, often world-wide. Sales conferences are therefore a convenient way of bringing to the attention of all representatives the new products and new models which are to be introduced in the forthcoming period. They also give an opportunity to review performance and procedures; to feature successful methods and examine weak points in the organisation. Often they can be followed—while everyone is available— by a public exhibition of the firm's products to which customers and influential buyers can be invited. Many hotel chains, such as the Penta Airline Hotels, offer conference and exhibition facilities at centres convenient to the main travel networks.

Public relations exercises of all sorts have a part to play in the organisation of most firms. One thinks of launching ceremonies for books, plays, films and sporting activities, designed to give the product or the entertainment press coverage which constitutes a free advertisement. Equally important are public meetings held to rebut allegations of anti-social behaviour, or to draw to the attention of the public developments which the firm intends to make, so as to forestall criticisms of the proposals.

Perhaps the largest gatherings of this sort are the international conferences held to consider questions of world-wide interest: conferences about the law of the sea, or the pollution of the atmosphere, about atomic waste disposal, developments in heart surgery, water resources and human rights. Such

150

gatherings are often organised by the national representatives of international bodies. A good example of such an organisation is the International Chamber of Commerce, which has its headquarters in Paris, but has national Chambers of Commerce in the capital cities of each member country, and Chambers of Commerce in every large town. A secretary working in the national head office of such an organisation will find much of the work consists in monitoring the activities of firms and government bodies in her own country and relaying information to headquarters. Each year a major conference on problems revealed during the year will be held somewhere around the world, and occasionally the chief burden of organising such an event will fall on her own national committee. This will need a year's intensive preparation along the lines described in this chapter.

The success of all such functions depends largely upon the preparations made. Not only must the topics to be discussed and the general programme be planned in detail, but the conduct of each part of the programme requires detailed arrangement so that those participating benefit from a complete package of experiences. Inevitably much of the work falls upon the executive secretary most directly involved, and the smooth running of the function will largely depend upon the detailed arrangements she makes.

Facilities for Conferences and Functions

Conferences and functions are intermittent activities, but their success often depends upon the availability of adequate facilities. Of course many firms do hire such facilities as and when required, and hotels and conference organisers usually offer a package of facilities which includes the provision of many of the most essential items. It is still necessary to accumulate and then safeguard display materials, lighting fixtures, visual aids, publicity material, etc., which is likely to be of use on future occasions. This type of material should be centrally controlled so that it is available for all departments, and should preferably be in the charge of a general handyman with a team of strong and willing assistants. A budget should be made available which will ensure the adequacy of the equipment provided, especially such things as spare bulbs for projectors, long leads able to reach distant sources of electricity, etc. The organiser and the general handyman should get together well in advance of the actual event to 'think through' the sequence of events and anticipate every requirement. Then facilities needed should be purchased or hired; notices should be prepared by suitable staff or subcontracted; fire precaution rules should be observed and any problems of security envisaged.

The failure of many conferences, and the chaos experienced at the start, usually reflects the inadequacy of the team made available to do the routine work. It is of little help to second staff from other duties to assist if they are resentful of the disturbance and uncooperative when the event takes place. There are usually some people in a department who enjoy this sort of activity. A secretary should get to know these cooperative souls, enlist their support in advance and then secure their nomination as assistants and release from normal duties. An early meeting of those to be involved is desirable. There should be an appropriate lead from someone of stature in the firm to impress the importance of the event and express the management's appreciation of the cooperation of staff. Then the sequence of events should again be 'thought through', allocating special responsibilities where appropriate but in a context of general cooperation to achieve a smooth operation.

Preparing for a Conference or Function

On each occasion when a conference or function is held a file should be opened which will contain details of all the conference activities. It may later need to be subdivided, perhaps by sectioning off into a separate file such items as the responses to invitations to attend the conference and the consequent issue of tickets and preparation of conference folders. Where strict costing is required the subdivision of the filing must include a separate file for each heading of expense.

A checklist should be prepared which contains details of all the arrangements to be made, with spaces to tick up initial activity, confirmation of the arrangements made, charges involved, etc. Activities omitted from the checklist but subsequently found to be necessary should be added, and the list preserved for reference on future occasions.

It is quite impossible to list here every requirement of such functions—each presents its own problems and needs—but a general list might include most of the following points:

(*a*) Preparation of a detailed programme with the appropriate executive who is acting as conference organiser or promoter of the function.

(*b*) Contact any speakers or guest celebrities and ensure that they are available and willing to appear. It may be necessary to sign a contract with their agents.

(*c*) Ensure the availability of any film, tape or other audio-visual aid that may be required, and the apparatus needed. If necessary buy or hire it.

(*d*) Book the accommodation and get the booking confirmed in writing. This may require a package of facilities, conference rooms, seminar rooms, overnight accommodation, a conference office, restaurant or canteen facilities, car parking space, toilet facilities, etc. Inspection of the accommodation is desirable, and if it in any way falls below the requirements—for example, rooms to be used may be inadequately signposted or numbered, furniture may be inadequate for display purposes, etc.—the booking should not be confirmed until attention to these matters has been promised.

(*e*) Consider the staffing situation for the period of the conference to ensure an adequate team. This may include handymen, porters, security guards and cleaners. An electrician is usually required at some time on these occasions. Reception staff, messengers, hostesses, waiters and other catering staff, clerks, typists and secretaries must usually be provided. Adequate notice to departments must be given and arrangements made to cover their normal duties so far as this is possible.

(*f*) Prepare the invitations and the programme, and check them very carefully to ensure that the invitation is complete in every detail. An omission of something like the date, or time of commencement, or the venue, means costly recirculation of the detail omitted, as well as telephone delays caused by the switchboard being flooded with enquiries. The incorporation of a simple tear-off application form will increase applications, as will a reply-paid envelope. Some measure of uniformity is desirable in all printed material, from the original invitation to the car stickers. An attractive logotype to appear on all printed material should be designed and incorporated. It gives a clear reference point for security purposes, and sets the overall style for tickets, passes, car parks and other authorisations.

(*g*) Advertising policy should be reviewed to ensure that advertising is effective. For example, controlled circulation magazines sent free of charge to all executives in a particular field may be the most effective way of contacting the customers you wish to attend. Some distinguishing code, which will enable you to evaluate the effectiveness of a particular advertisement, is helpful.

(*h*) Review the public relations aspects of the event. Is it 'news' likely to be of interest to the national press, or the local press? Will trade journals be willing to feature it and thus give free publicity? Is a press release desirable, and if so what deadline shall be set on it for publication? Will the press expect to be given an advance copy of speeches to be made by the leading personalities attending? Do we need to report speeches or contributions from the floor of the meeting verbatim? If so we must have stenographers available. Are some contributions likely to be in a foreign language? It may be necessary to hire interpreters and translators if foreign staff or visitors are to be kept 'au fait' with all that is going on. The conference office must be large enough to accommodate such staff.

(*i*) It is a common practice to supply each visitor with a conference folder which includes a number of relevant documents. The work of preparing such folders is considerable, since they have to be labelled and then stuffed with the appropriate contents. These may include name badges, details of restaurant seatings and hotel accommodation, brochures about products, sample packs perhaps, translations of speeches by foreign visiting speakers, notepads and pencils. A list of members and the organisations they represent may be included. (Note: A smooth system for giving out such folders is essential at the start of the conference. Sometimes this initial organisation is used again at the end when guests are given a souvenir present of some sort to take away.)

(*j*) The conference may require an office for the use of the organiser, or even the delegates. Brochures, news bulletins, etc., may be produced during the event, or to advertise side-line activities or recreational trips to be made in the evenings or at weekends. Supplies for this office must be estimated, allocated and transported together with equipment such as typewriters, duplicators, etc.

(*k*) Arrange transport for the various aspects of the conference, notably the initial setting up before the conference opens; for the proper conduct of any organised trips or outings; for the smooth processing of official arrivals and departures, etc.

(*l*) The costing of such functions can be very important. There is the initial costing of the programme; the passing of an initial budget for the event; the accumulation of costs and their comparison with the budget to ensure that they are kept within the budget if possible; and the final passing of accounts for payment by the accounts department.

Activities During the Event

The secretary to the conference organiser has a major part to play during the function. Not only will she be a general factotum expected to be on hand at all times to deal with any situation that arises, but in the smaller functions she may also play a 'hostess' rôle. It is essential to be well-dressed, well-groomed and manicured, with the necessary fund of polite greetings and interesting conversational remarks. The very start of the event is a difficult time, when an information desk needs to be fully manned by a team who are knowledgeable about the event. Many enquiries can be saved by adequate notices showing the disposition of various parts of the function, room numbers, etc. Such notices must be at a height which enables them to be seen above the heads of the crowd standing around in the foyer. Portable direction signposts which can be labelled to suit the function can be purchased relatively cheaply and form a permanent asset. Lists of accommodation, groupings for seminars, etc., must be placed at eye level, but the notice indicating their presence (of the 'Which study-group are you in? Please see below!' variety) should be visible above the heads of those studying the lists. Sets of preparatory notes for staff manning the desk are helpful—especially if they have been gone through beforehand in the run-up period to the conference. A wise secretary will appoint a deputy to assume her duties whenever she is absent, and before leaving will tell this deputy where she may be contacted if necessary. Messengers should also be at hand.

Genuine difficulties may arise which have to be dealt with during the course of the function. Notes should be made of these once they have been resolved, and the record preserved for reference on future occasions so that they can be anticipated and avoided.

Each part of the programme each day has its own particular arrangements to be made and its succession of deadlines to be met. The provision of 'orders of the day' for each group of employees will facilitate the smooth running of the conference, and secretarial staff will be thinking ahead to ensure that all the deadlines are met. Such matters as transport for key personnel, collection of completed documents if orders—or enquiry opportunities—are being received, arrangements for coffee breaks, luncheons, etc., are usually carefully timetabled. Equipment is sometimes moved from room to room during coffee breaks to meet the programme requirements; it must always be checked for efficient operation after such transfers.

Frequently a conference ends with all the delegates meeting together for a final session in the main assembly hall. This often takes the form of an 'any questions' session or 'Brains Trust' of all the major speakers still in attendance. It is a useful way to round off the conference, gives an opportunity for the presentation of bouquets or other gifts to guests, and for passing votes of thanks to groups of people involved in the work. To prevent such a conclusion falling flat it is a good idea to prime one or two delegates with appropriate discussion points, designed to remind other delegates of some of the major contributions to the conference made by the main speakers. By calling for a clarification or reiteration of some major point it gives the speaker concerned an opportunity to summarise his main contribution, and warm up the discussion.

Finally, at the end of the day or days, a great deal of clearing up must take place to vacate premises in reasonably neat condition. Two tendencies may be observed at such times: the tendency of staff to slope off without playing their fair part in closure procedures and the tendency for valuable equipment to vanish. With regard to the former, a gentle reminder to those concerned with the dismantling operation that they have duties to perform and must not leave until the dismantling operation is completed will save recriminations later. It is a good idea to record these reminders on a pad, so that staff concerned know you have given explicit instructions and there is no excuse for not pulling their fair weight. The disappearance of property is something that should be avoided at all costs. Nothing is easier when clearing up at exhibitions, etc., than for valuable equipment to be 'collected' by porters, put into vans and whisked away. Such items as display stands, tools, notice-boards, floodlights, chairs, typewriters, etc., are highly pilferable and at risk. All such equipment should be supervised at a central point on the stand where a deliberate invasion of the firm's territory will be needed if anyone is to make away with it. It should if possible be marked clearly to make it identifiable at a glance, and serial numbers should be taken of machines sent to the exhibition so that they are available to police if required.

A personal involvement in the dismantling operations is a great factor in ensuring goodwill and cooperation on future occasions. Since a great deal of the credit for a successful operation quite rightly accrues to the personal secretary of the organiser, and she usually receives some sort of recognition or tribute, the secretary's status is enhanced if those lower down the ladder believe such accolades to be genuinely deserved. It is worthwhile being one of the last to leave, if only to preserve this goodwill, and a quick word of thanks to those still clearing up the residue of equipment is even then desirable.

Follow-Up Operations

There are a wide variety of follow-up operations which are essential to the complete success of a conference or other event. These include such obvious items as letters of thanks to the various speakers, celebrities and distinguished guests. Less obvious, but just as valuable, are letters of appreciation to members of staff who have participated, and this includes very low level staff who have done the really hard work of the function. Sometimes this can be done through a house magazine article on the conference, and the actual naming of staff who participated is desirable. It is also important to ensure that no one is overlooked.

Equipment used should be returned to the appropriate store and a receipt obtained. Useful materials, notices, etc., should be filed away for possible use on some future occasion. Accounts of contractors, lecturers and other bodies should be passed for payment and the final costs compared with the budget. Copies of the final balance sheet should be supplied to the accounts department, the conference organiser and other interested parties. The sales department should be supplied with any names and addresses of interested parties and any other useful results of the function should be passed to appropriate persons.

A final appraisal for her own use, in the form of a review of the function, the way it was organised, the snags that arose, the names and addresses and telephone numbers of firms found to be efficient and helpful, the obstruction met with, etc., is well worthwhile to close the whole procedure. It will prove invaluable next time if this review is read through at the start of the proceedings and a flood of memories, both pleasurable and painful, is recalled to mind.

Social Functions

The chief types of social function are the formal luncheon or dinner, the dinner-dance and the cocktail party. Other activities such as staff parties are usually run by entertainments committees as part of the activities of a staff association.

The problems to be faced for social functions are very similar to those already described for conferences. We have to decide whom to invite, and to issue invitations. We have to prepare a programme, and invite speakers or entertainers. We have to reserve accommodation and provide refreshments, or a menu, wines, etc. We must arrange to receive guests courteously, announce them properly, introduce them to people we wish them to meet, etc.

The check list below will cover the main points, and should form the nucleus of a file opened to control the arrangements.

(*a*) Decide the type of function to be held, and the date and time.

(*b*) Prepare the guest list, and double check with departments, etc., if necessary to ensure that no one has been forgotten.

(*c*) Reserve accommodation at the venue and the package of facilities required. This may mean provisional booking of alternative dates.

(*d*) Decide on the guest of honour, chief speaker, etc., and ensure their availability. Confirm accommodation to suit this availability.

(*e*) Decide on a programme, draft the invitation and confirm its suitability with the committee or officials in charge of overall policy.

(*f*) Estimate the cost and secure a budget appropriation.

(*g*) Print and dispatch the invitation cards, receive the replies and prepare a seating plan if necessary.

(*h*) Think through and make detailed arrangements including:

  (i) Reception and hostess duties.

  (ii) Menu, wines, cigars, etc.

  (iii) Cars, car parking, entertainment of official drivers, etc.

  (iv) Press, publicity, photographers, security, etc.

  (v) Decide on a Master of Ceremonies; discuss continuity; prepare background notes on celebrities if required; decide on musical background if desirable and on any floral arrangements.

(*i*) Decide whether any awards, gifts or bouquets, etc., are to be presented either during or at the end of the function. Sometimes such matters as long-service awards, recognition of specialist achievements, gifts to celebrity visitors or presentation of bouquets form an appropriate close to an evening or lunchtime function.

Finally, each event of this type leads to its own sequence of follow-up duties, very similar to those already described.

Hostess Duties

Many secretaries may not become involved in the organisation of large-scale conferences such as are described in the early part of this chapter. More probable for every secretary is the need to act as hostess on innumerable occasions at smaller functions. These may range from meetings of departmental executives, called in her boss's office, to visits by customers, official delegations from overseas countries, interested members of the public, 'open' evenings, etc. Whilst the 'hostessing' of such occasions eventually becomes second nature, and their variety makes it difficult to select a set of rules which will apply invariably, the following suggestions will pinpoint many matters which usually arise:

(a) *Preparatory work.* Good preparation is essential for all such occasions and leaves the secretary free at the actual time that guests are arriving to receive them in an unflurried state. Essential features of this preparation are the arrangements for lower level staff, catering staff, porters, chauffeurs, car park attendants and security staff. If the VIP's are to be received in her boss's office the secretary should make sure it is tidy and uncluttered, with all papers and files put away. Check that all the light bulbs are working, that there are sufficient chairs, including one or two for the odd arrival who always seems to be called in at the last minute on these occasions. A nice bowl of flowers in the room, a conveniently placed drinks trolley and plenty of side tables with ashtrays help to add to the atmosphere.

It is useful if the secretary does a little discreet background research on the guest of honour and other leading VIP's. Their interests and hobbies should provide points of conversation during coffee breaks and lunch periods, while the opportunity to introduce them to others present with similar interests may give the executive just the excuse he needs to withdraw himself and clear up some uncertainty that is worrying him about the arrangements to follow. If the event is a luncheon or dinner date, it is advisable to find out if the guest has any special diet to follow, or any particular likes or dislikes if the menu is to be a set one. His method of transport may require some arrangements to be made. If he is not coming by chauffeur-driven car it may be necessary to meet him at the station.

The boss's speech should be prepared carefully and then produced in such a form that he can deliver it without fumbling. It may be necessary to print the main headings in quite large print if his eyesight is poor. Most people over the age of 45 need special reading glasses, or bi-focals which have two different sorts of lens built into one eyepiece. It can make a speech less effective if the speaker is manifestly struggling to make out his secretary's typing. Even block capitals are little help to such executives, who need a quarter-inch high headline at least. It is worthwhile doing a few dry-paper copies of these speech notes and putting them in convenient places so that if he mislays the original a duplicate is always to hand.

Before the conference begins a final check round the conference hall could be useful. The secretary will see at a glance whether the stage curtains are untidily drawn back or the chairs are not set out neatly. She should see that there is a covered jug of water and glasses on the main speaker's table, that any special 'reserved' seats carry a suitable 'Reserved' label, and if a junior member of staff can be appointed to keep an eye on the conference hall and usher guests to seats on arrival this is helpful.

(b) *Duties as guests arrive.* If the secretary has carried out her duties competently, on the actual day she will be at her station calm, smiling, confident and efficient. She will receive VIP's, perhaps taking their coats, bags and cases, and introduce them to her boss, handing out pre-conference coffee or sherry. When aperitifs are passed round in the boss's office it is always handy to have a bottle of squash, a jug of water and a small range of proprietary soft drinks in the cupboard, for teetotallers.

As the event proceeds she should ensure that everything is ready for the next stage. Thus after the guests have arrived and are conversing over a sherry, she might put through a quick call to the restaurant to tell them that guests will be down in fifteen minutes.

It is well to be prepared for the unexpected. All sorts of queries will arise during the event and the secretary should be willing to help wherever she can. This creates a good impression with the guests. Guests and VIP's will inevitably seek her out if they need help.

(c) *Duties at the conclusion.* The end of such a function is almost as important as the beginning, since an impression of a well-conducted occasion can be fortified by well-organised transport arrangements at the end and a courteous farewell. A secretary may be inundated with calls for local train times, bus service details, taxi rank numbers, etc. All such details should be to hand. Many guests, and often wives of guests, will make a special point of thanking the secretary for the arrangements she has made, so it is convenient and courteous to be available at this time should they wish to express their thanks.

Once again it is helpful, and fosters goodwill for future occasions, if staff who have been burdened with extra work, such as caretaking and security staff, are thanked for their efforts and assured that all went well.

Summary

1. Conferences and functions become increasingly important as firms grow in size. Morale is improved, information disseminated, criticism rebutted, products advertised and goodwill fostered by meetings and functions of all sorts.

2. Successful functions depend upon good organisation and adequate facilities. The secretary will play an important part in the preparations and must ensure that assets purchased to ensure the success of such intermittent activities are preserved for use on future occasions.

3. A checklist of the activities required must be prepared and action taken to implement them. This list should be preserved for future reference since functions tend to be repeated at regular intervals. It is essential to 'think through' the entire operation so that all the implications of the event are envisaged and the maximum advantage is secured.

4. Despite careful preparation all sorts of problems arise on the actual day. It is essential to have an adequate team on duty, and to man information desks from an early hour. Orders of the day for various groups are helpful. especially if they have been taken through the notes at a meeting earlier. The careful choice of staff to select willing and cooperative people is advisable.

5. Dismantling operations at the end of such functions provide an excellent test of character. Some people will cooperate manfully; others will evade any real work. It is necessary to control the latter, and express appreciation of the former. The loss of equipment at such time is highly probable and every attempt should be made to avoid this.

6. A wide variety of follow-up activities—letters of thanks, return of equipment, passing accounts for payment, etc.—has to be carried out to

complete the event. This includes the preservation of a full record in the files to make a similar event easier on the next occasion.

Suggested Further Reading

Planning Special Events, Institute of Public Relations.
Who's Who, latest annual edition.

16

EXECUTIVE TRAVEL

The Importance of Executive Travel

Today the world is not just a shrinking place; it has shrunk. The world is every businessman's oyster. We draw raw materials from every corner of the globe and sell our products in the remotest regions. Every businessman must travel, and every executive secretary must know how to organise itineraries and predict difficulties about travel so that they can be avoided as far as humanly possible. She should be prepared to accompany him wherever possible —an arrangement which often trebles the productivity of the trip. It is almost impossible to manage for any length of time without secretarial help, and an agency secretary in a foreign city is no substitute for your own secretary who knows your business, your products and your way of doing things.

The climate of business activity abroad is often very different from our own. In some countries Mark Twain's saying 'Never put off until tomorrow what you can put off until the day after tomorrow' really comes to life. The result is that appointments may be missed, telephone calls remain unanswered and time wasted locating contacts who are absent from their desks for one reason or another. Every effort must be made to raise the level of response, by such devices as last-minute reminders to contacts that the executive will be calling at the appointed time. A tip *on arrival* to the hotel switchboard staff may also do more to clear the lines for an executive than any number of complaints to management.

Preparation for an overseas visit requires decisions at a variety of levels, and the secretary may be involved in all of them. The chief points to be examined are:

(*a*) The objectives of the visit, its costs and likely benefits.
(*b*) The itinerary, and executive support while he carries it out.
(*c*) Practical travel details and documents.
(*d*) How is work to be handled in the executive's absence.

The Objectives of the Overseas Visit

A visit must have positive objectives if the considerable expense involved is to be justified. The preparatory work for an overseas visit should be particularly rigorous since the expense is greater and the event rarer than a visit to an inland market area, depot or plant. This preparation must be based on a careful review of performance in the area selected for a visit, an analysis of the operating and trading results and an examination of the strengths and weaknesses. This may lead us to the conclusion that the chief object of the visit is to build upon the strong position already established, or perhaps to cure the weaknesses revealed. It may include a comparison of the present organisation with an 'ideal' structure envisaged for that particular market.

160

Reviews of the type referred to have to be based upon evidence, and reports on the current situation may have to be called for well in advance. Planning must therefore start early, and a clear warning of the proposed visit will usually tighten up arrangements in a very desirable way at the start.

If the intention of the visit is to develop new markets and there is no earlier base to work from, it requires the most careful market research prior to the event. It may be advisable to employ a specialist market research agency, perhaps with government support. The *Export Handbook*, issued free by the British Overseas Trade Board, gives details of such assistance.

It is usually helpful to estimate the costs of the visit and the benefits to be derived from it. This will quantify the visit in financial terms and may lead to more rigorous action to increase the benefits or cut the costs.

The conclusion of this review is to draw up a list of precise objectives which are capable of being achieved, so that the progress of the visit can be assessed while it is actually taking place, and at the end some comparison between objectives and actual achievements becomes possible.

The Itinerary

The itinerary for any journey must depend upon the objectives to be achieved. These will decide which places are to be visited, which cities can best act as a temporary centre of operations, which executives and customers are to be visited, etc. Once these matters have been decided, a time allocation can be made between the various centres of operations to fit in the required visits, meetings, conferences, etc., which are envisaged. It is important not to have too tight a schedule, especially if the executive is calling on customers and must meet their convenience rather than his own. Four visits a day is often as much as can be managed in the tropics, and even then it is advisable to leave odd half days clear for follow-up arrangements, changes of programme, contacts with home, etc.

A careful check must be made to ensure that public holidays do not clash with arrangements. Books like Croner's *Manual for Exporters* include such details, or a telephone call to the appropriate embassy will confirm that the days selected are not public holidays. Where a public holiday cannot be avoided it should be planned as a day of relaxation and recreation.

The outline plan of the visit should now be clear and it is advisable to hand over the actual travel arrangements to an expert in the field. There are so many outside agencies who can assist in travel and hotel arrangements that there is little point in trying to do these things oneself. The charges are not high in a competitive field like this, and the specialist agencies have established links which can be made cheaply and effectively with a guarantee that the standard of facility will be adequate in relation to the price range used. Such arrangements can include car hire for the period required, and the reservation of rail travel and internal flights. It is desirable to use the car and public transport in any country visited, for both give real experience of the country concerned and broaden the executive's background.

While the travel agents are busy with these arrangements the secretary must turn to filling in the detailed programme on the outline itinerary. This may require the booking of actual appointments with customers; the calling of meetings and conferences to be attended by overseas staff; the delegation of arrangements to managers overseas so that all will go well on the day; and the allocation of budgeted funds to ensure that an adequate sum is available without exceeding the budget.

The whole itinerary must then be examined in detail so that every event, visit or function has been properly thought through. The following list of items that may be required to meet the needs of every event illustrates the diversity of requirements.

(a) *Visiting cards.* These should be as high-powered as possible, conferring a suitable degree of status on the executive.

(b) *Customer records.* These should be as detailed as possible and should highlight lines which the customer does not at present handle, new lines becoming available, quantity discounts to be offered as inducements for larger orders and suggestions for limits to which the executive may go in offering credit extensions on larger orders.

(c) *Sales literature.* Sales literature must of course be in the local language, and should cover the full range of products. Since only one or two copies of each can be carried it is necessary to have a back-up stock from which the executive's case can be replenished each day. Making this back-up stock into 'daily' packs so that a new pack can be slipped into the case without any waste of time is a useful idea.

(d) *Display equipment.* Today relatively light travel packs which include slide projectors, tape-recorded sales patter and even films can be made up relatively cheaply. This type of audio-visual package, if well prepared, takes a great deal of strain off the marketing executive and is interesting to the customer.

(e) *Visit briefs.* A 'visit brief' is a short account of the chief objectives of each visit, together with pertinent data based upon the customer's record. It may include details of the particular market area covered by the customer and information about the customer's special needs. Even his personality and general attitude may be hinted at, and his particular problems of finance, transport, warehousing or marketing may be analysed. Before departure each brief should be gone through, perhaps with a mini-conference of all who know the customers and their problems, so that the executive really understands his brief. Before making the actual call the executive reads through the 'visit brief' and recalls the relevant points. He then enters the interview knowledgeable about the needs of the particular customer and makes a more impressive impact as a result.

(f) *Speeches.* If the purposes of the visit include the holding of conferences and displays it will be necessary to plan these in detail or delegate their planning to senior staff abroad. The executive will certainly need speeches to be prepared which make the points that head office considers necessary. Such speeches will be based on reports already in existence or specially prepared, and this background material may need to travel with the speeches to give the executive a full package of background information.

(g) *Procedural routines.* It is important to plan in advance the routine procedures which the executive is to follow so that his secretary and other members of the back-up team can give the fullest possible support. Thus an 'Immediate Action' routine for any sales made should be devised so that they are followed up while the trail is still warm. Similarly, the executive may wish to dictate reports on the views expressed at any conference or meeting, as feedback to head office. Arrangements for tapes to be flown back for transcription, or for facsimile copies of reports typed abroad to be transmitted to head office may be finalised, including detailed arrangements for their appraisal at head office in his absence.

One routine that must be established is how the executive can be contacted for certain. Where the time lag is not too great—for example, when visiting European countries—it may be sound policy to fix a time, or perhaps two times, every day when the executive will try to ensure that he is in his hotel room. This will enable direct links to be established should they be required. If there is nothing to report either way the call can be terminated at once to save expense. With countries where the time lag is great it may be quite impossible to establish a link in office hours. Arrangements to have a telex link with one of the firm's agents may then be the most satisfactory method of contacting the executive, while the willingness of the secretary or some senior executive to accept calls at any time of the night will cater for real emergencies. The greater accuracy of a telex link compared with a conversation on a poor line is also an advantage.

(*h*) *Address and telephone lists.* A full list of all the business contacts in each itinerary area should be built up, with addresses and telephone numbers. It is convenient if they are in itinerary order, and it may be sound policy to prepare postcards in advance announcing arrival and confirming visit dates and times. These can be posted as soon as the executive arrives, although early appointments are better confirmed by telephone.

Friends and relatives (if any) should also be contacted, since they are often most helpful in assisting the visitor, and in addition enable him to relax by reducing the endless round of business that otherwise develops.

Practical Travel Details and Documents

Although travel agents or hotel agencies are to be used for the actual travel arrangements the executive must attend to many details for himself. His secretary should ensure that nothing is forgotten. Most of the points listed below are important.

(*a*) *Passport.* It is essential to have a valid passport with plenty of spare pages. It is taking longer these days to secure a new passport, except for the simplified 'British Visitors' type which only lasts one year and is inappropriate for a businessman who has to secure visas and entry permits. Order a new passport in good time if the pages are nearly all used up. It is wise to learn the number of the passport by heart, although it should also be recorded in several places. A few extra passport photographs may be helpful, and can be given up if required on entry to plants or depots where security is tight.

(*b*) *International Driving Licences.* The Automobile Association and the Royal Automobile Club are authorised to issue International Driving Licences at a relatively modest fee to those people travelling abroad who may find an ordinary United Kingdom Driving Licence unacceptable. The charge is quite small (£1.50 at the time of writing) and they are only issued to persons who possess already a valid United Kingdom Licence. A passport-type photograph must be attached.

(*c*) *Insurance.* Most businessmen who represent their firms abroad enjoy a high salary and have mortgages and family commitments to meet. It follows that they should insist on adequate insurance when travelling on their firm's business, for the risks of air travel and foreign travel generally are considerable. A policy for a realistic sum, say £50,000, for a short period is not very expensive, and may mean a great deal to a wife and children deprived of their breadwinner. Insurance against sickness, loss of property, etc., is usually taken out without hesitation by any traveller; life insurance at a sensible figure is not so frequently considered.

(*d*) *Credit cards.* While the major United Kingdom banks issue credit cards which have a very wide acceptability, it is regrettably true that not everyone will accept them abroad. This is partly due to the ways in which currencies are allowed to 'float' these days, so that a foreigner supplying goods and services to a UK businessman may find that the exchange rate has moved against him before he receives payment under the credit card. 'Bank of America' and 'American Express' cards are acceptable almost anywhere, and may be obtained relatively easily by businessmen. It is therefore desirable to carry one of these cards when travelling abroad.

(*e*) *Foreign exchange.* Adequate supplies of foreign exchange should be obtained before departure, and travellers' cheques or letters of credit which will enable cash to be obtained abroad should be also carried. Some of the earliest contacts with foreigners on arrival require small notes or coins. For example, one does not wish to give a 100 franc tip to the porter. It is therefore helpful to bring back from each trip a small amount of loose change and small denomination notes. Stored away in an envelope in the filing cabinet these small amounts will be useful on the next visit abroad.

(*f*) *Health aids.* Whilst in many foreign countries it is possible to buy products like antibiotics over the counter without a doctor's prescription, it often happens that ordinary medicaments like aspirin, ointments, etc., are difficult to obtain when required. A reasonable selection of health aids should be taken out. Such items as salt tablets and anti-malaria tablets may be necessary and a doctor's assistance should be sought in any difficulty. A full range of injections should be arranged against such diseases as yellow fever, bubonic plague, typhoid, etc., where embassies require or advise such precautions. A World Health Certificate certifying details of the inoculations obtained is essential in many countries. A doctor will supply prescriptions for any drugs required for the duration of the trip, or a letter advising foreign doctors of treatment being given.

One of the worst calamities of all is to break one's spectacles in a foreign country where it may be difficult to replace them. A second pair should be taken along, and also a prescription for their replacement if necessary. In some countries sun-glasses are essential, and a spare pair is also advisable.

(*g*) *Electrical equipment.* Variations in voltage, etc., sometimes render equipment such as display matter, portable electric-typewriters, electric razors, etc., unsuitable in some countries. Alternatively, it may be necessary to change over a switch from one voltage to another. Adaptors may be necessary and advice can often be obtained from travel agents or embassies.

(*h*) *Climatic aspects of the journey.* The secretary should check the climatic aspects to ensure that the executive has appropriate weights of clothing and sufficient changes to meet all likely needs. Books such as Croner's *Reference Book for Exporters* give such details for all countries in the world.

(*i*) *The secretary's personal requirements.* Where a secretary is accompanying the executive she must of course have appropriate smart clothing, be well groomed, be adequately supplied with such items as cosmetics, needle and thread, and able to appear at all times and on all occasions as a fitting companion for the executive. This will almost certainly include social occasions and formal functions, so that evening clothes are essential. She should demand an expense allowance to ensure she has a proper wardrobe and to enable her to visit the hairdresser, manicurist, etc., when required.

Covering the Executive in his Absence

The executive's normal programme has to be covered in his absence. If his secretary is not accompanying him she is the obvious person to cover his work, at least in its more routine aspects. She is obviously also the ideal person to know how the more difficult aspects of his work are to be covered and to relay them to the person designated to handle them. It is important to keep the work going as much as possible, so that his absence is no time to take 'French leave'. On the contrary, an even more responsible attitude is necessary, to ensure that his mail is opened, his calls answered and—should he need to make contact—that he will find the department manned.

If the executive is being accompanied by his secretary it is necessary to plan the handling of his work with real care. One way is to route his correspondence through to a secretary of equal status who should be fully briefed on the arrangements for delegating his work. Alternatively, a younger secretary should be inducted into the work for several weeks prior to their departure, so that she will know roughly what is required and to whom she should turn for help with each aspect of his work.

The office will usually be in contact with the executive much more regularly and directly than the executive's own family. The secretary, or if she is accompanying him, her deputy, should ensure that the family is told of his safe arrival at destination, and that any personal messages he sends are passed on accurately. If the secretary is accompanying the executive her own family should similarly be kept in touch with the progress of the visit.

Departure Day Minus One

It is of considerable help to the executive if a final review of everything affecting the trip is held on the day before departure. The secretary should go through the contents of his briefcase with him, explaining what he has and where it is packed. The location of his travel documents, itinerary, visit briefings, sales literature, etc., should be clarified and related to the checklist for the visit to ensure that nothing has been forgotten.

Finally the secretary should give the executive a checklist to use before leaving for the airport. It should list all those items to be taken with him, as a separate unit. Thus if his tickets are already in his briefcase, the words 'briefcase' on the checklist should be enough, but if his tickets are in his wallet then they should appear as a separate unit on the checklist. A typical list is shown in Fig. 16.1.

Summary

1. Every major firm has international links to secure raw materials and components, and to establish export markets. Executive travel is therefore inevitable, and the executive secretary should be prepared to travel too.

2. The overseas visit must be planned in great detail so that the objects of the visit are understood. The executive must be thoroughly briefed about each aspect of the visit and supplied with customer reports, proposals for future developments, etc. The costs and benefits of the trip should be estimated and compared.

3. The itinerary must be devised with great care to give adequate time at each centre to enable all contacts to be made. It should allow for changes of programme to meet customer needs.

```
                    Final Check List

Passport
Visa
International Driving Licence
World Health Certificate
Airline tickets
Foreign currency
Sterling
Credit cards
Travellers' cheques
House keys
Car keys
Medical pack (including spare spectacles)
Itinerary
Audio-visual pack
Back-up stock pack
Visiting cards
Spectacles
Briefcase
Personal suitcase
Hand luggage
```

Fig. 16.1. A final checklist.

4. To support the itinerary detailed plans for each meeting, conference or function should be made with speeches prepared in advance, and 'visit-briefs' drawn up to re-brief the executive about each meeting before he actually goes to it, so that he is au fait with the objectives of the visit and the background to it.

5. A wide variety of back-up facilities is necessary. Such items as sales literature, display equipment, business cards, etc., as well as essential paraphernalia such as passports, international driving licences, etc.

6. The various aspects of the executive's work should be delegated to appropriate staff for attention in his absence, and an adequate briefing of all concerned should take place beforehand. Immediately before departure the secretary should go through with the executive all the background material visit briefs, documents, etc., so that he knows where everything is and how it is packed.

Suggested Further Reading

Current literature of your local airport, seaport, travel agency, hotel chain, car hire chain, etc.

Pan Am's World USA Guide, Pan American World Airways Inc.
Penta Airline Hotels brochure, from the European Hotel Corporation (EHC) N.V.
 This body is partly owned by British Airways.
Reference Book for Exporters, Croner Publications, updated monthly.

MANAGEMENT APPRECIATION—MANAGEMENT IN THE FRAMEWORK OF PRODUCTION

The Secretary and an Appreciation of Management

One of the features which distinguishes the work of an executive secretary from that of a mere shorthand typist is the extent to which she is a part of the management team. She is not just a mere tool available to be used when required; she has a positive contribution to make and her own expertise to use in making it. This contribution lies chiefly in the communication field, where her unique position as a link between executive staff and ordinary staff enables her to offer a service to both sections. In the human and personal aspects of business she is similarly well placed to aid management in covering aspects of the working situation which may be of great importance in achieving and maintaining efficient operations. In social matters of every sort she will be an obvious reference point for all organisers of social functions, for staff associations and similar bodies.

For all these reasons the executive secretary needs to be well informed about management. She cannot operate effectively without an understanding of the structure of the firm for which she works, the principles which act as guidelines to the management and the legal framework within which all aspects of the firm's activities are conducted. Examinations for executive secretaries usually include a paper on management appreciation designed to direct the thinking of executive secretaries towards a broad appreciation of 'Management' at the executive level. Only such an appreciation enables her to understand the problems and responsibilities of the executive she serves and the pressures he faces. In this section of the book we consider the development of management thought, the organisation of businesses and the control techniques available, and the position of the executive secretary in the management team.

The Meaning of Production

We live in a sophisticated world which satisfies the needs of mankind by a complex system of production in which the goods and services required for a full life are produced by firms and institutions of all sorts. These firms and institutions all have their own specialist parts to play, and fit into the scheme somewhere, however varied their organisations or the operations they carry out. In trying to understand this complex pattern there are a number of basic ideas which we must get clear. The more important of them are listed and explained below, but a full understanding can only be gained by a detailed study of Economics and Commerce (see Suggested Further Reading at the end of this chapter).

Production

The popular idea of production is that it has something to do with factories, or farms, and is concerned with the production of goods which are made available for consumption. This is a very elementary view. More sophisticated views of production extend the meaning to include the provision of all mankind's needs—that is, both goods and services. We not only need food, clothing, shelter and other goods, but education, entertainment, medical care protection, etc. From this point of view every job is productive, and the work of the doctor, the teacher, the local government officer and the truck driver is just as essential as the work of the farm labourer, the factory hand or the motor vehicle assembler. From this viewpoint the executive secretary is a vital link in production. The letters she types and the telephone calls she makes will be key activities in the chain of communication. Not a factory starts up production until management approves the plans and finds the capital to build the works. Raw materials are purchased, finished goods distributed, strikes averted and wages paid by executives who use secretarial services as the medium of their activities.

Specialisation

Specialisation is the key to high productivity of goods and services. We do not raise our own sheep, shear them, wash and card the wool, spin it into thread and weave cloth from it. All these jobs are specialist jobs, carried on in the place where it is most convenient and logical. The sheep reared in New Zealand are shorn, and the wool sold in London to Bradford woollen manufacturers whose cloth eventually reaches the tailors and garment workers of the East End of London, etc., etc. Everyone has his part to play and receives his reward for the 'production' that results.

Money

Money is a veil that hides what is really going on. It is a means of exchange. We do not not want money for its own sake, for you cannot eat it, wear it, shelter under it or be entertained by it. Money is simply a convenient way of arranging rewards for services in the process of production. In return for the efforts we make in production we receive a sum of money which we exchange for the goods and services we require. Really we are exchanging our services for the goods and services of others, but the exchange is made through a money mechanism. That is why inflation is such a problem. It erodes money values and we do not know what the money we are paid for our services will eventually purchase when we come to spend it.

The Mixed Economy

There are two chief methods of producing goods and services. One way is to produce them by private enterprise, with people choosing what goods and services they will provide. The other is to produce them by nationalised industries; by some sort of state-run enterprise. A continual debate goes on as to which method is better, but in fact we have to have a 'mixed economy', with some private enterprise and some state-run services. For example, defence must be state-run; we cannot allow people to have their own private armies like the robber barons of the Middle Ages. In fact the United Kingdom has about a 50–50 mix, with many nationalised industries and many privately-run firms. Executive secretaries are of course active in both private and nationalised firms.

Primary, Secondary and Tertiary Production

In order to make the study of production simpler, economists divide it up into three types: primary, secondary and tertiary (third) production.

Primary production is the production of all the goods made available by nature. This includes all the agricultural products such as wheat, barley, oats, rye, root crops, vegetables, fruit, etc. It also includes animal products, such as beef, pork, wool, mutton, fish, poultry, etc., and also minerals in the earth, gases of the atmosphere, etc. **Secondary production** is the production of more sophisticated goods, such as are made by refining or improving upon the products of nature. For example, crude oil is refined into petrol, paraffin, solvents, etc. Skins are turned into shoes, and uncut diamonds into jewellery. Iron is turned into stainless steel and raw rubber into wet-suits. Primary and secondary production comprises then all the goods needed by mankind, whether in the natural state, like honey, or a more sophisticated state, like transistor radios.

Tertiary production is the production of services, and here it is important to distinguish two types: personal services and commercial services. Personal services are performed for us personally, as when the dentist repairs cavities in our teeth or the surgeon sets our broken limbs. Commercial services are performed on the goods made in primary and secondary production, to enable them to reach us in our own localities. The chief commercial services are transport (which moves the goods geographically), trade (which transfers their ownership from producers through wholesalers and retailers to us as the consumers), insurance (which carries the risks of losses), finance (which smoothes out money transactions) and communications (which keep everyone notified of the progress being made elsewhere). Executive secretaries are clearly part of this 'communications' aspect of tertiary production. Although some executive secretaries might work in the 'personal services' field—as medical secretaries, for example—the vast majority are employed in the commercial field.

It follows that every type of human activity fits into the pattern of production in some way. A trawlerman fishes for a catch on the high seas (primary production). A rivetter builds a ship (sophisticated secondary production). A banker arranges the clearance of cheques drawn upon him (a commercial service—tertiary production). A detective fingerprints the safe in our burgled office (a personal service). Only a very few people cannot be fitted into the pattern. The tramp sleeping under a haystack with a stomach full of raw carrots from a nearby field is a mere parasite on society. The retired pensioner is living upon savings made in more active times. The new-born baby is dependent upon his parents' efforts in the system of production, and when mature enough will in turn take his part in providing for his own needs. Like the vast majority of human beings he must work for his living, producing the goods and services required by mankind, as one of the **factors of production.**

The Factors of Production

The last part of this brief survey of the production process requires us to look at the factors, or agents, of production. Before we can have any production at all we must have three factors which will enable production to be carried on. These three factors are land, labour and capital. Each of these terms needs a word of explanation, as they have rather special meanings when used in this connection. By **land** we mean not only the surface of the earth itself but all the bounties of nature buried in it, or floating round it in the sea or in the atmosphere above it. Land therefore means the natural resources of the world. **Labour,** by contrast, means all the human resources of the earth, and the infinite variety of skills they display. Some have little more than brawn to offer, they can lift and push or pull. Others lift, push and pull with more intelligence so that they are more effective. Yet others invent cunning devices, mechanical and electronic contrivances which lighten labour, raise productivity and increase wealth. Some think sublime thoughts, sing blithely or entertain us with their wit. Whatever the part they play, labour when applied to the natural resources of the earth produces the goods and services we need.

The third factor of production, **capital,** is less simple to explain. Whatever the goods or services we produce, there is a time factor involved. We cannot decide we want a thing one moment and consume it the next. There is a growing period for plants, and a rearing period for animals. There is a planning period for every project and a construction period for every industrial plant before production can begin. During these time-lags we have to keep the people working on the projects alive and well, before production begins to flow. This means we must set aside before we start the project some of our wealth (goods and services) to support them. This is called capital—and it is collected in money form so that they can draw the money and exchange it for goods. So the system we operate is a 'capitalist' system, because it depends on keeping back some of our current production as capital to support new investment which is taking place. Even communist countries use the same system, though their money system is less well-developed than our own and much of the capital saved is saved at an official level.

A really good understanding of the relationship between current production and current consumption is essential to every manager. The difference between the two represents the amount available for investment. If we consume all we produce there is nothing left to 'invest' in new plant and machinery. If we cut consumption the rest of our output can be used to support workers in the construction and engineering industries to build new factories, plants, ships, aircraft, etc. In the early days of any capitalist system much of the wealth goes into investment in new industries. The early English trade unionists complained of 'jam tomorrow—never jam today'. Even today developing nations face the same problem. Once a broad industrial structure has developed, it is easier to finance new industrial plants while enjoying a reasonable standard of living, but the need to re-invest is always present. Over-consumption still means under-investment and a lack of growth in the economy.

A Fourth Factor of Production?

Some people hold that there are not three factors of production (land, labour and capital), but four. The fourth factor is the 'entrepreneur'. An entrepreneur is one who is in effective control of a business undertaking. Someone has to step out of the crowd and say 'Right, let's get this organised.' In the early days of the industrial system this entrepreneur was always the man who had accumulated some capital. He may have saved it up by self-denial, or obtained it by trading with distant places. He might have been a successful inventor or even an unscrupulous blackguard. The fact remains that he had capital with which to buy 'time' while he constructed a factory, or dug a mine or reorganised agriculture. The early enterpreneurs decided what to make, or what service to supply, and how to harness technology to assist the production process. They supervised much of the work directly, sought out expanding markets, hired specialist help to overcome problems, lobbied for legislation which would assist their activities and in general 'managed' much of the enterprise personally. Today such entrepreneurs still arise, but the scale of enterprises is so great that no one can control personally the diverse activities of our great companies. Instead the control of large firms lies in the hands of managers in a pyramid-like structure. The apex of the pyramid is the board of the company, making entrepreneurial decisions about what goods and services shall be offered, while at lower levels managing directors and managers make tactical decisions designed to implement the policies of the board.

In organising production there is, at least to begin with, a good deal of choice about the proportions in which the factors of production are combined. Generally speaking, we can vary the factors within certain limits anyway. For example, we can vary the quantity of land to be used. In New York City land is used more intensively than in Texas. Canadian farms are much less intensively used than English farms; the great wheat belt of the Mid-West is farmed extensively rather than intensively. We can usually reduce the quantity of labour we need to hire if we use extra capital to buy machinery. In old established industries, like the Port of London, it is very difficult to reduce the labour force and switch to a heavily capitalised port, and management has had to try to reduce it by a special system of severance payments to employees prepared to leave the industry.

When any business starts up one of the chief tasks of management is to decide the best 'mix' of land, labour and capital for the business. However, this mixture will vary as the firm grows in size, so that a periodic reassessment of the firm is essential. A host of other problems arises as well, problems caused by market trends, by competition from other firms, by official requirements relating to tax, manpower, health and safety, etc. All these problems make the task of management more complex. The secretary needs to appreciate the problems of management, and to keep abreast of developments in management thinking. Working as it does within a framework of production requirements which are dictated by the nature of the product or service it provides, management finds each of its requirements affected by a host of external influences such as the influences of world supply and demand, the influences of central and local governments, trade unions, etc. These influences are not static but dynamic, and constantly adjust to changing circumstances to which management must similarly respond if it is to remain competitive, or escape political, social, environmental or other censures. Many of the pressures exerted are mutually irreconcilable, so that it is impossible for management to escape censure by someone and it must do the best it can. Thus in the motor vehicle industry a new model to meet trends in public taste or fashion cannot be introduced without disturbing those engaged in the production of the old model to be rendered obsolete.

Some of these influences are illustrated in Fig. 17.1.

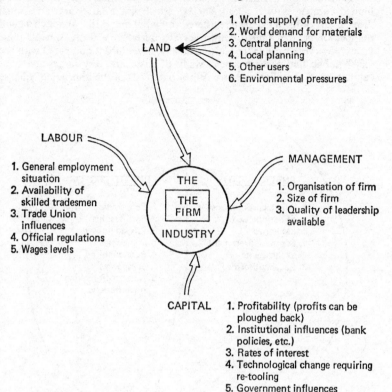

LAND
1. World supply of materials
2. World demand for materials
3. Central planning
4. Local planning
5. Other users
6. Environmental pressures

LABOUR
1. General employment situation
2. Availability of skilled tradesmen
3. Trade Union influences
4. Official regulations
5. Wages levels

THE
THE FIRM
INDUSTRY

MANAGEMENT
1. Organisation of firm
2. Size of firm
3. Quality of leadership available

CAPITAL
1. Profitability (profits can be ploughed back)
2. Institutional influences (bank policies, etc.)
3. Rates of interest
4. Technological change requiring re-tooling
5. Government influences
6. Investment reliefs (of taxation)

Fig. 17.1. Influences at work to affect management decisions on the employment of factors.

Types of Business Organisation

There are a number of forms of business organisation, ranging from small-scale businesses known as sole traders to large-scale organisations like multi-national companies and government departments. They may be divided into two sectors—the public sector and the private sector—which together make up the total national effort. These two sectors may be illustrated as shown in Fig. 17.2.

In former times the private sector formed about 90 per cent of the total national effort and government activities the remaining 10 per cent. In Gladstone's day the total income of the government was provided by the tax on four items—drink, tobacco, tea and stamp duty—and a small income tax of 1 per cent; £67 million in all. In the most recent year of statistics available the public sector took 46 per cent of the nation's wealth (£103,720 million out of £225,522 million) and the lowest rate of income tax was 30 per cent.

Sole traders and partnerships number about 1½ million firms, while private limited companies total about 600,000. Most of the latter are quite small firms, many of them having a registered capital of only £100, although a good number of private limited companies are fairly large firms. But all these firms, when totalled together, are relatively insignificant compared with the 6,000 public limited companies. Many of these are very large, and have capitals of £500 million or more. When one reads of the impending collapse

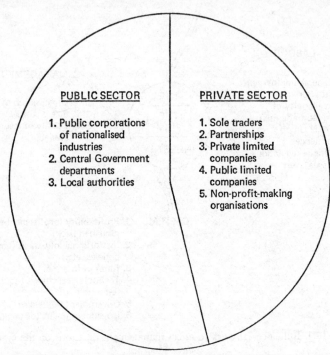

PUBLIC SECTOR

1. Public corporations of nationalised industries
2. Central Government departments
3. Local authorities

PRIVATE SECTOR

1. Sole traders
2. Partnerships
3. Private limited companies
4. Public limited companies
5. Non-profit-making organisations

Fig. 17.2. The United Kingdom economy.

of such a company, with tens of thousands of employees affected and firms all over the world supplying components for its products placed in jeopardy, one realises what large-scale business really means to the prosperity of the nation. Small wonder that cries are heard for official rescue operations by governments.

The typical organisation of modern business is therefore the public limited company. It is the type of business that really matters in the private sector, and most of the employment opportunities for top secretaries lie in this field. It is accordingly described in detail later in Chapter 19.

In the public sector the typical organisation was until recently the Civil Service, which recruited the staff required for all the great Departments of State, such as the Foreign Office, the Home Office, the Board of Trade and other Ministries. More recently, however, the nationalisation programme carried out in the immediate post-war years led to the establishment of many public corporations, such as the National Coal Board, the Gas Boards, etc. These bodies are very similar in organisation to the public limited companies in that they are autonomous bodies not subject, as is the Civil Service, to day-to-day Parliamentary control. Both the public corporations and the Civil Service Departments are large-scale organisations with many opportunities for executive secretaries.

The Development of Management Thought

The large-scale firms with whom the executive secretary usually finds employment are no longer run by entrepreneurs of the old sort like the men who founded the industrial system 200 years ago. Instead we live in what one observer called the era of 'organisation man'. Every organisation is managed by a hierarchy of upper, middle and lower management, guiding the business through the uncharted waters which surround it: 'uncharted' because the business scene is dynamic and restless. Even the best established firms have to contend with changing situations. At any given time one fifth of the products being marketed are made from materials not even invented a quarter of a century before. Today's breadwinning product is next year's has-been, and this year's has-been is next year's dead duck. In plotting its course management has been guided by a succession of philosophies devised to meet the difficulties facing it. Each of these philosophies reflects the needs of its times, and has developed from an earlier philosophy. In historical sequence they were (a) the doctrine of 'laisser faire', (b) scientific management, and (c) the human relations movement.

(a) *The Doctrine of 'Laisser Faire'*. 'Laisser faire' means 'leave it to work itself out'. The doctrine held that if a businessman was left to himself unhindered by any sort of regulation or control his natural inclinations would lead him to do things that were best for himself and created the greatest possible wealth. Since the creation of wealth is a praiseworthy process (wealth meaning an abundance of useful goods and services), in doing the best for himself he also would do the best for the nation and his fellow citizens. By creating employment opportunities he would spread some of the wealth he created around to others, and the general prosperity would be advanced. This philosophy fitted in very well with the times, for it was a period when discoveries were made largely by trial and error rather than by research. The entrepreneur, under the laisser faire system, was free to find a practical solution to the basic problems of production, and in so doing he developed the knowledge and expertise that has become modern technology. Those entrepreneurs who successfully solved their problems became rich. Those who did not succeed suffered the losses personally, as their resources were dissipated in unprofitable ventures. The increasing wealth of the nation in the years that followed the industrial revolution bore witness to the success of the 'laisser faire' system. The desperate poverty of some people, and the separation of society into classes of haves and have-nots was equally strong evidence of its failures.

As far as management was concerned then, the 'laisser faire' system meant a free enterprise system. The entrepreneur and his assistants ran the business in the way that seemed to them the most economic and efficient, and offered the best prospects of profitability. They used resources in such a way as to develop their businesses. They took little account of social and environmental criticisms, though many acted as much in the public interest as in their own. Even today, in many countries passing through their industrial revolution, the same disregard of social and environmental criticisms can be observed.

(*b*) *Scientific Management*. It was natural that a long period of trial and error in production and management should eventually be succeeded by a more scientific approach. The problem was to replace the mystery of an ancient craft system built up by trial and error by a more analytical process which sought to establish clear principles of production. The great exponent of scientific management in the early days was F. W. Taylor (1856–1915), who maintained that what was needed to revolutionise industry was that both managers and managed should cease to squabble about the division of the surplus wealth that they were creating, and should concentrate on increasing the wealth that was available to be shared. This would best be achieved by substituting exact scientific study of all aspects of the production process for the unsupported opinion of either the managers or the men.

During the first half of the twentieth century the greatest emphasis in scientific management was in the industrial field. Henry Ford said, 'Manufacturing is not buying cheap and selling dear. It is the focussing upon a manufacturing project of the principles of power, accuracy, economy, system, continuity, speed and repetition.' More recently the same principles have been applied to the other aspects of production. If a thing is not completely 'produced' until it reaches the final consumer, then the same scientific thought that goes into the industrial processes must be applied to transport and distribution, to warehousing and exchange, to documentation and communication. The control techniques are applicable not only to the factory, but also to the warehouse, the office; and even to the hospital theatre or the television studio. The great merit of scientific management is that in seeking to eliminate wastage, delay, under-utilisation of resources and low productivity it is in sympathy with the general aspirations of mankind to enjoy the highest possible standard of living without totally destroying the environment in which we live.

In terms of the human relations involved, scientific management substituted reason for authority. Whereas the entrepreneur did things his way in an authoritarian manner, scientific management did things in certain ways because it could be clearly shown that this was the best way to do them. The increased productivity enabled the surplus value created to increase and made a general raising of living standards possible. This is not to suggest that every venture into scientific management was a success. Everyone has heard of cases where 'time and motion study' produced such an increase in spoiled work or such an improvement in wages that the very existence of a factory was threatened.

The main groups of operations to be found in any organisation are five: technical, commercial, financial, accounting and administrative operations. Scientific management principles may be applied to each of these groups, and consist in analysing the process as follows. What is done? Who does it? Why do they do it? How efficient are they? How can efficiency be raised? At the lower levels most activities are technical; subordinates are carrying out activities which can be examined directly and the technical arrangements can be improved. At higher levels the production of technical activities is reduced, and administrative activities increase. These administrative activities must be subjected to the same close scientific analysis as the technical and other operations. Since they involve considerable preoccupation with human resources, and many of these activities cannot be examined in purely mechanistic terms, the problems require broad understanding by, and much administrative training of, top level executives.

(c) *The 'Human Relations' Movement.* The human relations movement sees the behaviour of any individual in employment as one aspect of the individual's behaviour in society generally. A person behaves cooperatively in a working situation if he is at ease with himself in all his social activity. The movement holds that even the most careful scientific appraisal of operations and procedures will be useless if the individuals who are to perform the operations are distrustful, uncooperative and unmotivated. One rather illiterate young lady described her situation more graphically than she intended when she told her personnel officer that she felt 'Like a *clog* in a big machine'. People resent being treated like cogs in a machine, and management must therefore get its human relations as right as its procedures and mechanical lay-outs, if it is to achieve the full benefits from scientific management.

All employees bring to their employment situation a basic personality, made up of three elements: temperament, behaviour patterns learned as a child and the background culture passed on by his parents. Temperament is largely inherited, but our understanding of the complexity of genetics these days leads us to believe that it is not necessarily just a matter of 'like father, like son'. It is just as likely to be 'like grandfather, like son' or even 'like great-grandmother, like son'. This inherited temperament is in any case modified by environment. Childhood circumstances may permit or inhibit the full development of inherited temperament, while child-rearing patterns of behaviour and cultural influences may suppress some inclinations and develop others which meet with parental or social approval. The employee therefore displays a basic personality, which motivates all his behaviour. He reacts to the work situation in a way that reflects his past experiences, and these reactions will be unique, for every individual is different. His reactions will be such as to satisfy his needs. These may be listed as primary needs, such as food, clothing, shelter, sleep and sexual satisfaction, and secondary needs, like companionship, self-esteem, respect of others and self-realisation. In advanced societies such as our own, primary needs are satisfied very easily by even the most routine employments, and a good deal of companionship follows. The really crucial aspects for the success of a business are the more sophisticated needs; self-esteem, the respect of others and self-realisation. The last of these refers to the total development of the individual, his attainment of the very best level of which he is capable.

The significance of these needs for management is that their frustration can cause enormous disruption of business activity. The worker who is unable to realise his own ambitions in the productive process will frustrate the best laid plans of scientific management. He must be treated like an individual and his problems and attitudes analysed. The good manager displays empathy, not sympathy. Empathy is the ability to 'feel with' the employee, and see the situation in the way that the employee sees it. If the manager is mature enough to see the situation from the employee's point of view he is more likely to be able to devise a policy that will ensure cooperation and acceptance by the employee of the system of work as one which he approves of. The human relations movement in management therefore seeks to replace 'reason' (the motivation behind scientific management) by 'self-realisation'. Every employee should feel that he is as interested as anyone in the productive process, for through it he will achieve self-esteem, the esteem of others and even the total realisation of his own natural capacities. This restores work to its natural place as an activity giving mental and spiritual satisfaction, rather than a tedious monotony of time to be endured.

(*d*) *Modern Influences and Styles of Leadership.* In the modern situation the style of leadership has to be such as to take account of the new aspirations of mankind and of mankind's increasing sophistication. In earlier days sophistication was a product of formal education and those who had achieved an appropriate level of formal education were the natural leaders. Today sophistication is still achieved to some extent in this old way, but the new technology of the mass media makes experts of us all. No longer is the field marshal's baton carried in every soldier's cartridge pouch. It is tucked away instead in the wiring of the television set he watches as a child. People are better informed about other life styles, observe from an early age how the other half lives, and can evaluate the rewards other people receive more accurately than ever before in history. To be a leader today requires manifest merit. It is impossible to lead without the confidence and respect of those around you. To get effective work from subordinates requires mastery of the job facing the group, and action in accordance with the needs of the situation and the views of all interested parties. Such parties can only form views of the situation if they are fully informed by an adequate system of communication and joint consultation. The manager who does not communicate or consult, and uses outdated authoritarian approaches, does a disservice to his company and becomes a pain in the neck to everyone above and below him. The sophistication of working people is such that they will usually see reason if they are fully informed. The election of unreasonable shop-floor representatives usually reflects intransigent authoritarian attitudes by management.

Management thought has therefore moved in the course of two centuries from the authoritarian control of ruthless entrepreneurs (Dickens called them the Iron Gentlemen), through scientific management based on reasoned appraisal of the best way to do things, to a system of leadership tending more and more towards egalitarian democracy. This seeks to secure an efficient economy by enabling each individual in the long chain of production, distribution and exchange to achieve maximum personal self-realisation in a system of work, which he understands, approves and appreciates.

In such a system the executive secretary has an important part to play. She is particularly well placed to assist self-realisation on the part of juniors and other staff with whom she has to deal. Equally, she can become a real source of frustration if she is insensitive to the true needs of enlightened management in such respects. The self-important secretary whose lack of tact damages human relations at all levels is frequently met with, and universally con-

Plate 9(a). The Dictaphone Dual Display word processor.

(Courtesy of Dictaphone Co. Ltd)

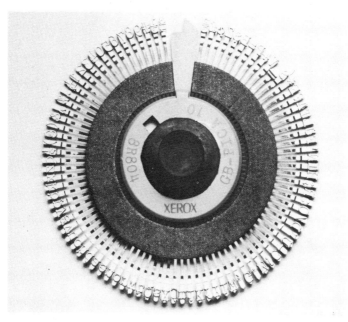

Plate 9(b). The Xerox 800 Electronic Typewriter 'Daisy'.

(Courtesy of Rank Xerox Ltd)

Plate 10. The Nashua 1218 plain paper copier.

(Courtesy of Nashua Copycat Limited)

Plate 11(a). A main telephone with one extension.

Plate 11(b). A keymaster 2×10 installation.

Plate 11(c). A cordless private manual branch exchange (4×18).

(a) Desk model 'direct speech' intercom.

(b) Desk model intercom with handset.

(c) Wall unit for workshops, etc.

(d) Pocket paging receiver.

Plate 12. The ITT 511 'direct speech' internal communications system.

(Courtesy of **ITT** Business Systems Ltd)

Plate 13(a). A loudspeaking telephone.

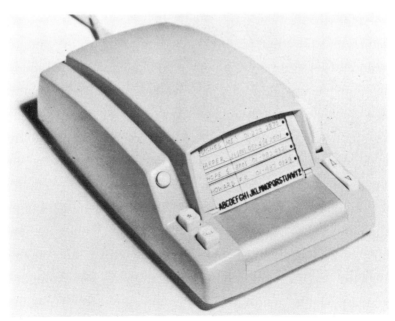

Plate 13(b). A tape callmaker.

Plate 14(a). A Shipton Telstor Autophone with playback facility.

(Courtesy of Shipton Telstor Ltd)

Plate 14(b). A Telex installation, showing the dialling unit, the keyboard and the copyholder.

(Courtesy of the Post Office)

Plate 15. A Shannon retractable door cupboard showing the flexibility of storage requirements.

Note: From the top, the cupboard is storing: 1st row, lateral filing; 2nd row, lateral filing and data printout; 3rd row, shelf filing; 4th row, a roll-out working surface and microfilm/computer cassette storage; 5th row, a roll-out tray to store index cards, literature or computer media; 6th row, lateral filing and magnetic tape storage.

(Courtesy of The Shannon Ltd)

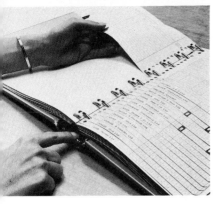

(a) A Shannoleaf book.

(b) A Shannovue book.

(c) A Shannovue cabinet.

(d) A Shannostrip desk unit

Plate 16. Visible index systems.

(Courtesy of The Shannon Ltd)

demned. The tactful, considerate secretary combines the complete mastery of her specialist skills with a generous ability to help others to make progress. At the same time she damps down situations likely to interfere with true efficiency in achieving management objectives. Such paragons are universally admired.

Summary

1. Production is a complex process in which the three factors of production —land, labour and capital—are harnessed by the management of firms to produce the goods and services required by mankind.

2. Business organisation is divided into two parts, the private sector and the public sector. The private sector includes firms run as sole traders, partnerships, private limited companies and public limited companies. The public sector comprises government departments, local government bodies, and nationalised industries run as public corporations.

3. Management used to be by authoritarian instructions issued by the entrepreneur in charge. This was later replaced by scientific management which subjected all procedures to a careful scrutiny designed to improve factory layout and plant performance. The same scrutiny was later applied to distribution and administration.

4. Modern management seeks to achieve harmonious operations by careful 'human relations' policies. These recognise the contribution made by each individual and seek to ensure the success of the firm by ensuring individual self-realisation in the work situation. The personal secretary has an important part to play in the management team.

Suggested Further Reading

Commerce Made Simple, G. Whitehead, Heinemann, most recent edition.
Economics Made Simple, G. Whitehead, Heinemann, most recent edition.
The Making of Scientific Management, L. Urwick and E. F. L. Brech, Pitman, 1955.
Management Made Simple, W. Coventry and J. Barker, Heinemann, most recent edition.
Pears Cyclopaedia (Section on Human Relations), Book Club Associates, most recent edition.

18

MANAGEMENT APPRECIATION—MANAGEMENT AND PLANNING

Objectives and the Formulation of Policies

The first requirement for sound management is to know what you are trying to do and how you propose to proceed in order to achieve your objectives. The objective is the most fundamental element in management, and operates at many levels so that objectives may be set for every level of activity to give targets which are attainable and can be observed to have been achieved. This system of management by objectives is discussed later in this chapter.

Every firm or other institution is set up with the intention of providing some good or service which will increase human satisfaction. It is this intention which forms the real objective of the firm, and which ensures the firm's profitability. Profit itself cannot be the objective initially, but is only a spin-off from the popularity of the good or service which is to be provided. Thus businesses are established to make shoes, or garments, or to catch fish or generate electricity. To the extent that the product or service required meets a popular need it will be possible to charge enough for the product to maintain the capital invested in the business and yield a profit. 'Maintaining the capital' means that we can replace equipment as it wears out in the course of production, and 'yielding a profit' means that something extra will be available to compensate the investor for surrendering the use of his funds while the business requires them.

Section 2 of the Companies Act 1948 requires all company promoters to draw up a Memorandum of Association, which is registered with the Registrar of Companies. One of the chief items in the Memorandum is a clear statement of the objects of the company, and a company must then keep its activities within the limitations imposed by its 'object clause'. Any acts outside the objects clause are said to be *'ultra vires'*—outside the powers—and are illegal. The effect of this clause can be very important, since contractual commitments entered into by a company acting outside its powers are unenforceable at law, except in the cases covered by Section 9.1 of the European Communities Act, 1972. These rules permit outsiders who did not have direct knowledge of the company's objects, and who dealt with the company in good faith in the normal course of business, to sue on the contracts they make. Those who supply goods knowing that the objects clause does not permit the company to trade in the item, will not be able to recover payment, for the contracts made are outside the powers of the company.

Within the limits set by its objects clause, the company has certain objectives to pursue. Management will define these objectives and once they are clear they can then proceed to agreeing policy. Policy is 'a body of principles underlying the activities of an organisation' (E. F. L. Brech). Such a body of principles constitutes guidelines to those charged with the conduct of the firm's affairs. It is usual to exercise a certain amount of discretion within a policy in

180

order to overcome practical difficulties that might arise in actual working, but in general matters are decided in accordance with policies laid down.

The responsibility for laying down policy rests with the Board of the company. It has a collective duty to enunciate the principles which guide the firm in its activities, and the decisions taken have to be recorded and passed down to staff at lower levels. This explains why the minutes of meetings are so important, and require to be accepted as a correct record. As she records the minutes the secretary is recording resolutions which become the policy of the company, to be followed by staff at lower levels who are carrying out the day-to-day activities. The authority of the board is carried down as 'policy' to the lower levels, in the form of instructions to executives.

One aspect of policy that will be clarified by senior management is the ethical element. This includes both the external standards of behaviour to be observed by the company in its dealings with suppliers, customers, competitors and the general public, and the internal standards to be observed by line managers in their relationships with one another and with subordinates. Other aspects are the principles of organisation which will eventually be reduced to detailed arrangements for the working of the firm. Such matters as the method of production, distribution and trade, and the functional pattern of organisation will be decided in principle and then passed down from the Board for detailed planning.

Planning

The term 'planning' may be defined as the detailed work necessary to bring an approved project or idea to fruition. The proposal has already been agreed by top management as a desirable and viable activity which has every prospect of profitability. Planning will ensure that what is envisaged in the original proposals is actually achieved. It will decide the broad outlines of operations; devise centres of activity and systems of work, and the interrelation of centres of activity so that products or documents flow through the system from start to finish in an orderly way.

Planning takes place at many levels. There is production planning which is concerned with the product itself, and its manufacture. It may be necessary to review the needs which the product is to meet, the likely development of demand for the product, the activities of competitors and the market trends. The product proposals may then need to be reviewed to ensure that it is ahead of its competitors; that it is an economic proposition; that the engineering and assembly arrangements meet the cost requirements of the market, and so on. Marketing planning seeks to ensure that the products of a firm meet the requirements of the market place, and are presented at such times and in such ways that they evoke a maximum response from customers.

Part of the planning process will be the prediction of costs and benefits, not only from the final output from the activity but from each alternative way of working. There are usually several alternative methods of work for each stage of a project and part of the planning process is to arrive at the best method from all points of view. Cost-benefit analysis is of great assistance in making such decisions.

It is also necessary to appoint a project leader and to allocate particular tasks to particular departments or members of the team. This inevitably involves some measure of *coordination*, to secure harmony between the various parts of the team; a function exercised by the team leader, or in major projects by the managing director.

Secretarial work in the planning stage is usually onerous, for there will be many meetings to attend, decisions to be recorded and reports to be made. Coordination calls for constant checks by telephone, etc., to ensure that one group does not delay the work of others or proceed impossibly fast for others with more exacting responsibilities.

Forecasting

While planning seeks to turn the proposals for viable products and projects into detailed arrangements to achieve the desired objectives, forecasting examines the whole future trend of a company's activities. It is essentially more long term than planning, and attempts to predict the pattern of activities in the years ahead, certainly five years and possibly ten years ahead. Inevitably forecasts are more inaccurate than plans, because there are more unpredictable factors to be taken into account. The background influences which are at work in the economy as a whole have to be considered. Such matters as the growth in the Gross National Product; the elasticity of demand resulting from the changes of income of our citizens; the course of international trade; the extent of foreign competition, etc., have to be taken into account.

When a firm attempts to forecast business activity for several years ahead it is dealing with a complex set of variables. Whilst it is possible to discuss many of them a brief glance at one or two may help. Take the firm's existing products. Each of these has its own share of a particular market and will display some sort of trend. How will each of these trends develop? Will the product forge ahead of, or fall behind, its competitors? Will it be faced with new competition from similar products, or from an entirely different range of goods which comes on to the market and diverts customers from one activity to an entirely different range of interests? How will each of them react if a depression period reduces customer incomes? Are they likely to be in inelastic demand, or elastic demand? The demand for a product in inelastic demand does not change much whatever happens to incomes. A product which is in elastic demand is more volatile—it sells well when people are well to do but they give up buying the product in hard times.

A second example is the policy of a firm towards capital expenditure. It is usual to evaluate the purchase of new machinery, etc., on a basis of discounted cash flow. This is based upon the fact that £1 received today is more valuable than £1 in two years' time, which is itself more valuable than £1 in ten years' time. If we set down the cost of a machine now (or perhaps payable in instalments) against the probable benefits to come from the use of that machine over the years ahead, we can compare the two to see whether the sums payable will be less than the sums receivable, (discounted, of course, to present value). Yet even if we do this type of forecast we are using a very precise type of mathematics on a basis of rather imprecise data. Most of the estimates of future income are only guesses, and in an inflationary climate even the best guesses can be hopelessly out.

It follows that while the exercise of thinking ahead is valuable in that it keeps management awake to the possibilities of competition, aware of dynamic situations in the real world and alive to the necessity to develop new products and keep ahead of the competition, it is important to bear in mind that a forecast is only a forecast in the end. A rolling programme which relates the long-term possibilities to the shorter-term possibilities and the trends actually being revealed by current business activities is most likely to keep forecasts in perspective.

Management by Objectives

Management by objectives is a system of management which aims to motivate individual members of staff, departments, divisions and indeed the whole corporation by setting objectives to be achieved.

All firms have objectives which they were established to achieve, and management policies and plans arising from them. Experience shows that if objectives can be precisely quantified and expressed in simple terms not only for the company in general but for each department or even each individual employee, then the motivation to achieve the objective may be increased considerably. Thus the objective 'To become a leading firm in the electronics industry' is too vague an objective for many line managers, and may not be within their power to achieve. The objective 'To increase sales in the department to a quarterly total in excess of £100,000' is much more interesting as a target. It must be a realistic and attainable target. The short time-scale requires staff to get busy now if they are to achieve the objective by the end of the current quarter, and considerable enthusiasm may be generated in the scramble to achieve it.

Management by objectives requires the establishment of measurable objectives, not objectives stated in general terms. There are two categories: corporate objectives and individual objectives. The former must be decided by the Board, and constitute a review exercise in an established company. 'Where are we going, and what are we trying to do?' When this has been decided the organisation of the company will usually need to be changed in order to achieve the clear targets established by the Board. So far as possible a quantity (or standard of achievement) and a time-scale should be built into the objective. How much improvement is to be achieved by a certain time, and relative to what levels of achievement at what base date? Thus if the objective is based on current output levels being raised by 20 per cent in two years' time, the objective can be compared with the actual attainment as the two-year period proceeds. Effort can then be called for to achieve the objective if we appear to be under-achieving at any time during the period. A passive prediction is no good, it has to be a challenging goal which can be reached by planned performance.

With the tools available to management today—data processing in the form of 'models' based upon mathematical expressions of the constraints existing on a company's activities—it is possible to evaluate alternative strategies and choose objectives which are both attainable and desirable.

Individual objectives should be achieved by a process of supervisor–employee negotiation which takes an adult view of the employee and his ability to contribute to the setting of targets and the achievement of objectives. The essential thing is for the employee to set down his own targets and for these to be matched by his superior's view of targets in the light of corporate objectives. The resulting discussion no doubt leads to the rejection of some items and possibly even to feedback to higher levels. For example, the worker's view that a certain aspect of corporate objectives is quite unrealistic unless a particular machine is replaced may lead to the necessary capital being made available. The agreed personal objectives should be written down, and copies made available to both the supervisor and the employee. They then form the standard of anticipated performance with which actual results can be compared in due course. The individual knows and understands where his personal efforts fit into corporate strategy, and his manifest success (or otherwise) will be obvious to both parties, and will call forth its justified measure of praise (or blame).

Summary

1. A company is set up with definite objectives which are stated in the 'objects clause' of the Memorandum of Association. These objects will be pursued by management, which will lay down policies designed to achieve the objectives. These policies are principles underlying the firms' activities.

2. Planning is the detailed work necessary to carry out a project which has been approved by management. It seeks to establish centres of activity and systems of work which will be effective.

3. Forecasting is the long-range appraisal of business trends for a number of years ahead. It seeks to envisage market trends, capital investment programmes, future project developments and future products. It is inevitably less precise than short-term planning, but serves to keep management alert to the need for innovation in, and adjustment to, a changing, competitive world.

4. Management by objectives seeks to establish clear targets for attainment at all levels of business activity. By setting realistic and measurable objectives which can be seen to be achieved it generates enthusiasm for the corporate aims. By agreeing with individual members of staff personal objectives which advance corporate aims, personal initiative and cooperation is achieved to secure the success of the proposed plans.

Suggested Further Reading

The Arts of Top Management, A McKinsey Anthology (Ed. Roland Mann), McGraw-Hill, 1970.

Management. Its Nature and Significance, E. F. L. Brech, Pitman, most recent edition.

Management Made Simple, W. Coventry and J. Barker, Heinemann, most recent edition.

MANAGEMENT APPRECIATION—ORGANISATION AND DIRECTION

Principles of Organisation

The organisation of any firm is usually the result of long periods of slow growth interspersed with shorter periods of reappraisal and modification. It is rare for an opportunity to arise to start an enterprise entirely from scratch, and reappraisals of organisation take time to plan and put into effect. They then need even longer to work themselves out in practice; too frequent innovation can cause serious problems.

Equally serious problems can arise if a pattern of organisation is too rigidly prescribed, as when a neat chart is presented showing the most important members of staff at the top and the juniors at the bottom, or the key figures in the centre with everyone else ranged in orbit around them, and the least important people at the greatest distance. It rarely happens that there are enough tiers of management in the diagram to place everyone in his proper position, and people with quite different qualities and ranges of duties finish up on the same level. All such charts should carry a footnote emphasising their inherent limitations.

Organisation consists in determining what **duties** have to be performed to achieve the objectives of the management; allocating these duties to certain designated posts so that the holders of the posts assume **responsibility** for seeing that the duties are performed; determining the individual characteristics necessary for success in the range of posts decided upon; finding suitable people for appointment to these posts and conferring **authority** upon them as they are appointed. The extent of the authority will vary for each post, and each appointee will be told where he fits into the general pattern, so that he knows who is above him and who is below him.

To the extent that the plans were correctly made and the individuals correctly selected the organisation will be effective. Modifications may prove to be necessary, but they should be fairly limited if the plans have been carefully thought through.

There are three main types of organisation. They are known as:

(a) 'line' relationships
(b) 'functional' relationships, and
(c) 'staff' relationships.

(a) *'Line' Relationships.* Here the implication is that authority starts with the person at the head of the line and moves downwards in an unbroken sequence to the lowest employee. Each individual knows to whom he should look for leadership and to whom he should give orders. It is a 'military' style of organisation which is all right on the field of battle but breaks down when a complex pattern of activities has to be carried out. Since most companies have a wide variety of functions to be performed all at the same time, the 'functional' relationship is more appropriate.

(b) *'Functional' Relationships*. In most large companies a number of main functions have to be performed simultaneously, and each requires its departmental head. This gives a chain of command which is not in a single line, but has a number of strands in the chain, led by a production manager, a marketing manager, a chief accountant, a general administration officer, etc. These functional responsibilities vary with each type of firm, but the pattern is the same. Each departmental chief will have section heads below him while each section will have a small chain of command down to the lower levels.

(c) *'Staff' Relationships*. These are arrangements which supplement the other relationships with specialist staff assistance. They are more appropriate perhaps to the 'line' relationships so that we often hear of 'line and staff' relationships. What happens is that each line manager at higher levels has a staff of assistants who are either general factotums making smooth the path of their chiefs, or specialist advisers with particular skills to offer. They may be computer experts, or statisticians, or work study practitioners, etc.

Organisational Charts

A chart showing the organisation of a company will have at its apex the Board of Directors. The Board of Directors will convert the 'objects' of the company as stated in the Memorandum of Association into a body of specific objectives. These will be attained by a programme of action planned within a framework of policies laid down by the Board.

Usually one of the directors will be appointed as Managing Director, on such terms and remuneration as the Board may decide. He will then be instrumental in putting the Board's policies into effect, and departmental chiefs will draw their instructions from, and report back to, him as Managing Director.

The question then arises as to which 'span of control' is best. Naturally this varies with the capacity of the individual selected as Managing Director and the size of the organisation. A very gifted Managing Director may be able to control as many as eight departmental heads. If there are 15 departments he will probably be unable to control them all. At some point it may be necessary to introduce Assistant Managing Directors, each controlling a group of managers. The appointment of personal assistants may be necessary to ease the burden on senior staff. Many top secretaries are given PA status and a small staff to relieve them of routine secretarial duties, so that they can give real assistance to the senior member they are to serve. Fig. 19.1 shows some typical chains of organisation (see pages 188–9).

Delegation

It is a major principle of organisation that work must be delegated from higher levels to lower levels, and preferably as far down the organisational 'tree' as possible in conformity with efficient performance. This means that whatever work is performed is being performed as economically as possible by the cheapest grades of staff. We do not want top secretaries addressing bulk envelopes.

Delegation usually has two favourable effects. It gives greater job satisfaction to those lower down the tree if they are given a job to do and the responsibility that goes with it. It goes without saying that they must be given the chance to do the work in their way and the support they need in terms of staff, equipment and funds if necessary. They must then be called upon to give an account of the work and an evaluation must be made of their success. The second favourable effect is the progress made by staff while performing work delegated to them. They become more responsible; recognise their limitations and seek to overcome them; seek wider training, etc. Thus grows within the firm a body of future middle management which knows the firm, has loyalty to the organisation and can be promoted as required to more onerous responsibilities.

Decentralisation

As firms grow they set up branches and plants at some distance from head office and it eventually becomes necessary to move the administration of routine matters away from head office. This process of decentralisation is really a development of the delegation process, to shorten communications on all but the most important matters. Policies are still determined and plans made at head office. The allocation of capital and other resources will still be made from head office, but decision-making on production or marketing activities of a routine nature will be handled locally in plant or depot.

With the very largest firms, generally those with diverse products, a further increase in delegation leads to autonomous divisions specialising in product areas or market areas and the link with head office is purely one of general accountability, and liaison with data likely to be of use in planning and policy formulation.

Committees

A good deal has already been written in Chapter 14 about meetings, and the chief types of committee have been referred to there (see page 140). A committee is a group of people appointed by a higher-level group to consider particular facts or aspects of a situation in detail, with a view to making recommendations to the higher body, or dealing directly with a difficulty so as to resolve it satisfactorily. In limited companies the powers of committees are usually drawn eventually from the Board of Directors, which at some earlier date must have passed resolutions to set up the main management committees from which other committees are evolved.

Management committees are set up to run major activities within the company. They are usually standing committees, but they may be *ad hoc* committees if the particular activity to be considered is a single event—such as an issue of shares. Standing committees usually have coordinating functions or consultative functions. Coordination seeks to ensure that all departments, plants, depots, etc., take similar action and pursue similar policies on the matters under discussion. Consultative committees are usually concerned with a particular aspect of the firm's work—for example, social and welfare activities, staff development and training, etc. *Ad hoc* committees tend to be concerned with resolving particular problems or organising one-off events. Thus a committee dealing with a particular accusation of professional misconduct would hear the views of those directly concerned and report back with its recommendations.

It is always important to have clear terms of reference, and these should

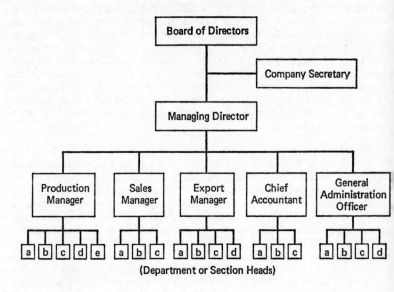

(i)

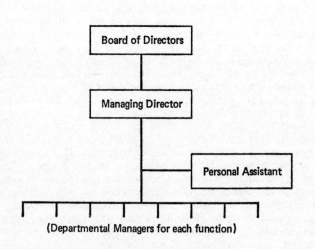

(ii)

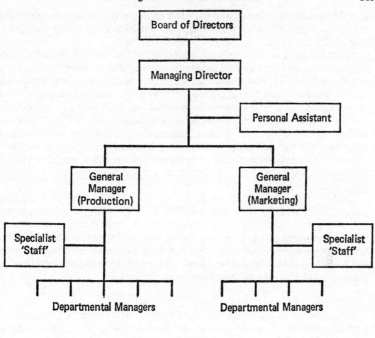

(iii)

Fig. 19.1. Some typical organisations.

Notes:

(i) This is a functional organisation. The managing director's span of control is not too great and each function is controlled by a manager whose subordinates are similarly not too numerous.

(ii) Here the span of control is wider, but the burden on the managing director is eased by giving him a personal assistant.

(iii) Here the managing director has been freed of the direct management by delegating major functional groups to assistants called general managers. The span of control is reduced by putting in an extra tier of management, but communication chains lengthen. Each general manager has an appropriate specialist 'staff'.

(iv) The reader should join in the exercise by drawing up for personal reference an organisational chart for his/her own firm. This will show how difficult it is to fit everyone into a chart at the correct level.

preferably be in writing and embodied in the minutes of the meeting setting up the committee. Clear terms of reference act as guidelines to the Chairman, who is charged with the responsibility for conducting the committee meetings. He can easily see where discussion is going off the lines if his terms of reference are straightforward. A Chairman must be a strong personality, well informed on the matter in hand and independent in his views. He must not be a member of any particular faction; must be a good listener and quick to detect trends in a discussion which gets away from the main point. He must be literate, so that he can quickly rephrase a proposition which is carelessly worded or incorrectly expressed.

Members of a committee must represent all the known points of view, otherwise the decisions arrived at may be unacceptable to some people. Those who have particular expertise which may be of use to the committee should be told that they have been appointed for that reason, and asked to make their services available wholeheartedly to promote the work of the committee.

The secretarial activities essential to any committee must be efficiently performed. The circulation of minutes and reports; the tabling of late reports; the preparation and circulation of agenda; the adequacy of seating and other accommodation facilities and the minuting of the meetings are of crucial importance to the success of the committee's work. These have already been fully explained in Chapter 14.

To the extent that a meeting is properly organised and conducted it should achieve the aims for which it was established. If it is poorly conducted it may be either a waste of time or even a disruptive influence. It may undermine the authority of office holders who are forced to abide by its decisions when they believe them to be of disservice to the firm. It may become a rallying point for dissidents anxious to achieve some other result than the one envisaged by the body which set up the committee.

Direction

The direction of a company is in the hands of the Board of Directors. The first director/s must be named with the first secretary/ies in a special 'Statement of First Director/s' attached to the Memorandum of Association made out when the company first registers under the Companies Acts. Most companies have several directors; the minimum number is two for a public company and one for a private company. Subsequent directors are appointed in the way laid down in the Articles of Association; for example the articles may say that the company in general meeting may appoint them, or the Board may appoint additional directors. Every company must keep a Register of Directors at its registered office, giving their names, former names, addresses, nationalities and other details.

Some directors are full-time directors and others are part-time. The latter only attend perhaps one meeting a month, when they bring an outside viewpoint to the Board Room. They usually read documents and reports during the month, and are available for consultation at any time on points where their expertise may be relevant. They often have specialist knowledge of a technical nature to offer the Board, or links with financial or professional institutions, and their objective viewpoints on trends and situations are usually of considerable value to the company.

Other directors are full-time employees under contracts of service with the company, and are known as executive directors. Their functions are explained below.

The Chairman may be named in the Articles of Association, or he may be elected by the directors at their first meeting. They may also elect a Chairman from among themselves should the Chairman fail to arrive or be unwilling to serve on a particular occasion. The Chairman conducts the meeting in accordance with standard rules of procedure and has discretion in closing a particular discussion even when some people still wish to speak. On a 'show of hands' those present have one vote each, but if a poll is called for the voting is one vote for each voting share held.

The Managing Director may be appointed by the directors, who fix his powers and his term of office. He is usually given a service contract, so that he is both a director and an employee.

The directors' powers are generally set out in the Articles of Association and the clause usually gives them the exclusive right to manage the affairs of the company, though the members assembled in a general meeting have the power to replace directors or even dismiss the whole Board. It is the right to manage the company which is so important. It is at this point that the specialist feature of limited liability companies appears—the separation between ownership and management. The shareholders own the company; the directors manage its affairs, and although directors usually own at least some shares the number held may be small compared with the total issued.

When the directors act they do so in a meeting called the Board Meeting, unless the Articles allow them to act otherwise. The main function of the Board is to decide policy, but usually at least some members of the Board will be executive directors charged with putting the policy into effect. The most obviously executive director is the Managing Director, but where other managers such as the Works Managers, the Sales Manager, the Chief Accountant, etc., are directors they are 'executive' directors and will actually carry out the Board's decisions in their departments. Executive directors are employed under conditions of service, so that they are both directors and employees. Part-time directors, who are from outside the business, bring their own expertise to the service of the company and offer an objective point of view in the discussions. An executive director, fully engaged in company work, may find it difficult to take such a view.

Responsibilities of the Board

The Board of Directors has many responsibilities which reflect its position as both the representative of the shareholders and the body authorised to manage the company's affairs. It also is the only active, functioning body which represents the corporation or legal entity created by the Certificate of Incorporation, and it must therefore ensure compliance with the law. Listing its duties we find these to include the following:

(*a*) The determination of policy, the clarification of the company's objectives and the formulation of plans to achieve them.

(*b*) The provision of capital, not only initially but on a continuing basis. This includes the control of dividend distributions to ensure that adequate funds remain available for the company's activities.

(*c*) Compliance with legal requirements. These include the control of business activities to keep them *intra vires* (within the powers granted); compliance with the Companies Acts, which require statutory meetings to be held and statutory records to be maintained; compliance with taxation regulations and a whole host of regulations such as Factory Acts, Health and Safety Regulations, environmental statutes, etc.

(*d*) Preparing and establishing a proper organisation, with a suitable executive structure; appointing executives to fill the posts available and vetting their qualifications and credentials.

(e) Considering the results achieved by all aspects of the firm's activities, evaluating their profitability and reporting back to the shareholders on the results as discovered.

(f) Ensuring the morale of the organisation by effective and positive leadership. This requires intangible qualities of leadership. A manifest harmony at Board levels; enthusiasm for the firm's products, projects and programmes and confident appeals for effort and initiative on the part of subordinates will do much to raise morale and foster discipline. Adequate communication channels, along the lines already described in detail in Chapter 4, will assist the maintenance of morale.

Social and Economic Responsibility

Today the direction of the affairs of a large company involves more than just manufacturing and marketing a range of products or providing a service that is in popular demand. In fact, it might be said that these major preoccupations of management in former times have now been subordinated to other 'higher' requirements. Today management is held responsible for advancing the economic, social and environmental well-being of the entire local and national community.

These are daunting responsibilities, since the communal well-being may conflict with the interests of the shareholders, and so may the interests of the employees. Examining the problem historically we can say that at one time the directors of a company had only one master to satisfy—the shareholders. The interests of this group were easily satisfied by the provision of a regular, steady dividend, and a figure of about 10 per cent was usually reckoned to be adequate and fair—although of course many dividends were much higher than this. In recent years a general claim on behalf of employees to share more fairly in the fruits of industry has led to considerable pressure to raise wages. Executive directors have themselves benefited from this changed attitude. The results have been not only a squeeze on profits, but increases in prices, which have generated a measure of inflation. This pressure from those employed within the industry has been reinforced by a host of pressures from outside the industry. Some of these pressures have been from environmentalists seeking to raise the quality of life, not the economic rewards. Campaigns for cleaner air, cleaner rivers, noise abatement, lorry re-routing, access to countryside, etc., have been largely justified and highly successful. In the process they have increased costs, squeezed profits and assisted prices to rise. The general inflationary trend has then called the government into action to defend those on fixed incomes, pensioners, etc., by raising taxation or controlling prices and dividends.

It seems inevitable that companies must accept and bear with these legitimate interferences with their activities. The company that cooperates in eliminating the undesirable social and environmental effects of its activities is most likely to be successful in the end. Goodwill is easily lost when national and even international discussion of its activities is featured on television and in the press. (Some reference to these problems has already been made in Chapter 13 on public relations.) A measure of social and economic responsibility must be assumed by the directors if the campaigns of environmentalists, the legitimate aspirations of the workforce, and the well-being of customers and the general public are to be given proper consideration. In so doing they must also seek to preserve what they can of their traditional responsibilities to the shareholders whose funds they are using. It is a question of achieving an acceptable balance between the various claims.

The Companies Act, 1980, lays upon directors in S. 46 a duty to pay attention to the interests of the company's employees. This statutory requirement has led to 'worker-directors' on some Boards. This raises difficulties, but it may also provide some solutions. Since a chief criticism of United Kingdom management is that it is failing to invest sufficiently in new equipment, it can hardly do any harm for workers to be fully informed about the impact of wage claims, taxation to improve social welfare and inflation on the pool of resources available for investment and dividends. The need to attract capital by paying a reasonable rate of dividend will become obvious to those appointed to the board. There is much to be gained by ensuring the widest participation of the workforce in the decision-making process, and spreading a proper knowledge of the company's affairs among its personnel.

Summary

1. Organisation consists in determining the duties necessary to achieve the objectives of the company; making each part of these duties the responsibility of some office-holder; deciding what qualities the office-holder will require; finding someone with the right qualities to fill each post and conferring authority upon him on appointment. A system of checks and control techniques must then be devised to measure the success of the organisation that has been established.

2. Three main types of organisation are 'line' organisations, 'line and staff' organisations and 'functional' organisations.

3. Organisational charts are useful in giving a picture of the organisation of a particular firm, but charts can rarely be made completely clear, or show sufficient tiers of organisation. Organisations are necessarily dynamic, and a chart may ossify the organisation if it is adhered to too rigidly.

4. Delegation is an essential part of any organisation, and seeks to free top management from the more routine tasks. With large firms it extends to decentralisation (which leaves head office free of routine matters), and divisionalisation (which sets up autonomous divisions within a group).

5. The direction of a company is in the hands of the Board of Directors, appointed to manage the affairs of the company. They determine policy, ensure compliance with the law, appoint such executives as are necessary, review achievements and control dividend policy, and ensure the adequacy of the capital available. The morale of the organisation stems largely from the leadership they give.

6. Besides the traditional duty which the directors owe to the shareholders of the company, they are increasingly required to acknowledge and make provision for an adequate participation of the workforce in the fruits of production. They are also under increasing pressure to observe social and environmental codes of behaviour which promote the general welfare at both local and national levels, and to broaden the administration to permit employee directors to participate in management.

Suggested Further Reading

The Arts of Top Management (A McKinsey Anthology), Roland Mann (Editor), McGraw-Hill, 1970.

Code of Best Practice, British Institute of Management, 1974.

Committees: How They Work and How to Work Them, E. Antsey, Allen & Unwin, most recent edition.

Management Made Simple, W. Coventry and J. Barker, Heinemann, most recent edition.

MANAGEMENT APPRECIATION—CONTROL TECHNIQUES

The Problems of Control

While organisation and planning are essential preliminary activities to production, the real test for management comes when operations have actually started. From that point on we are not involved in controlling a static organisation but a dynamic one. Each part of the organisation is developing at its own pace, but exerts influences upon the other parts, and is itself affected by them and by outside forces in the real world. These influences need to be controlled, or taken account of if they are uncontrollable.

Brech defines control as 'the process of checking actual performance against the agreed standards or plans, with a view to ensuring adequate progress or satisfactory performance, and also *recording* such experience as is gained as a contribution to possible future need'.

This definition makes it clear that control is a comparison activity in which what we hoped to achieve in a particular field is compared with the actual achievements. What we hoped to achieve may be regarded as the 'standard' with which we will compare the actual achievements. The difference between the two is known as a 'variance', and 'variance analysis' is the process of examining a variance to see what caused it and what action needs to be taken, if any. The Board of Directors looks to the managing director and the other executive directors to bring forward control information which will enable the Board to assess progress and pinpoint weaknesses in their overall plans. In the course of collecting such information the executive directors will incidentally correct any adverse tendencies which are revealed and require immediate attention. Thus if quality control checks reveal a high proportion of substandard work they will at once investigate the problem and resolve it. The result is a planning-control feedback cycle of the sort illustrated in Fig. 20.1.

The variations which may occur in any large-scale enterprise are so numerous that few people will be able to understand them all. We have had to develop expertise in all sorts of management fields to control the various types of changes that may occur—in other words, managers have had to specialise. Control techniques which may be helpful to the cost accountant may have little relevance to difficulties on the production line, and so on.

One of the problems of control, therefore, is to have a sufficient body of expertise available to control the various aspects which need to be monitored If the plans set the standards from which progress is to be judged, systems must be devised to follow up the plans and ensure that the rules and procedures laid down are in fact being followed; what are the actual results and do these call for any corrective action or any modification of the plans in the light of experience? Such systems must be devised by those who have the necessary expertise. Sometimes this expertise can be obtained on a short-term basis from outside consultants. Thus a work study consultant may be called in to deal with a particular problem where the failure to meet a planned programme appears to be due to poor plant layout. Management consultants may similarly be called in for an objective view of the systems of work being used.

Another problem of control is that the modifications to working, or the acceptance of changed plans, have to be secured in an atmosphere of personal relations. We are not dealing with machines, but with men and women. The adjustments to the daily round which will optimise corporate achievements

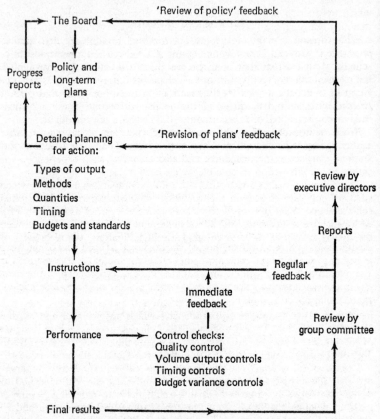

Fig. 20.1. The 'planning-control' feedback cycle.

can only be achieved by willing cooperation of those concerned. This has to be achieved by some process of encouragement to the meritorious, stimulation of the apathetic and censure of the ineffective or obstructive.

It is sufficient for the purposes of a management appreciation course if we now examine briefly some of the techniques which are most widely used. These are:

(*a*) Progress control (production control)
(*b*) Critical path analysis
(*c*) Stock control

(*d*) Quality control
(*e*) Statistical controls
(*f*) Budgetary controls
(*g*) Management information
(*h*) Computer appreciation

Progress Control (Production Control)

Progress control is the general process of checking up on the extent to which production plans are being put into effect—what progress is being made in realising the plans. A production plan has many aspects to be considered, and in each of these fields we need to compare the planned programme with the actual achievements day by day. The programmes or schedules may be in the form of charts, and the actual figures, when set against the planned figures, reveal at once any shortfall. Corrective action may then be taken to boost output if that is necessary or to soft-pedal if we are up to schedule. We can transfer extra staff in to help, or reduce machine loadings in favour of other activities according to the situation revealed by the charts.

Where serious difficulties are revealed, it may be necessary to warn other departments of the difficulties. Customers may need to be advised, export shipping dates re-negotiated, extra staff taken on, etc.

Critical Path Analysis (Network Analysis)

Where a project is a major undertaking, such as a large construction job, the multi-facet operation is controlled by a process known as critical path analysis. Other names for the same general approach are network analysis and PERT (programme evaluation and review technique). The problem is to devise the most economical method of working so that each part of the work is begun at the optimum moment and is ready for use when it is required in the overall plan. This will ensure that the work is approached in the most direct way so that the journey to final completion is as short as possible—made along the critical path.

Critical paths are arrived at by drawing a special type of diagram called a **network**. By convention a network is drawn from the left-hand side of the page, where the events and activities start, to the right-hand side of the page, where they finish. Each event is numbered, and each activity is indicated by a line with an arrowhead at the right-hand end where the activity finishes. Against each activity line the expected duration of that activity is shown. The general idea is best understood by looking at a simple network, such as Fig. 20.2.

The critical path is that series of essential events which has the longest time path; in other words, the project cannot be completed in less time than the critical path indicates. Thus events numbers 3, 4, 6, 7 and 8 are the ones that decide the critical path in Fig. 20.2. The project will take 22 days to complete. Activities on the critical path have to be carried out in the time stated. Activities which are not on the critical path can be allowed to 'float'—we can get activity 1–4 done at any time during the 10 days that 1–3 and 3–4 are being completed, so long as we start it by day 6 so that it gets done in time.

Clearly, critical path analysis is an art which has to be learned. The actual stages in planning a project may be listed as follows:

(*a*) State clearly what has to be done.
(*b*) Break this down into events, activities and duration times.

(c) Draw the network.

(d) Analyse the network and decide how to schedule the activities.

(e) Check the schedule against the network.

(f) Institute progress controls over the project as it moves through to completion.

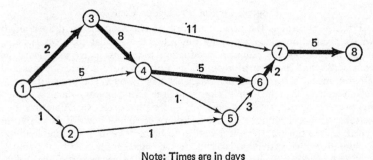

Note: Times are in days

Fig. 20.2. A simple network showing the critical path.

Notes:

(i) Each event is shown by a circle and they are numbered from left to right of the page, in the time sequence in which they occur.

(ii) An event is not reached until all the activities leading into it have been completed. The only event that has no activities leading into it is the starting event 1.

(iii) Activities are shown as arrows. They are clearly identifiable tasks to be performed, usually by one man or one team of men. The length of the arrow has no connection with the duration of the job, it only helps to join up the network. The duration of the activity is marked alongside the arrow in agreed units, like hours or days.

(iv) An activity cannot begin until the event it starts from (the tail event) has been 'reached'. (See (ii) above.)

(v) An activity is described by naming its tail event and its head event. Thus activity 1–2 takes 1 day and activity 1–3 takes 2 days.

Stock Control

Stock presents particular problems to management. We never want to be out of stock of a particular item, but it costs money to keep stocks and there are all sorts of losses associated with them, such as theft, dessication, infestation and deterioration due to age, dampness, etc. Another major consideration is that idle stock ties up working capital, and yields no profit. If we have an excessive stock of slow-moving items the **return on capital invested** which is one of our major control figures, will be smaller than we hoped.

Some of the considerations which enter into stock policy are the re-order time and the optimum order. The re-order time is the time required by our suppliers, or by our factory if we are making up goods for stock, before they can fill the order we place. This time decides the minimum stock level. Suppose it takes three weeks before an order can be fulfilled, and we need 3,000 items per week. Then the minimum stock will be 9,000 items. As soon as stocks fall close to this figure a new order must be put through. Some firms bag up the minimum stock, or set it aside in some special way. This minimum stock may not be broken into for use until a purchase requisition marked URGENT has been made out and sent to purchasing department. An order will now be placed, but for how much? If we could be absolutely sure of our supplier's delivery dates, so that the replacement order arrives just as we run out of stock, then an order for 9,000 units would be enough. But this order may be inappropriate for several reasons. It may be too small to interest our supplier, who perhaps only finds it economic to supply a batch of 30,000 units. He may offer better terms if we order 50,000 or 100,000. So the **optimum order** depends upon discounts allowed for quantities—when balanced against losses due to deterioration or theft while in stock.

Quality Control

Quality control is a process which seeks to maintain quality by testing the product of a manufacturing process, either by testing every unit or by testing a random sample of each day's output. For example, we cannot test all the cement we manufacture, but we can test a few pounds of each batch made. The use of random sampling methods is a statistical process, which seeks to prevent any bias in the choice of a particular sample for testing. In establishing quality we have to bear in mind the purpose for which an article is required. If we take the same pains to produce a bicycle chain as we take to produce a chain to be used in the complex machinery of an atomic power plant, we shall probably waste our time and skill. It is uneconomic to make things better than they need to be.

Many firms now work on a **quality assurance** basis which seeks to build the quality into the product rather than rely solely on final inspection.

Quality control seeks to reduce customer complaints, and wasted or rejected units of output, It looks for errors, and follows them through until the cause of the error is discovered. It may be human error, or machine failure, or substandard material, or incorrect processing, mixing, firing, etc.

Statistical Controls

The branch of mathematics known as Statistics has many implications for management, and most advanced business courses include a study of this subject. One of its methods, random sampling, is referred to above and others are used in the control techniques described later.

Statistics is the science of numbers. It uses 'raw' data collected from actual experience in the real world and then manipulates these numbers first of all to make them simpler, and then to relate them to one another so that a more digested range of figures—secondary statistics—can be derived. For example, suppose we produce 527,294 units of a particular product in a year. This is a difficult number to comprehend. If we round off the figure to the nearest thousand and call it 527,000 we are leaving out a very small number— 294 units—so small compared to the 527,000 as to be quite unimportant. Suppose that last year we produced 418,000 units. Clearly output has risen by 109,000 units in the year. If we work this out as a percentage increase, we get

$$\frac{109,000}{418,000} \times 100 = 26 \cdot 1\%$$

A 26·1 per cent increase is easier to understand, and gives a clear picture of how much more effectively the factory has been working this year than last.

Many of the policy decisions which management has to make are assisted by statistical techniques. Market demand can be judged by a knowledge of the population, its wealth, its habits and the growth trends in the economy. International influences affect export trade. Market research is largely a statistical examination based on sampling data. Site location for depots and territories for salesmen can be planned with statistical techniques; so can the layout of warehouses, supermarkets and service areas like railway stations, hospital waiting rooms, etc. Perhaps the most influential statistics are those prepared by accountants in providing management information.

Budgetary Control

A budgetary control system is one where figures are worked out, usually for a year ahead, with details of estimated income and expenditure, preferably for each department. It is often a good idea to have departmental heads draw up this sort of budget for their departments. Usually such figures then need to be scrutinised to pick out unrealistic estimates, where costs tend to be understated (increase them) and outputs or sales tend to be exaggerated (reduce them). Within the budget we must then look for likely expenditure profiles and income flows, since they rarely coincide. Thus a department might spend a lot of money on stock in August to October, and then buy very little at all in November and December although takings in those months would be very high. We could have a shortage of cash developing in September and October so that an overdraft had to be negotiated, to be repaid as cash flowed in with the pre-Christmas boom in trade. Similarly, we may have a department which is given a budget to spend over the twelve months at a steady rate, but within the first three months has spent nearly half its allocation. The budget controller must be able to pinpoint such trends. A quick note to the head of department warning him of the danger will cut the orders being placed until such time as the department is back to its target expenditure.

Of course budgetary control becomes meaningless if those who overspend can simply apply for a 'Supplementary Estimate'. This type of request must be scrutinised with the greatest severity. It sometimes happens because of circumstances totally out of control of the head of department. Thus a natural disaster may put a local government relief organisation's budget totally out, and yet the disaster has to be dealt with. When the government designates an area a disaster area this always means that special funds can be diverted to assist the budgets of the organisations dealing with the problem. If, by contrast, a supplementary estimate is made necessary because of poor control by the head of department he has to be reprimanded and only the most essential future requirements met, while the next year's progress will be watched to see that there is no repetition.

There are very few areas of business activity that are not susceptible to budgetary control. We have sales budgets, purchases budgets, distribution budgets, production budgets, research and development budgets, manpower budgets, cash-flow budgets, administration budgets, advertising budgets, training budgets, and many more. The work involved is considerable, but the effect on those who have to justify the expenditures and forecast the receipts is salutary. When the master budget, which coordinates all the department budgets, reveals manifest disparities the departmental managers are forced to think realistically and relate their own ideas to corporate strategy. The corporate control that is established, and the integration achieved, is invaluable.

Management Information

An enormous amount of management information can be made available these days. Not only raw data, but ratios and percentages which enable us to compare one period with another, and thus discover trends in business. These trends can then be examined and corrective action taken. For example, a trend to lower profit margins may be found to be due to severe competition, and some diversification of products to avoid the worst effects of this—phasing out projects where we manifestly cannot compete and increasing sales in more profitable fields—may correct the trend. The most fruitful source of management information is **management accounting.**

Accounting is the process by which profits are calculated. The basic principles of double-entry book-keeping are used to keep records of the firm's activities. These principles depend upon the fact that whenever goods, services or money change hands, two accounts are affected. One of these accounts must receive value, and is said to be debited. The other account gives value and is said to be credited. So the basic rule of double-entry book-keeping is: debit the receiver and credit the giver of goods, services or money. For example, the Cash Account is a very busy account in many businesses. When money is received, as when customers in supermarkets pay for the purchases at the check-out counters, the Cash Account is receiving money and has to be debited. When cash is spent—for example, when the workers' pay packets are made up—Cash Account is giving money, and must be credited. At the end of the day, or the week, etc., the account can be balanced to see what the outstanding sum left in the cash tills should be. We can check the book-keeping by counting the actual cash.

By using the accounting records we can discover the profits of the business. This is usually done in two parts. First the Gross Profit on Trading is found. This is done by taking the total Sales in the year, and deducting from it the Cost of those Sales. The resulting Gross Profit has now to be reduced by the overheads of the business, i.e. the expenses such as rent, rates, light and heat, etc. When the total of these expenses is deducted from the Gross Profit we find the Net Profit or clean profit. Using imaginary figures this calculation may be shown as follows:

	£
Proceeds from Sales (Turnover of the business)	100,000
Less Cost of Sales	60,000
Gross Profit	40,000
Less Overheads	25,000
Net Profit	£15,000

From these figures many control figures can be produced. These control figures are called **management ratios,** and are most often worked out in percentage form. For example:

$$\text{Gross Profit Percentage} = \frac{\text{Gross Profit}}{\text{Turnover}} \times 100$$

$$= \frac{40,000}{100,000} \times 100$$

$$= 40\%$$

$$\text{Net Profit Percentage} = \frac{\text{Net Profit}}{\text{Turnover}} \times 100$$

$$= \frac{15,000}{100,000} \times 100$$

$$= 15\%$$

Expense Ratio (say staff salaries were £8,500)

$$\text{Staff Salaries Expense Ratio} = \frac{\text{Salaries}}{\text{Turnover}} \times 100$$

$$= \frac{8,500}{100,000} \times 100$$

$$= 8.5\%$$

The significance of these control figures is that they should remain roughly constant from year to year, even if turnover is quite different. Thus suppose everything next year is 50 per cent up on this year. Figures would now be:

	£
Proceeds from Sales (Turnover)	150,000
Less Cost of Sales	90,000
Gross Profit	60,000
Less Overheads	37,500
Net Profit	£22,500

However, the Gross Profit Percentage is not changed:

$$\frac{\text{Gross Profit}}{\text{Turnover}} \times 100$$

$$= \frac{60,000}{150,000} \times 100$$

$$= 40\%$$

Similarly Net Profit Percentage still works out to 15 per cent and Expenses Ratio (expenses are now up to £12,750) works out to 8·5 per cent.

It therefore follows that if our business is still adding on the same margins to Cost Price to fix its selling prices the Gross Profit Percentage should be the same no matter how much business we do. If Gross Profit falls—say, from 40 per cent to 37 per cent—we should find out why. Is the manager stealing the takings? Are the check-out assistants stealing the takings? Is someone taking the stock (a smaller Stock figure will affect the Cost of Sales which is partly worked out by taking Stock into account).

There are many things to know about management accounting, which is a major study in its own right. Expense ratios can reveal that certain aspects of a business are becoming more expensive and others less expensive. This may help us to detect dishonesty, theft, unfavourable stock items, bad buying, and many other things.

Computer Appreciation

The increasing use of computers and the introduction of mini-computers make some measure of computer appreciation essential for executive secretaries. An explanation of the basic units in a computer is given in *Office Practice Made Simple* and it is not necessary to repeat it here. (The reader who has no experience of computers is urged to read the chapter concerned.) Here it is proposed to say something about mini-computers.

As computer technology advances, the size of the systems becomes smaller and smaller. Mini-computers and micro-computers must eventually replace mainframe systems. The first small business machines were called VRC's— visible record computers. They use as their main medium for the storage of information cards with printed information on the front and computer-readable information in magnetic strips on the back. Costs continue to fall, and the range of facilities to improve. At the start of the 1980s a micro-computer with a printer and other essential ancillary units cost as little as £2,500.

The modern range of mini-computers offers a wide variety of services to small businesses, under the general name 'small business systems'. A significant development is the growth of agency arrangements between hardware manufacturers and software suppliers. As the number of small computers in use increases it becomes more difficult for hardware suppliers to provide the back-up service required. They have turned increasingly to the business equipment suppliers to provide the software. Users of mini-computers therefore do best if they identify their needs, in terms of inputs, outputs, file sizes, processing, etc. This will indicate what sort of equipment is needed. They should then invite proposals from suppliers able to satisfy both the hardware and software needs, and evaluate them in terms of costs and benefits, bearing in mind training needs as staff are converted to the new system or redeployed on other work.

As an alternative to the purchase of mini-computers an increasing number of firms are turning to computer packages supplied by specialist firms. The advantages of such a system are that the more sophisticated computers available can analyse aspects of the firm's situation which are not susceptible to analysis by mini-computers. Some idea of the range of services which can be offered by a sophisticated computer bureau is given below, by courtesy of Computer Power. (Computer Power is the trade name of Compower Ltd, a wholly-owned subsidiary of the National Coal Board. With almost 20 years of experience it has developed a comprehensive range of over 60 commercial and technical computer applications.) The Integrated Business Service illustrated in Fig. 20.3 is designed to handle the bulk of any firm's clerical and accounting procedures. Systems such as Payroll, Purchases Accounting, Sales

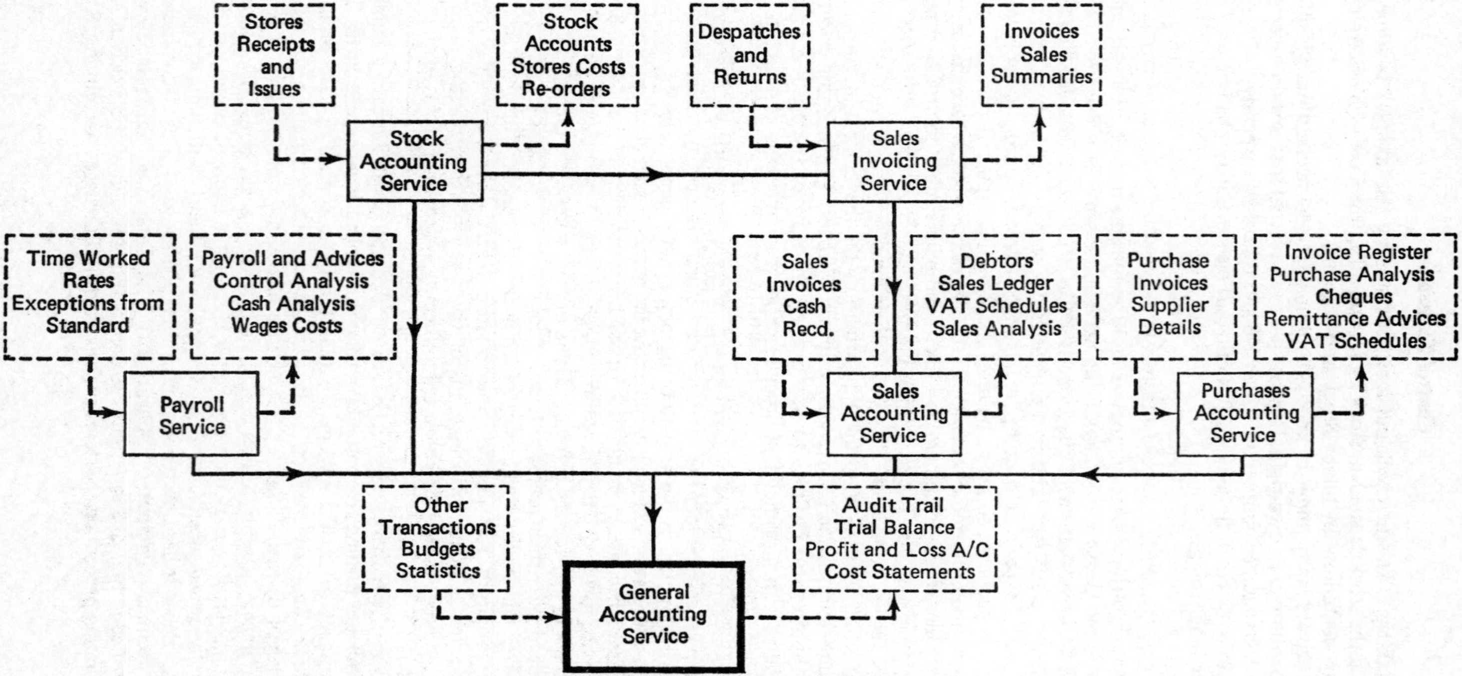

Fig. 20.3. An integrated computer accounting service.

(Courtesy of Computer Power, Compower Ltd, Cannock)

Accounting, Sales Invoicing and Stock Accounting can be provided as individual systems, or as part of an integrated General Accounting Service which maintains the full books of account.

Other services provided by the bureau include special business applications such as Production Control, Distribution Control, Vehicle Parts Distribution, Road Transport Fleet Services, Securities Management, a Rents Accounting Service and Trade Association Services. Under the general heading of Technical Services, Computer Power offers programs for Traffic Engineering, Highway Engineering, Land Survey, Structural Engineering, Construction Industry Network Analysis, Electrical Engineering Network Analysis and Linear System Analysis, and a range of statistical analysis programs. Terminal services can be supplied to give direct links with the main computers through an appropriate range of terminals, including visual display units, typewriter terminals, line printers, etc.

Summary

1. Control in business is a process of comparing actual performance with planned performance, and taking such measures as are necessary to achieve the planned programme or modify the plans if they prove to have been unrealistic. Control is effected by a planning-control feedback cycle, which brings appropriate measures to bear at a series of levels as required.

2. Critical path analysis is a technique for dealing with major projects where a number of activities are taking place at once. By identifying these activities and the events to which they contribute, the stages of progress may be discovered and the activities scheduled to ensure that no stage is delayed. The critical path is that sequence of essential events that has the longest time requirement. If we follow the critical path we shall complete the project in the minimum time possible.

3. Stock control seeks to ensure that stocks are adequate, but inexpensive in that as little capital as possible is tied up in unnecessary stock.

4. Quality control tests the quality of output on a statistical sampling basis.

5. Budgetary control seeks to control departmental expenditure by drawing up department budgets which can be used as a standard against which actual expenditure can be compared. By taking account of expenditure profiles an alarm note can be sounded if departmental heads authorise purchase requisitions which seem likely to exceed the proposed budget.

7. Management information includes a wide range of statistical ratios which pinpoint trends in business that may prove adverse to the success of the firm, so that corrective action can be taken. Such information is most easily provided by computerised data processing.

Suggested Further Reading

Management. Its Nature and Significance, E. F. L. Brech, Pitman, most recent edition.
Management Made Simple, W. Coventry and J. Barker, Heinemann, most recent edition.

MANGEMENT APPRECIATION—PERSONNEL MANAGEMENT

The Personnel Function

The rôle of the personnel officer has received increasing recognition over the last quarter of a century. While other kinds of management are engaged in such activities as buying, production, marketing and accounting, the personnel manager seeks to discover staff of the right type, with appropriate knowledge and skills for the work in hand. The personnel function is concerned with every aspect of a firm's work, for it deals with the staffing of all departments, and the human and social problems which arise within the firm. While the work of the firm proceeds in a framework of organisation designed by the management, this framework has to be staffed with real human beings. It is rarely possible to find staff with the exact requirements hoped for, and plans may need to be modified in the light of the actual skills possessed by those appointed.

A popular misconception is that the personnel department is a sort of social service which looks after the welfare of staff. It may in fact do this as an incidental activity to its management function, but this is a minor rôle. **The true personnel function is to recruit and select people of the right type**; to induct them adequately and train them effectively; to plan for their long-term development; to arrange schemes of pay and conditions of service which meet legal and trade requirements; to advise on health and safety aspects; and to promote welfare and pension schemes such that the climate of relations between management and personnel is conducive to cooperation and mutual endeavour. The personnel manager provides the necessary specialist knowledge to enable the Board to obtain the staff it requires and make the best possible use of them. As a national average over 70 per cent of the funds received by UK firms in the course of their business activities are used to pay staff, This emphasises the importance of the personnel rôle.

The chief aspects of personnel work are as follows:

(a) personnel planning
(b) selection and recruitment
(c) staff development and training programmes
(d) management training and development
(e) wages and conditions of employment
(f) industrial relations
(g) personnel records

Each of these aspects is dealt with below, but personnel management is a full study in its own right and it is not possible here to do more than refer to the salient features of each aspect.

Personnel Planning

Personnel planning is the process of forecasting manpower requirements in the future, in the light of developing technology, economic growth, etc. It is essentially long term, and looks at the likely situation five, ten and fifteen years ahead. What skilled tradesmen will be required; in what numbers? How can they be produced, and what training and re-training programmes will best meet the needs anticipated?

A more specific activity is 'succession planning'. This seeks to ensure that the sudden departure of any individual will not affect the firm unduly, since his successor is already present and has been trained in many of the duties which he will now be called upon to perform. This activity requires us to review the present organisation and establish the number of key posts needed in the future according to the plans already under consideration. We then examine existing personnel and consider their respective potentials. Training and development programmes to assist promising individuals to realise their potentials must then be undertaken, and recruitment and selection policies adjusted to recruit staff of the right type, where a shortage of a particular type of skill seems likely to develop.

Under this heading it should be emphasised that the executive secretary may be able to contribute to the personnel officer's understanding of particular situations. Inter-personal relations may not be amicable in a particular area, or working conditions may be unsatisfactory, and cause a higher than average labour turnover. Similarly, a particular area of labour stability reflects some favourable aspect of employment in that particular area. If this can be isolated it may be of benefit to a larger circle within the firm. Has the supervisor in that area a capacity for deft control of staff problems which merits an expansion of his/her influence? There are always times when a review of the work of an individual employee gives an opportunity for judicious enquiries about his sense of job contentment. These may reveal that a particular way of working is popular, or that an *esprit de corps* exists which was not previously appreciated.

Selection and Recruitment

A firm is only as good as the staff it employs. It follows that a policy for recruitment and selection is essential if the number and quality of staff is to be maintained. Whilst this is particularly true at times of full employment it is also true of less prosperous times as far as skilled staff are concerned. One essential element of such a policy is the firm's attitudes to filling vacancies. If vacancies are to be filled from within the organisation, employee morale will be high because promotion prospects are good. Staff will also tend to stay on in the hopes of promotion, thus reducing labour turnover and induction training costs. The chief danger of such a policy is the development of an in-bred management, each member of which has climbed a ladder in his predecessor's footsteps. The result can be a lack of awareness of developments in competitive firms, and a lack of preparation for new situations and conditions. It is usual therefore for management to admit the general principle of promotion from within, whilst reserving the right to advertise for staff where the range of abilities available within the organisation seems inadequate for the particular post under consideration.

Recruits may be obtained in a number of different ways. Many firms use their own staff as recruiters, giving priority to anyone recommended by an existing member of staff. There is some sense in the arrangement. A good worker will hesitate to recommend anyone who might let him/her down, and a family connection eases induction problems and develops solidarity within the organisation between department and department.

Many firms receive unsolicited applications from members of the public. Such letters are a useful source of recruits, particularly for less skilled staff. The large firm, with an established public image, benefits particularly in this way and may thus avoid expensive advertising.

A common point of entry to employment is the school leaving age, when those who are unable or unwilling to continue their education become available. Such young people may be most easily recruited through the local Youth Employment Office, which holds 'Careers Conferences' annually, and liaises continuously with schools about careers lessons, work experience schemes and similar activities. Many firms could do more to help themselves by assisting in such events, particularly by offering to speak to pupils and students about their own particular needs. Many trades and sub-trades have never even been mentioned to school leavers, perhaps because schools' careers staff are themselves not aware of the enormous range of employment opportunities.

In recent years the development of **Job Centres,** a sort of job supermarket where posts on offer are displayed so that unemployed people may consider the various opportunities, has improved the appearance and efficiency of the local employment exchange. These official centres run by the Employment Services Agency, under the general umbrella of the Department of Employment, are the most important source of semi-skilled and unskilled recruits. They make no charge to employers and the expertise they offer can do much to reduce selection procedures and ensure that only worthwhile candidates for a particular post are interviewed.

For higher-level staff, colleges and universities are major sources of specialist recruits, and the range of skills is enormous. Such staff need careful selection and induction before they can be fully effective, but bring knowledge and expertise acquired in a different way from the experience of the ordinary employee. They therefore have much to contribute in new attitudes. They may be recruited by the circulation of brochures or other informational material, and by liaison with college administrative departments which are prepared to assist students to find posts. Often accommodation for a film-show or display of a firm's activities will be provided at little cost, and an opportunity to meet interested students will thus be provided.

Today there exists a wide range of specialist journals published on a controlled circulation basis. Each is sent free to all members of a particular profession or trade who wish to receive it. Thus *Accountancy Age* contacts almost everyone of real importance in the accountancy field. Not only is it an ideal advertising medium for an employer in that field seeking staff, but it is the natural medium to which employees who are considering a move will turn. Whilst advertisements are competitively priced, the chances are greatly increased that the right sort of staff will see an advertisement. Such papers are ideal for securing specialist staff at all levels of experience.

Selection is a process which sifts through the available applicants to arrive at the most suitable. Where the number of applicants is large it is usual to require them to complete an application form which will then be reviewed as part of the selection process. This results in the preparation of a 'short-list', which consists of those who are apparently best suited for the post. The preparation of such a list from a file of several dozen applicants proceeds by stages. The first page of the application form usually consists of basic information. This will weed out many of the applicants because they do not have appropriate qualifications or experience, or their job record indicates inability to stay a reasonable course. It then becomes more difficult to select between those who do appear to be suitable. If the **job description** indicates certain attributes which will be a recommendation for the post it may be possible to rate the applicants on these points and thus discover the best applicants. These will then form the short-list, and actually be invited to sit a selection test, and attend an interview. **References** should be taken up, preferably before the interview is held, and qualifications claimed should be verified by the inspection of certificates.

For many posts which are of a routine nature, or where job turnover is high, staff agencies may be used. Clerical staff agencies, hotel and catering staff agencies, and nursing staff agencies are some of the commoner types. The agency charges for its services, anything between one week and one month's salary, but this rarely comes to much more than the cost of advertising in the national press. The time and expense incurred in writing copy for advertisements and responding to the many totally unsuitable applicants are also saved by the use of these agencies. At a higher level, when seeking professional staff, it is possible to use the services of selection consultants. These specialise in finding staff of a particular type—accountants, chemists, engineers, transport managers, etc., etc. They will advertise in the appropriate journals, distribute application forms and check references and qualifications. They will set up interviews and attend as one of the selection team to advise on the particular qualities of the candidates. At this sort of level staff often prefer to make application to such an independent consultant. For example, if there are only a few firms in a particular industry a process engineer who is thinking of a change may hesitate to apply for a particular post for fear his own firm finds out that he is disgruntled with his present position. Selection consultants usually enquire if there is any particular firm to which the applicant does not wish his application to be submitted.

Staff Development and Training

Staff development and training are processes which go on all the time, in the endless search to maintain a firm as a competitive unit in a changing world. They should not be looked upon as mere steps to promotion, for in many cases promotion cannot be given and would not be deserved anyway. What is true is that the successful completion of a number of training courses followed by practical application of the skills acquired in the service of the firm will usually fit an individual to take a more responsible position when the opportunity for advancement occurs.

Staff development as a personnel activity arises from the 'succession planning' already referred to. In evaluating the potential of an individual, the personnel officer seeks to sum up the qualities that individual displays, and to point him in a direction that is likely to offer him job satisfaction and secure prospects. This type of appraisal and counselling service will probably be operated by the personnel department, but in liaison with line staff in the departments, who will advise personnel about the particular attributes of an individual and give their views on his potential. The personnel officer must enlist the support of the individual, who should know why he is being guided along a particular channel. If the employee then actively participates in the development process, becoming a self-starter as far as his pursuit of relevant studies and works experience goes, the success of the programme is almost assured.

Each training course on such a path of development concerns itself with the performance required by the individual in the working situation. It may well be that a background atmosphere has to be understood as well, so that the particular activity can be understood as one element in an intricate pattern of activities. The fundamental aim of any training programme is that the course members shall acquire some skill. A successful training scheme is a communication exercise based on **skill-analysis,** which will enable the employee to acquire the skill. Certain training methods will be generally appropriate, others may be more suitable to one trainee than to another. The package of methods must point up the parts played by verbal, manual, spatial, aesthetic and other abilities in performing the job. It must then offer an opportunity to practice these abilities so that they may be developed. The skills must be taught in such a way that they will be reinforced in practice later on. The trainee who returns from his course to be told by his supervisor 'Never mind all that stuff they told you at the training course; this is what we really do' is bound to feel frustrated. The training scheme must lead directly into the real world of practical application, or it is humbug.

The **Employment and Training Act** 1973 set up the **Manpower Services Commission** with a broad field of responsibilities in the promotion and co-ordination of training services. Its two arms, the **Employment Services Agency** and the **Training Services Agency,** seek to find employment and train for employment respectively. The Manpower Services Commission took over control of the system of Industrial Training Boards set up under the Industrial Training Act 1964 and advises the Minister about the establishment of Industrial Training Boards. There are about 24 such Boards at present, financed by levies on the industries concerned. Their thorough and comprehensive reviews of the needs of each particular industry, and their specification of the types of training required, have transformed the training scene in each industry where they have been established.

Management Training and Development

Management skills are less easy to analyse than other skills. They operate in the fields of human and social relations, where circumstances differ from day to day. A correct decision in one set of circumstances may be an incorrect decision where the circumstances have changed. It is difficult to assess success, and impossible to know when a course of training is complete. What the individual has to do in any management situation is to assess the situation, decide what the problem is, decide what will be the best remedy, and then take action to defeat the mischief and advance the remedy. Learning such skills is a very personal matter, and must proceed largely on the job, which is its own training ground. Management training can only provide a framework of skills, such as the principles of communication and problem solving. The

training officer can introduce the aspiring junior manager to the human relations orchestra. He can demonstrate the basic features of each of its sections,
and run through a series of trills and arrangements. What he cannot hope to
do is to demonstrate its gentle pianissimos or the awesome thunder of its full
arousal. It is for the individual, over a period of years, to learn how to tune it,
to control it and to bring forth a sweet harmony.

For many firms the training of junior management staff and the up-dating
of senior staff is best handled by specialist management training centres. A
network of regional management centres covers the country, each county
having either its own centre or a centre shared with neighbouring localities.
Since these centres are self-financing in that they recoup from firms whom
they serve the expenses they incur, they are less affected by cuts in educational
budgets than other aspects of education. They are already staffed by knowledgeable and experienced personnel who can devise courses, or tailor an
existing course, to meet the exact needs of a firm. They will conduct the course
either in-plant or in-college, to suit. Moreover, the network is so extensive
that the services of a real expert in a particular field can usually be secured to
meet a special need. Firms could save money by making much more use of
this service than they do, and an alert secretary in the personnel department
should get to know the staff at her local technical college management centre
and ensure that her executive is furnished with their current literature.

Wages and Conditions of Employment

The establishment of a fair wages system is one of the most difficult aspects
of management. Today there are so many pressures exerted on the wages
structure that it is almost impossible to reach an agreed concensus. The chief
problem is to evaluate jobs relative to one another, and relative to the availability of the particular skills required. The importance of the post to the
entire organisation will enter into the job evaluation, as will the pleasantness
or otherwise of the working conditions; the unsocial nature of the hours; the
length of time taken to acquire the skill and knowledge used and the degree of
personal flair arising from the employee's innate capacities. All these must be
balanced within a framework constructed of government restrictions, trade
union views of differentials, disincentive taxation and domestic and international competition.

In evaluating jobs the tendency is to measure the job in some objective way,
and avoid judgments where possible. Thus the degree of unpleasantness
might be graded from 0 to 5, the higher point ratings going to the more unpleasant jobs. The influence of the job on other people and its importance to
the company might be graded in the same way. The job is isolated from the
individual doing the job. Later, when the individual comes to be taken into
account, a system of merit gradings and of long service increments attempts
to take account of the way a particular individual fills his position.

The problem is to maintain a consistent and balanced policy, in line with
the Board's basic philosophy, but taking account of particular situations,
shortages of certain types of skill, the market price for similar types of labour
in the real world and the purchasing power of the actual take-home pay.

Flexible Working Hours

An important development in the general field of wages policy, with important side effects on industrial relations, is the development of flexible working hours. One of the earliest firms in this field, Hengstler Flextime Ltd, who own the trade mark 'Flextime', have kindly provided background material for this section.

The principle of 'Flextime' is that a degree of choice is available to all employees about the actual hours they work, subject only to the exigencies of the job itself. The needs of the job must be met, and the completion of the work is the most important consideration, but this need not prevent an employee from adjusting his/her duty to meet personal needs and tastes. Some people are at their best early in the day; others prefer to rise late and stay on into the early evening. It is usual to specify two or more periods of **core-time** when all staff must be in the building. Other periods are **'Flextime'** periods when staff may choose whether they will take a break, or continue working. Figure 21.1 illustrates some common arrangements for core-time and 'Flextime'.

Clearly, if meetings are to be called which require the presence of several staff it is best to time them during core-time. Alternatively, by giving adequate notice, staff will be aware that their presence is required and will not absent themselves even though it is 'Flextime'.

It is usual to specify a total **'bandwidth'** between which all working hours occur. For example, it may be forbidden to start work before 8 a.m. or continue after 7 p.m. (except for overtime arrangements).

The advantages to both staff and management are enormous. Gone are all those tedious problems which arise when staff are adjudged to be late, or alleged to have sneaked off early. We do not have hundreds of cars trying to leave the car parks at the same moment as staff go home. An awkward dental appointment can be covered without the need to ask for time off, or to negotiate leave of absence with some petty tyrant. Even a full day off for a special need, such as a hospital visit or even a shopping expedition, can be earned by working a little extra time to accumulate an entitlement to **'Flex-leave'**.

Perhaps the most valuable effect of flexible working hours is the maturity it brings to the employment scene. No longer are employees dragooned into premises by a particular time like schoolchildren hurrying to beat the school-bell. Instead they plan their commitments weeks ahead, if necessary, so that they cover the work they need to do and the personal arrangements they have to make. Communication between staff is usually found to improve considerably because staff plan their days more carefully. Only a relatively short period after a transition to flexible working is needed before the pattern of attendance settles down. Certain people usually arrive early, and others usually stay late.

Under the 'Flextime' system each employee has an individual key, which also serves as an identity pass in buildings where security is important. The use of this key in the key acceptor starts the clocking-up of the hours worked. Removal of the key on departure disconnects the pulses from the master clock. These occur every 36 seconds; one hundred pulses per hour. Insertion or removal of the key also lights up or extinguishes a **'presence indicator lamp'** on the key acceptor. This lamp can also be connected to **remote lamp indicator panels** situated at convenient points—in Reception, for example—to indicate to switchboard or other sensitive communication areas the presence or absence of the individual.

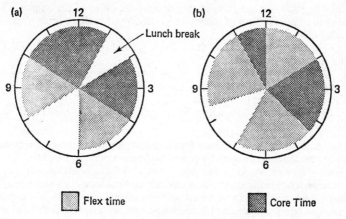

Fig. 21.1. Core-Time and Flextime.
(Courtesy of Hengstler Flextime Ltd)

Notes:

(a) This diagram is an example of the introduction of Flextime. People may arrive and leave their work at any time during the flexible hours at either end of the working day. The extent and precise times of the flexible hours can be selected in accordance with the wishes and individual circumstances of each organisation. The employee's responsibilities are to be present during core-time, to work the mandatory number of hours during the accounting period, whether it is a day, week or month and, most importantly, to ensure that the work does not suffer. Responsibility is the essence of a Flextime system.

(b) It depends on the individual circumstances of each place of work as to whether it is preferable to have a fixed lunch break or one which is converted into flexible hours. The diagram shows another possible configuration based on a different organisation's criteria.

Industrial Relations

For some years industrial relations has been a major subject of debate in the United Kingdom, and a succession of laws has been passed. The major statutes are the **Trade Union and Labour Relations Act, 1974** (as amended by the **Employment Act, 1980**), and the **Employment Protection Act, 1975.**

The 1974 Act repealed the Conservatives' controversial Industrial Relations Act, 1971. It enacts that an employee who has been employed for more than 26 weeks has the right not to be unfairly dismissed, and if he is so dismissed he may appeal to an Industrial Tribunal. The tribunal may then order his reinstatement, and if it is not complied with compensation will be awarded against the employer. The Act affirms the basic right of an employee to withdraw his labour. The Act also provides that the Code of Industrial Relations Practice agreed under the 1971 Act shall continue in force. It is not legally binding, but breach of the code may be used in evidence at an industrial tribunal.

The Employment Protection Act was implemented in the late 1970s. It gives employees fundamental new rights. These include:

(a) The right to a guaranteed payment in the event of the employer's inability to offer him work of the kind he is employed to do or some alternative employment.

(b) Females have a right to maternity pay, and to reinstatement after the baby is born.

(c) The right to payment while suspended on medical grounds. Suspension on medical grounds arises under a number of statutes; for example, statutes referring to exposure to radiation.

(d) The right not to have action taken against him by reason of trade union activity, etc.

The Acts also set up machinery for promoting improved industrial relations, notably the **Advisory, Conciliation and Arbitration Services (ACAS).**

With such a strong legal framework within which industrial relations are conducted it has become extremely difficult in some industries to reach agreements which are acceptable to all sections of a strongly unionised labour force. The British tradition of specialist unions representing crafts within an industry, rather than the industry as a whole, aggravates the situation. Even so, about 98 per cent of all firms never have an industrial dispute, and reach agreements quite satisfactorily through joint consultation procedures.

Personnel Records

A comprehensive, accurate and up-to-date set of personnel records is invaluable in ensuring the adequacy of human resources in a firm. Without these basic facts all recruitment programmes, training schedules and manpower forecasting become haphazard activities, while absenteeism and poor health records go undetected. Conversely, all records cost money to maintain, and it is wasteful to maintain an elaborate set of records which are not likely to be used.

The most basic types of personnel record are those which contain a store of information about a particular employee: his qualifications and experience before joining the firm; his record of employment within the organisation, showing advances in salary and status over the years; his health, timekeeping and training records and periodic appraisals of his performance. Often a simple manual record is quite adequate for these purposes, and a well-designed folder may not only accumulate all the details succinctly but serve as a storage file for such items as the Contract of Employment, training reports issued at the conclusion of courses, correspondence arising from disciplinary incidents, etc. The basic records reproduced in Figs. 21.2 and 21.3 show typical rulings which meet most requirements.

A strip-index record containing basic details is helpful in discussing allocation of staff with departmental managers. A department may be fully described in a single leaf from the wall panel containing strips for each member of staff, colour-coded to pinpoint their skills and functions. Transfers are easily accommodated by moving the transferee's slip from one department to another and re-positioning it at the correct point to indicate status, skills, etc.

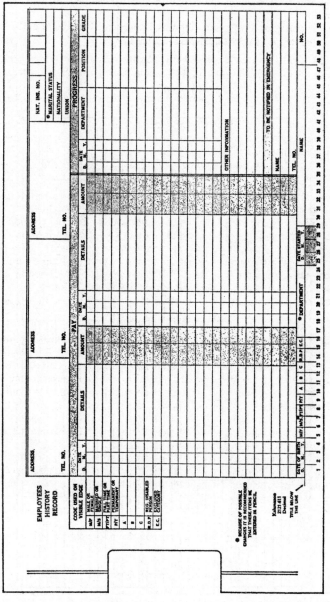

Fig. 21.2. Personnel records.

(Courtesy of Kalamazoo Ltd)

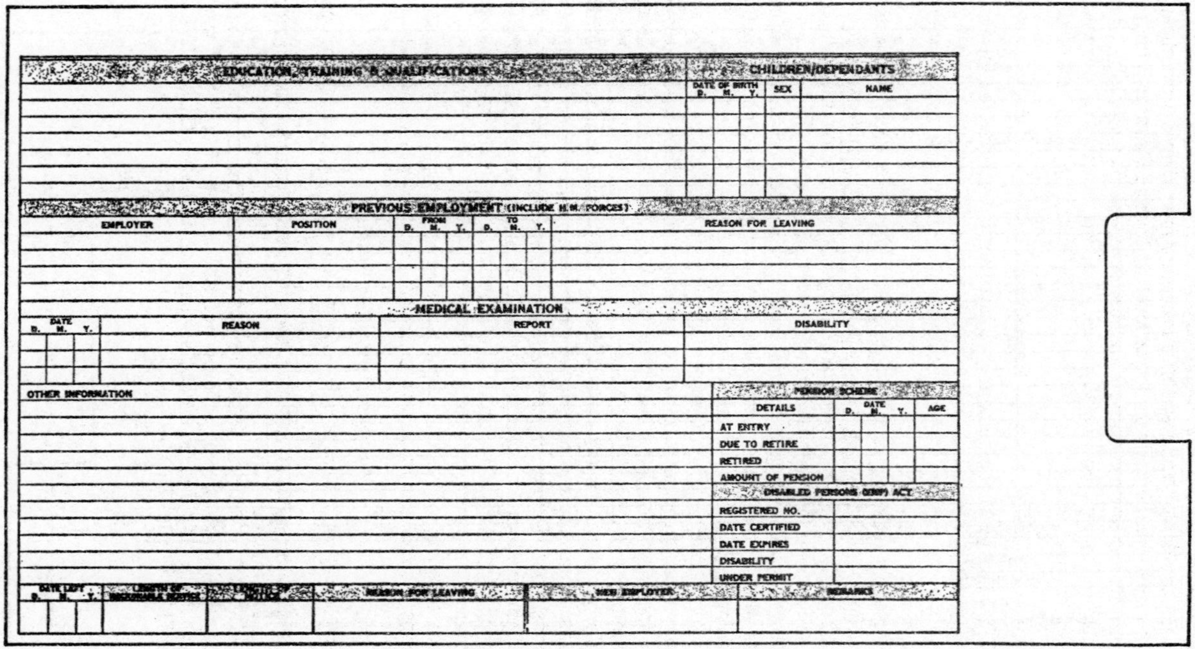

Fig. 21.3. Personnel records.

(Courtesy of Kalamazoo Ltd)

Visi-index records such as Kalamazoo personnel records (which are illustrated in a companion volume, *Office Practice Made Simple*) are a cheap and efficient system, particularly for lower level staff where turnover is high and a long-term record not necessary. Kalamazoo also market simple systems for Time and Absence Records, Pensions, Training Records and Employee History Records.

Summary

1. The function of the personnel department is to secure for the firm the human resources it requires, with the necessary degrees of skill and knowledge. It must then induct them effectively and foster their development and advancement.

2. Personnel planning is a long-term activity which keeps personnel requirements for the future under constant review. It seeks to ensure both that the right number of staff of the right quality are available, and that a successor for each important post is being trained.

3. However staff are recruited they should go through a systematic selection process which includes the completion of an application form, the taking up of references, checking on qualifications claimed and an interview.

4. Training and staff development are essential activities if firms are to maintain their competitive position and have adequate human resources. The cooperation of trainees is an essential element in the success of training programmes.

5. The personnel department will have a major rôle to play in industrial relations. It must ensure compliance with major statutes like the Industrial Relations Act 1974 and the Employment Protection Act 1975. Most major firms also have joint consultation procedures which provide a forum where discussions can take place about all aspects of the employer–employee relationship.

6. An adequate system of records is essential to the personnel office, and forms the basis of manpower planning and development programmes.

Suggested Further Reading

Personnel Management Made Simple, S. Tyson and A. York, Heinemann, London, 1982.

The Institute of Personnel Management issues a range of literature which is authoritative and up to date.

The Department of Education issues a range of free leaflets on personnel matters.

A comprehensive collection of employment forms covering all aspects of personnel records is available from Formecon Services Ltd, Gateway, Crewe, CW1 1YN, England.

22

SOURCES OF REFERENCE

Introduction

No range of reference books can hope to be complete, and the range available in any office must necessarily be smaller than the range available at a reference library, particularly a specialist 'Business Library'. In preparing this chapter I am indebted to Susan Drury, who researched most effectively to cover the chief fields required.

English Language and Correspondence

1. A good English dictionary, e.g. *Chambers Twentieth Century Dictionary* or the *Concise Oxford Dictionary*.

2. Any translating or specialist dictionaries appropriate to the work of the particular office, e.g. *Chambers Dictionary of Science and Technology*, *Pitman Dictionary of English and Shorthand*.

3. Fowler, H. W., *Dictionary of Modern English Usage* and/or Partridge, E., *Usage and Abusage*. These are guides to the formally correct use of the English language, including points of grammar, punctuation, idioms, etc.

4. *Roget's Thesaurus of English Words and Phrases*. This is a thesaurus or 'treasury' of English words and phrases, classified into groups of similar meaning. It can be helpful for finding the right word to express an idea exactly. With a dictionary one starts with a word and finds its meaning. With a thesaurus one starts with an idea and finds the best word to convey that idea.

5. *Black's Titles and Forms of Address*. A guide to the correct way of addressing people of rank, or holding official positions, both in writing and in speech. It also includes a guide to the pronunciation of certain surnames.

Post Office Services

6. *Post Office Guide*. An essential guide to all the services of the Post Office, including information on savings, licences, etc. A useful feature in the telecommunications section is the statement for each overseas country of the differences in time from Greenwich Mean Time.

7. *Post Offices in the United Kingdom*. A useful list giving hours of opening and the latest times for the receipt of telegraphic communications.

8. *Postal Addresses and Index to Postcode Directories*. This indicates where a correct postal address may differ from the usual administrative address, depending upon the nearest main sorting office.

9. *London Post Offices and Streets*. A publication serving similar purposes to the two previously mentioned, but for the London postal area.

10. *Telephone Directories*. As well as providing telephone numbers of subscribers, unless they have chosen to be 'ex-directory', these also cover the range of services available through the use of the telephone. Directories for areas outside the immediate locality can be purchased, together with an index.

11. *Telephone Dialling codes.* An essential booklet providing STD (subscriber trunk dialling) codes available for this country and overseas.

12. *UK Telex Directory.* This appears twice a year and lists subscribers to the Telex service alphabetically and by their answer-back codes.

Meetings

13. Curry, T. P. E., and others, *The Conduct of Meetings* (21st edition, 1975). A guide to the conduct and procedure of meetings, edited by a team of barristers and covering statutory regulations.

14. Graham-Helwig, H., *How to take Minutes* (8th edition, 1975). This deals with both the arranging and recording of meetings, both formal and informal.

15. Perry, P. J. C., *Hours into Minutes* (revised edition 1972). A brief guide to minute taking.

People

16. *Who's Who.* Provides information on prominent people in this country, e.g. Members of Parliament, peers, well-known personalities from entertainment and sport.

17. *Debrett's Peerage* or *Burke's Peerage.* A more comprehensive guide in each case to peers and their families.

18. *Directory of Directors.* This is an alphabetical list of prominent directors, giving a little biographical information and indicating the companies with which they are associated.

19. *Medical Directory.* As well as listing doctors alphabetically, this also provides local listings, a guide to hospitals and other data about the medical profession. The official list of recognised medical practitioners is the *Medical Register*, and there are similar lists for related professions, e.g. dentists, opticians, etc.

20. *Crockford's Clerical Directory.* This is the guide to the Anglican Church, both at home and abroad, and its clergy. Both an alphabetical list and indexes by parish are provided.

21. *The Law List,* which used to be the standard guide to the whole of the legal profession, was discontinued in 1976. It is now necessary to consult *The Bar List* for judges, barristers, etc., and *The Solicitor's Diary, Almanac and Legal Directory* for solicitors.

There are many other lists of personnel in particular professions and trades. The work of the office concerned will dictate which of these are necessary. In some cases the electoral roll for the locality might be useful. These are available for consultation in the local library or Post Office if not otherwise obtainable.

Trade and Industry

22. *Kelly's Manufacturers and Merchants Directory.* This includes both a classified and an alphabetical listing of manufacturers and merchants, and a list of exporters. United Kingdom and international volumes are available.

23. *Kelly's Post Office London.* As well as providing classified and alphabetical trades lists for the London postal area, this publication has a street directory for commercial concerns and information on official, legal, ecclesiastical and local government offices and personnel in the area. (*N.B.* Kelly's local directories *other* than London have been discontinued.)

24. *U.K. Kompass.* The first volume provides a very detailed guide to products and their manufacturers; the second volume gives information on the firms included. International volumes are also available.

25. *Yellow Pages* provide a handy guide to local suppliers and manufacturers and also to specialised services available. Some volumes are issued separately and others are bound in with the alphabetical telephone directory for the area.

26. *Stock Exchange Official Yearbook.* This gives financial information on firms as well as facts about their history and structure, and the names of directors.

According to the work of the office, specialised directories might also be required, e.g. *Benn's Hardware Directory, Food Trades Directory, Sell's Building Index.*

Travel and Conferences

27. *ABC Rail Guide.* A monthly publication which indicates the principal rail services from London to all areas of the United Kingdom. Bus connections are listed for places not served by rail. There is a detailed timetable section for the London and South-East region. Continental ferry services and rail connections are also given.

28. *British Rail Passenger Timetable: Great Britain.* This provides the detailed timetables for the whole country. A separate international section is available for overseas connections.

29. *Cooks Continental Timetable.* A guide to the principal rail services of Europe, North Africa and the Near East. It also covers local shipping services in the area.

30. *ABC World Airways Guide.* Complete guide to all the latest timetable and fares information for the airlines of the world, in two parts, monthly.

31. *Airport Times.* A much smaller monthly guide giving an outline of air travel services.

32. *ABC Air/Rail Europe.* Air and rail services for Europe are shown together for easy comparison; monthly.

33. *ABC Shipping Guide.* Another monthly publication which shows details of regular sailings throughout the world and covers European car ferries.

34. *National Express Guide to Express Services.* A guide to coach travel within Britain.

35. *RAC Guide and Handbook.* A handbook produced by the Royal Automobile Club covering Great Britain. There are maps and town plans, and accommodation and garage facilities are given for towns listed in the gazetteer section.

(The Automobile Association issues a similar handbook to its members and both organisations publish continental guides for motorists.)

36. *Britain: Hotels and Restaurants.* A guide published by the British Tourist Authority, in which places listed should conform to certain minimum standards. Indicates hotels able to provide conference facilities.

37. *Good Food Guide.* Published by the Consumers' Association and aims to be completely impartial. Does not therefore necessarily include establishments for every major town.

38. *Hints to Businessmen.* A free series of booklets covering the countries

of the world, produced by the Department of Trade. Advice on travel, entry regulations, customs control, consular facilities, hotels, etc., is included.

39. *Personnel and Training Management Yearbook and Directory.* The directory section includes a list of conference centres and a section on conference services such as equipment hire, reporting services, conference organisers, etc.

40. *London A-Z.* This or a similar street atlas of London is an essential aid in London offices, but also useful elsewhere if there is any likelihood of members of the firm or organisation having to visit the capital city.

A general world atlas is always useful and other maps and street plans may be required according to the work of the office.

The Press and Public Relations

41. *Writers' and Artists' Year Book.* If items have to be prepared for publication, this can be a handy guide, covering copyright, specialist publishers, typing services, proof correction, etc., as well as listing many magazines and journals.

42. *Newspaper Press Directory.* As well as listing national and local newspapers, and providing details of them, including advertising rates and circulation figures, this also covers magazines and directories. Some foreign publications are dealt with.

43. *Willing's Press Guide.* A more compact guide to newspapers and magazines.

44. Black, S., *Practical Public Relations* (4th edition, 1976). A comprehensive textbook rather than a reference source for public relations practice in the United Kingdom.

General and Current Affairs Information

45. *Whitakers Almanack.* An annual publication giving a great variety of facts and figures relating to this country and to some extent for other countries too. A useful source for names and addresses of asssociations and societies, of government offices and other national institutions.

46. *Britain: An Official Handbook.* Another annual publication giving an up-to-date description of Britain—its governmental, legal, financial structure, etc.—and providing some statistics and sources of further information.

47. *Annual Abstract of Statistics.* A compilation of national statistics from a wide variety of fields, such as trade, production, health, population, crime, weather, etc.

48. *Statesman's Yearbook.* A guide to current information on the countries of the world, and to international organisations.

49. *Pears Cyclopaedia.* This is a small annual encyclopaedia which, amongst other information, has a useful world gazetteer.

Consultancy and Advisory Services

50. *Register of Management Consultants and Advisory Services to Industry* (Gower Press). A public listing of British management consultants and advisory organisations.

51. *Personnel and Training Management Yearbook* (already listed for conferences—see reference 39). This includes a section on advisory and consultancy services.

The British Institute of Management and the Confederation of British Industry jointly run the Management Consulting Services Information Bureau, which will compile lists of appropriate consultancies for specific assignments for BIM member organisations.

Office Equipment

52. *Business Equipment Guide* (BED Business Journals Ltd). Published twice a year, this guide gives a comprehensive coverage of the whole business equipment field, with special charts on each class of equipment to pinpoint the features of each firm's product, and consequently its limitations.

53. *Business Equipment Digest* (BED Business Journals Ltd). A monthly management magazine for executives responsible for the selection or purchase of business equipment, materials and services.

54. *Business Systems and Equipment* (Maclean-Hunter Ltd). A monthly magazine which brings up-to-date and comprehensive news about business equipment and practical advice on its application in working systems.

55. *Index* (Maclaren Publishers Ltd). A controlled circulation magazine reaching 60,000 middle-management readers each month, containing details of new equipment as it appears and monitoring trends and developments in office practice.

Other Sources of Information

The efficient secretary will make herself aware of the resources available at the nearest reference library, which will supplement the office library. In London there is easy access by telephone to the City Business Library, and in provincial cities there will often be a library which has a specialist business collection. Some reference materials which are unlikely to be in office collections are worth remembering for use if they are accessible elsewhere.

56. *British National Bibliography*. A weekly publication with regular cumulative volumes listing British publications year by year, with subject indexes.

57. *British Books in Print*. Author and title listings of publications currently available.

58. *British Humanities Index/British Technology Index*. For tracing articles which have appeared in newspapers and magazines.

59. *Keesing's Contemporary Archives*. A file of world current events brought up to date with weekly supplements. The information is gathered from newspapers, parliamentary proceedings (Hansard) and official publications.

60. *Vacher's* (pronounced Vasher's) *Parliamentary Companion* gives the names and addresses of all members of the House of Lords, the House of Commons and Government departments of every sort.

61. *Vacher's European Companion* provides similar information to the above for the European Economic Community.

QUESTIONS

Chapter 1

1. What is meant by the term 'mixed economy'? What opportunities for top secretaries exist in the various organisations that are to be found in societies having a mixed economy?

2. 'The executive is a key person; his secretary must therefore also be a key person in any firm or institution.' Discuss this statement, giving your own view of the importance of the executive secretary.

3. Discuss the qualities which a top secretary should have if she is to play a full part in her firm.

4. What is office practice? How does it differ from secretarial practice? A young copy typist tells you that she has passed examinations in office practice yet she did not even have a reply to four applications she sent in for posts described as 'private secretarial' posts. Explain to her why this happened, in your opinion.

5. 'Not a wheel turns without a top secretary giving the vital push.' Explain.

Chapter 2

1. The personal secretary should be seated in the same room as the executive she serves. Discuss.

2. Discuss the merits of the L-shaped desk configuration for personal secretaries. What alternative desk and seating layouts are found in offices?

3. What means are available to reduce noise in the office?

4. What minor office aids are essential to the efficient conduct of a personal secretary? Explain their contribution in terms of cost-effectiveness.

5. Draw a layout (viewed from above) of a secretarial work station to suit a busy personal secretary. Design the layout to suit your own personal preferences, labelling the items of furniture you include and the ancillary equipment you expect to have provided. Then write a few short paragraphs explaining why you positioned units in the way that you did.

Chapter 3

1. What is meant by the term 'executive–secretarial partnership'? Discuss whether a partnership arrangement is likely to be more effective than an employer–employee relationship.

2. How crucial are secretarial skills to a personal assistant in a major company? Explain the terms 'secretarial skills' and 'personal assistant' in the course of your answer.

3. An executive secretary complains to you that her job gives her little satisfaction, and that she is thinking of going elsewhere. How do you think such situations arise, and how can they be solved? Include in your answer possible criticisms of the executive, the personnel arrangements and the girl herself.

4. Explain the terms 'Year Planner' and 'Follow-up System'. How could they be useful to an executive secretary?

5. An executive who is fastidious and painstaking in everything he does is seriously overworked. What steps might be taken to overcome this problem by (a) the executive himself, and (b) his secretary?

6. What is meant by the term 'a cost-effective secretary'? In what ways might a secretary increase her cost-effectiveness?

Chapter 4

1. Define communication. What is the importance of communication to a large company today? In your answer refer to both internal and external aspects of communication.

2. 'Verbal communication is direct and informal, written communication is indirect and formal.' Explain these statements and illustrate their truth from your knowledge of the modern communication scene. Are they absolutely accurate?

3. What difficulties might be met in giving instructions to junior staff about a particular office procedure? Outline a suitable method for giving instruction to temporary junior staff.

4. A proposal to management by time and motion study experts has suggested the ending of a personal secretary status and their replacement by a pool of secretaries working for a wider range of executives. Prepare a statement to be delivered to a meeting of staff, in which you either support or oppose the suggestion. Do not write out the full statement, merely a list of headings and notes of the points you would make under each heading.

5. What is an NCR memo-set? Why is it more effective than an ordinary written memo? Illustrate your answer by drawing up a typical memo on this type of form.

6. What is a report? Outline the style that should be followed in making a report. Imagine in your answer that you are preparing a report from a firm of independent consultants about financial proposals regarding the purchase of capital equipment for a major producer of chemical products.

7. Write short notes (10–15 lines each) about three of the following:

(*a*) Quick-reply letters   (*b*) Circulars
(*b*) Press statements   (*e*) Tele-notes
(*c*) Summaries   (*f*) Bulletins

8. 'The rapid communication to staff of the results of negotiations between management and trade unions on hours, pay, conditions and reorganisation presents major difficulties.' What means of communication are available to ensure that staff are rapidly informed about such developments?

Chapter 5

1. Distinguish between direct dictation, recorded dictation and shorthand dictation. Discuss the appropriateness of each as a method of imparting the contents of business letters to a typist.

2. Why do many executives still prepare material for the typist in manuscript form? What are the advantages and disadvantages of this method?

3. A proposal to replace secretaries by a recorded dictation system is being debated in a large business organisation. Discuss this proposal from the point of view of the managing director's secretary.

4. 'I dislike taking dictation from Mr Smith; he's so disorganised!' List ten ways in which Mr Smith's efforts might fall short of a satisfactory performance.

5. Draw up a list of ten suggestions to a young secretary about her preparations before taking dictation from an executive and her actual performance during the dictation session.

6. A young executive has never used dictation machines before, and asks you to explain the more important points. After doing so you decide to type out a list of suggestions for use in the future, should a similar situation arise. Draw up this list of suggestions.

Chapter 6

1. What is the meaning of transcription? A new secretary is starting work at your office and you have been asked to draw up a list of points that she needs to know so that correspondence she produces will meet your firm's high standards. List the points you would cover to help her.

2. Why is the use of English an essential skill for a secretary, even though all the material she types has been dictated to her and she only has to transcribe it?

3. An executive complains to you that his new secretary presents work to him with several mistakes in every letter. He asks you to help her overcome this serious shortcoming. What advice would you give her?

4. What is the link between the salutation and the complimentary close of a letter? Suggest suitable salutations for letters to different individuals and the complimentary closures which are appropriate to each.

5. Explain 'fully-blocked style' and 'modified fully-blocked style' in correspondence. What is the meaning of 'house style'? Discuss its advantages and disadvantages.

6. Write short notes about any four of the following:

(a) References (in business correspondence)   (e) Marking instructions
(b) Paragraphing   (f) Attention lines
(c) Enclosures   (g) Subject headings
(d) Continuation Sheets

7. Why do firms use headed notepaper? What legal requirements must letter heading comply with, and what problems exist in the control of headed notepaper?

Chapter 7

1. Discuss the relative merits of (a) manual typewriters, (b) electric typewriters and (c) portable typewriters.

2. What is an electronic typewriter? How does it assist productivity in the stenographic field?

3. What is meant by 'word processing'? How is word processing of use to a skilled secretary?

4. Explain the use of a word-processing system in each of the following cases:

(a) To produce letters on routine matters by means of standard paragraphs;
(b) To produce a final report from the first rough draft, through successive critical appraisals of it in which alterations, deletions and additions are made.

5. What are the difficulties in introducing word processing into a busy office? How may they be overcome?

6. Explain what is meant by the terms 'automatic typewriter' and 'word processing'. Discuss the benefits from, and limitations of these facilities.

Chapter 8

1. Explain the following abbreviations:

(a) STD   (b) PMBX   (c) PABX.

2. You are about to instruct a new member of staff about the use of the telephone. What points would you make to her about (a) her voice, (b) her attitude to the caller, (c) note-taking, (d) follow-up actions after a call has been concluded—supposing that any action is neccessary?

3. You are often forced to use more than one telephone at a time. How do you overcome the difficulties?

4. List and then describe eight items which a secretary would find useful in the course of her duties in so far as they affect the telephone.

5. Why is a telephone-answering machine a great asset to any secretary? Suggest how she could use it if it had a 'playback' facility.

6. Write a short account of three of the following: (*a*) a telenote, (*b*) direct speech intercom systems, (*c*) loudspeaking telephones, (*d*) key callmakers.

7. What is a PABX? Explain the following terms in connection with a PABX: (i) trunk offering, (ii) trunk call barring, (iii) hold for enquiry.

8. Describe and comment briefly upon the uses of: (i) facsimile telegraphy, (ii) telephone answering services, (iii) the Telex service, (iv) telenote systems.

Chapter 9

1. Draw up a checklist to be used by a young secretary to ensure that letters are correctly dispatched, by the most appropriate mail service, and that nothing is left out or overlooked.

2. How should incoming mail be handled in the interval between its arrival on collection from the Post Office and its final distribution to the staff for whom it is intended?

3. Internal mail in a large organisation is as important as the mail received through the Post Office system. Outline a procedure for ensuring that internal mail is handled efficiently. Mention in your answer (*a*) collection, (*b*) distribution, (*c*) economy and (*d*) confidentiality.

4. Describe the procedures an executive secretary should follow who has received the mail for her executive at a time before he has arrived.

5. What is a mail inwards register? What is a postage book? What is a posting list?

6. Rule up two sheets of petty cash paper similar to Fig. 9.6 and complete the exercises given below on it.

(*a*) Enter the following items in a Petty Cash Book which is kept on the Imprest System. At the end restore the original Imprest. Use analysis columns for Fares, Postage, Sundries, Stationery and Ledger Accounts.

19..
Oct. 1 Drew Imprest from cashier £50.00
     2 Paid fares £7.50; paid for stamps £2.80
     3 Paid for office teas £4.42; paid for envelopes £3.65; paid for string £0.65
     4 Paid fares £5.15; paid for glue for office use £0.85
     5 Gave proprietor £10.00 from till for his personal use
     6 Paid J. Thomas £4.36; paid cleaner £7.50

(*b*) A Petty Cash Book is kept on the Imprest System, the amount of the Imprest being £50.00. It has four analysis columns: Postage and Stationery; Travelling Expenses; Carriage; Office Expenses. Give the ruling for the book and enter the following transactions:

19..
Jan. 4 Petty cash in hand £1.50; received cash to make up the Imprest; bought
       stamps £3.50
     7 Paid railway fares £3.25; bus fares £1.26; telegrams £2.50
     8 Paid carriage on small parcels £1.15; paid railway fares £7.00; bought
       envelopes £2.89
   10 Paid for repairs to typewriters £12.75; paid carrier's account £8.75

Balance the Petty Cash Book as on January 11th and bring down the balance.

Chapter 10

1. Discuss the importance of filing in a modern office. Include in your answers an appraisal of departmental as opposed to centralised filing systems.

2. 'Staff salaries are the hidden cost in an antiquated filing system.' Discuss this

statement by a leading business equipment manufacturer, bringing out the implications of the sentence.

3. Why is flexibility important in the filing system of a small office? How can flexibility be achieved without excessive expenditure on capital items?

4. Write brief notes on *four* of the following:

(*a*) Suspension filing
(*b*) Index tabs
(*c*) Powered filing

(*d*) Rotary filing
(*e*) Post binders
(*f*) Lever-arch files

5. Explain the process of microfilm filing and the pieces of equipment needed to achieve an adequate system. What are the advantages of the method?

6. 'Unless the filing clerk has chosen the filing system herself she will never be happy with it.' Comment on this statement, bringing out your own views on the selection of a filing system.

Chapter 11

1. What is reprography? What is the importance of an adequate reprographic system in modern business?

2. Two executive secretaries are preparing reports for their executives about adequate reprographic facilities for their respective offices. One is the secretary to a personnel officer, the other to the head of department in a teacher training college. Choose one of these positions and discuss the sort of reprographic needs that might exist, and the ways in which they could be met.

3. 'Our house journal is a splendid means of informing staff and building *esprit de corps.*' Explain this sentence, referring in your answer to the reprographic problems that might arise in the regular production of a house journal.

4. Write short notes about four of the following:

(*a*) Spirit duplicating
(*b*) Xerography
(*c*) Heat transfer copiers

(*d*) Collators
(*e*) Ink stencils
(*f*) Dual spectrum copiers

5. Explain the advantages and disadvantages of sophisticated electrostatic plain paper copiers.

Chapter 12

1. What points would you make to a young member of staff who is about to take her first post as a personal secretary, with regard to the diary of the executive she is to serve?

2. What is a follow-up system? Explain how it improves executive and secretarial efficiency.

3. Explain how to introduce a visiting female fashion consultant to a male executive who is the chairman of the product design committee of your firm.

4. What constraints affect the secretary in planning her own working day? What measures might she take to ease the burdens these place upon her?

5. What is visual planning? How might it be used in the following situations? (*a*) Holiday rotas. (*b*) Allocation of staff to classes in a technical college or school.

6. What points are important in the reception of a visitor who has arrived for a pre-conference discussion with your executive? His hotel accommodation is not available until 6 p.m. and he is arriving from the local airport for an 11.30 a.m. appointment. His plane lands at 10.45 a.m.

Chapter 13

1. 'Every secretary is in the front-line as far as public relations are concerned.' Explain this statement, referring particularly to a secretary who works in the public relations department of her firm.

2. A firm is about to launch a new product in the kitchen equipment field. The public relations officer is asked for his comments upon (*a*) the product and (*b*) the promotion of the product, which is to include a television promotion and press advertising. Suggest a number of points he might consider, and explain the 'public relations' aspect of each point.

3. You are called upon to arrange a tour of teenage schoolgirls around a fashion house workshop. Consider the steps you would take to ensure that this was an enjoyable and memorable occasion.

4. A letter is received by your public relations department which claims that an article purchased was so badly rusted that it is almost totally useless for the purpose intended. It gives the serial number of the unit purchased, the name of the retailer who supplied it, and calls for its immediate replacement. It is in fact a model which was discontinued several years ago. Write (*a*) a letter to the consumer promising some action as soon as the complaint has been investigated, and (*b*) a letter to the retailer asking for an explanation.

5. What is office protocol? Discuss whether it is a useful feature or not of office life. What part should the executive secretary play as far as protocol is concerned?

Chapter 14

1. Discuss the importance of meetings in a large-scale organisation. Contrast the position in a large limited company with that in a small firm run by a proprietor.

2. Write a short paragraph (5–8 lines) about four of the following:

(*a*) An Annual General Meeting   (*d*) An Ad Hoc Committee
(*b*) A Board Meeting   (*e*) A Statutory Meeting
(*c*) An Extraordinary General   (*f*) A Briefing Meeting
    Meeting

3. What duties would the secretary to a committee perform in the period shortly before her committee meets, to ensure a successful meeting?

4. What is an agenda? How should an agenda be prepared and circulated? Draw up an imaginary agenda for a meeting of the safety committee controlling safety aspects of an oil refinery.

5. 'The secretary's rôle is to assist the chairman, take minutes and serve refreshments.' Comment on this definition of the secretary's rôle at a meeting, and suggest your own definition.

6. Explain the following terms used in connection with meetings:

(*a*) Motion   (*d*) Resolution
(*b*) *Nem con*   (*e*) Proxy
(*c*) Quorum   (*f*) Adjourned *sine die*

Chapter 15

1. Why are conferences and public relations functions a feature of modern business? Outline the part played by the secretary to a conference organiser.

2. What are the chief functions of the personal assistant to a conference organiser on the actual day of the conference?

3. Describe the arrangements necessary for a cocktail party to launch a new range of cosmetics.

4. Write short notes (8–10 lines) about each of the following:

(*a*) Invitation cards   (*c*) Orders of the day
(*b*) Car parking problems at   (*d*) Dismantling exhibitions
    functions

5. What are 'follow-up' activities? Describe the likely follow-up activities after (*a*) a convention on 'Problems of Port Operations', (*b*) a formal 'Chamber of Commerce' luncheon.

Chapter 16

1. Why is executive travel a regular feature of modern business? How should such a journey be planned?

2. What is meant by the term 'itinerary'? What decisions must be taken before an itinerary can be arranged? Explain how the difficulties of a tight schedule can be reduced.

3. Consider what travel details must be arranged if an overseas visit is to be trouble-free. Explain the arrangements necessary for each item in the list.

4. In six weeks' time your chief is to leave the country for one month on a business trip. He does not expect to be bothered during this period with his normal programme of work, since he will be fully concerned with the specialist activities of the trip. Explain how you will ensure that the work of his department continues in his absence.

5. What facilities are necessary to support a salesman on an overseas visit? Refer in your answer to (*a*) his selling activities, and (*b*) follow-up facilities.

6. An overseas visit by a senior executive is to involve a stay of seven days, commencing with his arrival on Thursday evening. The country is Islamic, and no business is done on Friday. Saturday and Sunday are to be used for visits to seven business contacts. Monday and Tuesday are to be devoted to a conference of agents from all over the territory, concluding with a social gathering on the Tuesday evening. Wednesday is to cover a visit to a plant in the southern region, and a detailed review of its operations in the light of developments in living standards throughout the region. The return flight is booked for 3 p.m. local time on Thursday. Prepare an itinerary inventing such names and places as you feel necessary to fill in the details of the programme.

Chapter 17

1. What do you understand by the term 'production'? Would you regard the services of a doctor or a dentist as 'production'?

2. What are the 'factors of production'? Explain in detail the resources each factor makes available to management. How does management use them to create goods and services?

3. Why is the public limited company so important in the modern business scene? Describe the organisation of such a company.

4. What is meant by scientific management? Explain how scientific management might improve (*a*) a factory, (*b*) the system used in a busy office to prepare correspondence.

5. 'Tina has virtually ruined the plans we made for the new publicity mailing by failing to complete the work allocated to her, which she maintains is excessive and unfair.' What sort of solutions are available to deal with Tina, who cannot be dismissed because she is a relative of the managing director?

Chapter 18

1. What is the 'objects clause' as far as a company is concerned? Explain its importance to contracts made by the company in the course of business.

2. Explain what is meant by the phrase 'As a matter of policy the Board declares. . . . .'. Define policy and explain how it is laid down.

3. What is 'planning'? What part does planning play in the realisation of corporate objectives?

4. What is meant by the term 'management by objectives'? How is this type of management achieved, and why is it held to be appropriate in modern circumstances?

5. Some firms try to forecast their business activity well into the future, as long as ten to fifteen years ahead. Is such forecasting valuable in your opinion? What criticisms might be made of such forecasts by the man on the shop floor?

Chapter 19

1. Distinguish between 'line and staff' organisations and 'functional' organisations.

2. Compile an organisational chart for any firm with which you are familiar. If you are not in employment, compile a chart for the college or school in which you are studying.

3. What part is played by delegation in a large organisation?

4. What is the basis of the powers of a Board of Directors? Describe a typical structure of such a Board, and explain the importance of each type of director to the success of the company.

5. Write short notes (7–10 lines each) about any four of the following:

(a) Environmental responsibility	(d) duties and responsibilities
(b) A Memorandum of Association	(e) Executive directors
(c) Management committees	(f) Span of control

6. 'A reappraisal of organisation is always valuable.' 'Too-frequent reappraisals of business systems can be counter-productive.' Discuss these two viewpoints.

7. Assess the value of the appointment of 'worker-directors' to the board of a large manufacturing company.

8. What factors in your opinion motivate staff to display loyalty to the company which employs them?

Chapter 20

1. What is meant by the term 'planning-control feedback cycle'? How is control achieved, and at what points does it feed back into the planning–production process?

2. Many firms are introducing mini-computers. What sort of applications has a mini-computer? Where would such applications achieve cost-savings? How can the advantages of computer operations be achieved without the purchase of a computer?

3. 'Capital tied up in excessive stock reduces the return on capital invested.' Explain this statement, and suggest how excessive stocks can be avoided.

4. Why are secondary statistics more use in controlling aspects of business than primary statistics collected from department reports? In your answer refer to (a) sales figures collected from year to year, (b) 'expense' figures collected from year to year.

5. Define 'critical path analysis' and explain how it might be used to control a redevelopment project in which five units for a chemical plant have to be assembled and installed, and access paths and landscaping to the existing premises improved. Invent such events and activity times as you feel are necessary.

Chapter 21

1. What are the functions of a personnel officer? What status does he usually have in the firm, and what qualities are required for such a post?

2. What are the meanings of the terms 'personnel planning' and 'succession planning'? How much does the success of these activities depend upon the cooperation of staff being groomed for more onerous activities?

3. Write short paragraphs (8–10 lines each) on four of the following, bringing out their significance to the personnel officer:

(a) Job centres	(d) Careers conferences
(b) References	(e) Application forms
(c) Interviews	(f) Selection consultants

4. What is meant by the term 'flexible working hours'? Explain how a flexible working hours system operates and discuss the advantages to staff and management compared with the normal 'fixed day' system.

5. What part does industrial relations play in modern industry?

PROFESSIONAL ORGANISATIONS FOR EXECUTIVE SECRETARIES

Career Prospects as a Private Secretary

There is no doubt that there is a continuing shortage of well-qualified private secretaries. The papers are full of advertisements for executive secretaries; secretarial agencies are constantly on the look-out for staff who are able to take immediate charge of an office; the variety of work available is enormous. Yet at the same time colleges are at full pressure turning out secretaries of reasonable competence, the schools are producing a flood of lower-level typists and shorthand typists, and bodies like the Training Services Agency are using official funds to sponsor suitable mature applicants for TOPS (Training Opportunities Scheme) courses all over the country. How is it that, with so much output from all these sources, there is such a shortage of really top-level staff?

There are several answers. First, one does not become a top secretary overnight. This book is called *Secretarial Practice Made Simple*, yet anyone who has read its hundreds of pages will appreciate that secretarial practice is not as simple as all that. There is much to learn; the general background knowledge required is very extensive, and when a particular post is taken up by the secretary she finds that this post has its own extensive background to be learned before she can be fully effective. Second, the secretarial skills which have to be mastered take time and practice. They have to become automatic responses which can be performed instinctively. Only when the secretary can take dictation at high speeds, and then transcribe impeccable correspondence, can she hold down the most onerous posts without strain. At this level the secretarial skills become the least of her worries, and management and supervisory responsibilities occupy her mind to the exclusion of the skills she has so laboriously mastered.

The chief reason for the shortage of top private secretaries is that the acquisition of private secretarial skills is not an end, but only a beginning. The first post the secretary takes up reveals a distant horizon ahead of her. In trying to reach that horizon she only reveals a more extensive vista ahead. Her secretarial skills may lead her in directions she did not envisage for one moment when she undertook this study. An enormous range of industries, and of commercial activities, is open to her. She may find herself playing a management role in an industry she did not even know existed. The more responsible she is, the more she is likely to be tested, and the greater the opportunities ahead. Secretaries do marry their bosses, or at least they tend to marry the people with whom they work. This inevitably means a loss to industry and commerce at some stage or other. As they move on to higher things, or to marriage, they vacate posts which have to be filled. There just never are enough good secretaries to meet the demand.

It follows that career prospects for well-trained private secretaries are excellent. The student who successfully completes a secretarial course can look forward to securing a first post as junior secretary without much real difficulty. Employers and secretarial agencies are looking for her, rather than her needing to look for them. This first post will usually lead to a secretarial post at middle management level. This gives the young secretary experience in running a small department, possibly working for a small group of young executives. This again leads either to promotion with an executive to top management level, or to transfer to serve an executive at this senior level. She may become a personal assistant to a senior executive, or to a professional person. Finally, she may secure an executive position in her own right, either within her present company or elsewhere.

Professional Organisations

It is desirable that the executive secretary should join and play an active part in one of the professional organisations for senior secretaries. There are many other professional institutions which may be appropriate as well, such as the Institute of Public Relations and the Institute of Personnel Management.

The Institute of Qualified Private Secretaries Ltd

Enquiries to the Assistant Secretary, 126 Farnham Rd, Slough, Berks., SL1 4XA

Full Membership is available only to holders of the London Chamber of Commerce Private Secretary's Diploma. Holders of the Private Secretary's Certificate are eligible for Associate Membership and this class of membership is open also to holders of certain other qualifications which the Council of the Institute feels are comparable to the Private Secretary's Certificate. Diploma and Certificate examinations include an interview, and applicants for Associate Membership must be prepared to attend for an interview before their application can be considered.

A leaflet is available giving details of the organisation, its aims and activities.

The Executive Secretaries Association

Enquiries to The Secretariat, 45, Milford Close, Abbey Wood, London, SE2 0DS

The Executive Secretaries' Association is an organisation for secretaries working at director and company chairman level. The association does not hold examinations for its members. The Association is for those who are already proven executive secretaries and junior secretaries who hope to become top secretaries.

A leaflet is available giving details of the aims of the Association, and an application form is incorporated.

EXAMINATIONS FOR PRIVATE SECRETARIES

There is such a wide range of secretarial training available in the United Kingdom that it is impossible to describe the full scene in an appendix of this sort. This book was written with the syllabus for the Private Secretary's Diploma of the London Chamber of Commerce and Industry chiefly in mind. This may be described as a top-level qualification. Of comparable status is the Diploma for Personal Assistants, awarded by the Royal Society of Arts. Both these examinations are intended for students who are carrying out 'post A-level' studies in private secretarial practice. This phrase, of course, includes students taking secretarial courses as post-graduate studies, and those taking secretarial courses after completing BEC National Diploma and National Certificate courses in Business Studies.

It is not suggested that only 'post A-level' students can attain the top ranks in secretarial work, and the Private Secretary's Diploma is open to those who have started secretarial studies earlier than A-level, if they have passed the Private Secretary's Certificate, a slightly lower level examination.

In view of the importance of languages in secretarial work, reference is made below to Language Examinations for Secretaries, run by the Royal Society of Arts.

The Private Secretary's Certificate (London Chamber of Commerce)

Students must be at least 18 years old in the calendar year in which they take this examination, though certain exceptions are made to this rule. The subjects of the examination are:

Private Secretarial Practice Part I (Communication)
Private Secretarial Practice Part II (Private Secretarial Duties)
Office Organisation, Equipment and Services
Structure of Business
Shorthand-Typewriting Duties
Audio Typewriting Duties
An Interview (The purpose of the interview is to satisfy the Board that candidates have the personality and aptitude of mind considered necessary in a secretary to middle management.)

Details are contained in a brochure, *Private Secretary's Certificate* obtainable from The London Chamber of Commerce and Industry, Commercial Education Scheme, Marlowe House, Station Road, Sidcup, Kent, DA15 7BJ.

The Private Secretary's Diploma (London Chamber of Commerce)

Candidates must be not less than 21 years of age in the year they sit this examination (except that holders of the Private Secretary's Certificate may enter in the year they attain 20 years of age).The subjects of the examination are:

Private Secretarial Practice Part 1 (Communication)
Private Secretarial Practice Part II (Private Secretarial Duties)
Shorthand-Typewriting Duties
Meetings
Management Appreciation
An Interview

Details are contained in a brochure, *Private Secretary's Diploma*, obtainable from The London Chamber of Commerce and Industry, Commercial Education Scheme, Marlowe House, Station Road, Sidcup, Kent, DA15 7BJ.

The Diploma for Personal Assistants (Royal Society of Arts)

This top-level examination is for 'post A-level' students, and is designed to ensure that students not only have a good standard of shorthand-typewriting and audio-typewriting skills, but also that they can use these skills intelligently in the office. The subjects studied are:

Communication
Office Administration
Economic Aspects of Business
Law and Procedure of Meetings
Practical Correspondence
An Oral Test

Details are given in a brochure, *Diploma for Personal Assistants*, available from The Royal Society of Arts Examination Board, Murray Road, Orpington, Kent, BR5 3RB.

Language Examinations for Secretaries

There are several examination boards offering qualifications in languages for secretaries. The Royal Society of Arts, for example, offers three qualifications. These are:

(a) The Certificate for Secretarial Linguists
(b) The Diploma for Bilingual Secretaries
(c) The Certificate in French for the Office

The languages examined are French, German, Italian and Spanish.

Details are available in a brochure, *Language Examinations for Secretaries*, obtainable from The Royal Society of Arts Examination Board, Murray Road, Orpington, Kent, BR5 3RB.

Index

ACAS, 214
AGM, 140
AOD, 120
Acoustics, 9
Address lists, 163
Advisory, Conciliation and Arbitration Service, 214
Advisory services, 221
Agenda, 141–2
  items, 142
  preparation, 142
  schedule of recurring items, 142
Air conditioning, 9
Answering machines, 78–80, Plate 14
Appointments
  confirmation of, 125
  diary and, 122
  preparation for, 131
Attention line, 52
Audio-typing, 40
Automatic
  centring, 67
  overlay device, 120
  repeat keys, 13, 62
  underscoring, 67

BED Business Journals Ltd, 222
Bandwidth, 212
Bell and Howell Ltd, 107
Board of Directors, 140, 190–2
  responsibilities, 191
  social responsibilities, 192
Brief instructions, 39
Budgetary control, 200
Buffer memory, 63
Bulletins, 34
Bureaucracy, 138
Business
  knowledge of, 3
  organisations, 173–5
Business Aids Ltd, plate 4, 36
Business Equipment Digest, 222
Business Equipment Guide, 222
Business Systems and Equipment, 222
Busy-person index, 125

Cables, 81
Card call-makers, 73, 78
Careers conferences, 208
Carriage return
  automatic, 70
  mandatory, 64
  optional, 64

Carson Office Furniture Ltd, Plates 1 and 2, Fig. 2.1
Centralisation
  filing, of, 98
  reprographics, of, 112
Centring, automatic, 67
Chairs, 12
Charts, 118–19, 186
Chat areas, 9
Circulars, 33
Circulation
  correspondence, of, 57, 89
  reports, of, 143
Clichés, 26
Climate, 164
Collators, 120
Committees, 140–1, 187–90
  ad hoc, 140, 187
  special, 140
  standing, 140, 187
  steering, 140
  sub-committee, 140
  terms of reference, 187
Communication, 24–38
  bulletins, 34
  chart of, 25
  circulars, 33
  correct form of, 24
  correspondence, 29
  debates, 28
  definition, 24
  discussions, 28
  facsimile copying, 73, 82
  house journals, 35, 142
  industrial relations, and, 213
  instructions, 27
  letters, 29–33
  meeting of minds, 28
  memoranda, 33
  nature of, 24
  notices, 34
  press releases, 37
  quick-reply letters, 31
  recipient and, 24
  reports, 35
  requests, 28
  secretary, and, 24–38
  sincerity, and, 26
  spoken, 27
  standard form letters, 32
  statements, 28
  summaries, 36
  telecommunications, 38

Communication—*cont.*
  telenotes, 37
  timing of, 24
  veracity and, 26
  written, 29
Company secretary, 1
Complimentary close, 52
Compower Ltd, 203–5
Computer appreciation, 203–5
Computer Power, 203
Conditions of employment, 211
Conference areas, 9
Conferences, 150–5
  activities during, 153
  checklist, 152
  facilities for, 151
  follow-up activities, 155
  importance of, 150
  preparations for, 152
  public relations aspects, 153
  reference books, 220
Constitution, 140
Consultancy services, 221
Consumer relations, 134–5
Continuation sheets, 58
Controls, 195–205
  budgetary, 200
  critical path analysis, 197–8
  definition, 195
  expense ratio, 201–3
  feedback cycle, 196
  gross profit percentage, 201–2
  net profit percentage, 201–2
  network analysis, 197–8
  optimum order, 198
  production, 197
  progress, 197
  quality, 199
  return on capital invested, 198
  statistical, 199
  stock, 198
Cooperation with executive, 20
Coordination, 181
Core time, 212–13
Correction
  keys, 13
  ribbon, 62
  transcription, 59
Correspondence
  attention line, 52
  circulars, 33
  clarity in, 29
  completeness of, 30
  complimentary close, 52
  consistency in, 30
  continuation sheets, 58
  correction of, 59
  correctness of, 29
  courtesy in, 30
  date in, 51
  display, 53–6
  enclosures, 57
  house style, 58

  internal address, 52
  letterhead, 50
  mailing instructions, 51
  memorandum, 33
  preparation of, 30
  quick reply, 31
  reference books, 218
  references, 51
  salutation, 52
  signature, 56
  standard form, 32
  subject headings, 52
  transcription of, 48–60
  word-processing, 63–70
Credit cards, 164
Critical path analysis, 197–8
Current affairs, 221

Data processing, 110
Datapost, 93
Date
  letters, on, 51
  meetings, of, 141
Datel services, 83
Debates, 28
Decentralisation, 187
Delegation, 186
Desk configurations, 9–10
Diaries
  harmonisation of, 123–4
  keeping of, 18, 122–5
Diazo copying, 117
Dictaphone Co. Ltd, Plates 6, 7 and 9
Dictatimer, 45
Dictation, 39–47
  art of taking, 42
  brief instructions, 39
  dictatimer, 45
  direct, 40
  interruptions, to, 43
  machines, 44, 46
  multi-bank systems, 44, 45–6
  outline notes, 39
  preparation for, 41–2
  recorded, 40, 43
  sessions, 40–43
  short forms, 43
  thought-tank systems, 44
Dictionary, 218
Diploma for Personal Assistants, 234
Direct speech, 75
Direction of business, 190–1
Discussions, 28
Display
  correspondence, in, 53–6
  equipment, 162
Distribution
  correspondence, of, 57
  mail, of, 89
Drafts, 39, 40
Drawers, 11–12
Dry copying, 117
Dual spectrum copying, 117

Duplicating, *see* Reprography
Dyeline, 117

Economist, 129
Education, secretary, and, 3, 4
Electric typewriters, 13
Electrostatic copying, 117
Employment Protection Act, 1975, 213
Employment Services Agency, 210
Employment and Training Act, 1973, 210
Enclosures in correspondence, 57
English
  clichés, 26
  command of, 18, 24–6
  dictionary, 218
  jargon, 26
  language, 218
  mastery of, 18
  reference books, 218
  slang, 26
  thesaurus, 26, 218
Envelopes, typing of, 59–60
Envoy Public Relations Ltd, Foreword
Equipment
  electrical, 164
  small items, 15
Error
  correction key, 64
  literal, 59
European Hotel Corporation, 150
Examinations
  Diploma for Personal Assistants, 234
  languages, 234
  Private Secretary's Certificate, 233
  Private Secretary Diploma, 233
Executive
  absence of, 165
  action, 2
  cooperation with, 20
  diary, 122
  dictation sessions, 41
  directors, 190
  efficiency and, 21
  expectations, of, 16
  functions, 19
  partnership with, 21
  priorities, 19
  reminder index, 125
  Secretaries Association, 232
  –secretary relationship, 2, 16–23
  travel, 160–7
Expense ratio, 201–3

Facsimile copying, 73, 82
Factors of production, 170–1
Feedback cycle, 196
Filing
  aids, 108–9, 110
  alphabetical, 99
  binder, 101, 104, 105
  box, 103
  cabinets, 14, 102

  card index, 99
  centralised, 98
  chronological order, 100
  data-processing, 110
  departmental, 98
  geographical, 100
  indexing units, 100
  lateral, 102
  lever arch, 103
  mail inwards, and, 89
  microfilm, 106–7
  mobile, 103
  name, 100
  numerical, 101
  post, 104
  powered, 103
  principles of, 99
  rotary, 103
  secretary, and, 97
  shelf, 101, 103
  side, 102
  specialist, 101, 105–10
  subject, 100
  suspension, 100, 102
  thong, 104
  vertical, 102
  visible index, 101, 104, 105, Plate 16
  wallet, 103
Flexible working hours, 212–13
  bandwidth, 212
  core-time, 212–13
  Flexleave, 212
  Flextime, 212–13
  presence indicators, 212–13
  remote-lamp indicator panels, 212–13
Flexleave, 212
Flexowriters, 62
Flextime, 212–13
Flipover units, 73
Follow-up systems, 19, 126
Forecasting, 182–3
Foreign exchange, 164
Franking machines, 92
Freighting World, 208
Friden Flexowriter, 62
Functional relationships, 186
Functions, *see* Conferences *and* Social functions
Furniture, 9–15
  chairs, 12
  configurations of, 9–10
  drawers, 11–12
  versatility of, 9

Graphics and word-processing, 66
Gross profit percentage, 201–2

Handouts, 134
Health aids in foreign travel, 164
Heat transfer copying, 116
Hengstler Flextime Ltd, 212
Herman Miller Ltd, 56
House journals, 35, 142

House style, 58
Human relations movement, 177

ITT Business Systems Ltd, Plate 12
ITT Terryphone, 73, 80
Impression controls, 13, 62
Index
    strip, 105
    telephone, 73
Indexing units, 100
Industrial relations, 213
Input media in word processing, 67
Institute of Public Relations, 133
Institute of Qualified Private Secretaries,
    232
Instructions, 27
Insurance, 163
Intercom, 14
Internal address, 52
Internal mail, 89
International driving licence, 163
Itineraries, 161

Jargon, 26
Job Centres, 208
Job description, 209
Job evaluation, 211
Justified margin, 13

Kalamazoo Ltd, 126, 215–17
Key call maker, 78

Laisser faire, 175
Language examinations, 234
Layout of correspondence, 50–9
Letter bombs, 85
Letterheads, 13, 50
    Company Acts, and, 50
    European Communities Act, and, 50
Letters, 29–33
Lift-off ribbons, 62
Line-length adjustment, 67
Line relationships, 185
Line-selection, 116
Literal errors, 59
Loudspeaking telephone, 73, 78

Machines
    dictation, 44–6
    franking, 92
    multi-bank, 45–6
    portable, 44
    thought-tank, 44
    typewriters, 62
    word-processors, 67
Maclaren Publishers Ltd, 222
Maclean Hunter Ltd, 222
Mail inwards, 85–91
    collecting, 85
    filing, 89
    letter bombs, 85
    opening, 86

register, 90
    routines, 85
    top secretary, and, 90
Mail outwards, 91–5
    franking, 92
    postage books, 92
    top secretary, and, 93
Mailing instructions, 51
Management
    accounting, 201
    appreciation of, 168
    Board of Directors, and, 191
    budgetary control, 200
    business organisations and, 173
    charts, 186
    committees, 187–90
    computer appreciation, 203–5
    controls, 195–204
    coordination, 181
    critical path analysis, 197–8
    decentralisation, 187
    delegation and, 186
    development of, 175
    direction, 190–1
    economic framework to, 168–73
    economic responsibility in, 192
    ethical element in, 181
    factors of production and, 171
    flexible working hours, 212–13
    forecasting, 182–3
    functional relationships, 186
    human relations movement, 177
    industrial relations, 213
    information, 201
    'laisser faire', 175
    line relationships, 185
    managing director, 190–1
    mixed economy, and, 169
    money, rôle of, 169
    network analysis, 197–8
    objectives, by, 183–4
    organisation, 185–93
    organisational charts, 186
    personnel, 206–17
    planning, 180–4
    planning-control feedback cycle, 196
    policy, 180
    production, and, 168–73, 197
    progress control, 197
    quality control, 199
    regional centres, 211
    scientific management, 176
    social responsibilities, 192
    span of control, 186
    specialisation, and, 169
    staff relationships, 186
    statistical controls, 199
    stock control, 198
    styles of leadership, 178
    technical college centres, 211
    training, 210–11
Managing director, 190–1
Manpower Services Commission, 210

Manuscript draft, 40
Master preparation in word-processing, 67
Matters arising, 130, 145
Meeting of minds, 28
Meetings, 130, 140–9
  AGM, 140
  activities before, 141
  adjournment of, 146
  agenda, 141
  amendments, 146
  any other business, 146
  Board, 140
  briefing, 141
  committee, 140
  conduct of, 144
  constitution, 140
  date of, 141
  departmental, 141
  extraordinary general, 140
  importance of, 140
  matters arising, 130, 145
  minutes, 130, 142, 145, 146
  motions, 145
  nem con, 146
  operational, 141
  orderly conduct at, 144–5
  points of order, 144
  preliminary activities, 141
  propositions, 145
  proxy, 146
  quorum, 144
  reference books, 219
  resolution, 146
  rider, 146
  rules, for, 144
  sine die, 146
  standing orders, 144
  statutory, 140
  venue, 141
Memo, 33
Memorandum of Association, 180
Memory in word-processing, 69
Microfilm filing, 106–7
Minutes, 130, 142, 145–6
Mixed economy, 1, 169
Money, rôle of, 169

NCR sets, 33–4, 115
Nem con, 146
Net profit percentage, 201–2
Network analysis, 197–8
Notices, 34

Objectives
  business travel, of, 160
  management by, 183–4
Office equipment reference books, 222
Offset copying, 120
Optimum order, 198
Organisation, 185–93
  authority in, 185
  charts, 186, 188–9

  duties, and, 185
Organising ability, 18
Outline notes, 39

PA, 7
PABX, 75
PMBX, 75
Partnership with executive, 21
Passports, 163
Penta Airline Hotels Ltd, 150
Per pro, 57
Personal assistant, 7
Personal qualities of secretary, 3, 5
Personnel management, 206–17
  careers conferences, 208
  conditions of employment, 211
  function, 206
  industrial relations, 213
  Job Centres, 208
  job description, 209
  job evaluation, 211
  planning, 207
  promotion, 209
  records, 214–16
  recruitment, 207
  references, 209
  selection, 207
  selection consultants, 209
  staff agencies, 209
  staff development, 209–11
  staff selection, 207
  succession planning, 207
  training, 209–11
  wages, 211
Petty cash book, 93–5
Plain paper copying, 117
Planning
  personnel, 207
  production, 181–2
  succession, 207
Planning-control feedback cycle, 196
Pool typing, 66
Post Office, Plates 11, 13 and 14, Figs. 8.1, 8.2, 8.3
  Guide, 92
  reference books, 218–19
Postage books, 92
Presence indicators, 212–13
Press
  reference books, 221
  releases, 37
Printing heads, 67
Priorities, sense of, 19
Priority switch, 45
Private secretary,
  Certificate, 233
  Diploma, 233
  executive and, 2
  importance of, 2
  mixed economy, and, 1
  qualities of, 3
Private sector, 174
Problem situations, 130

Production control, 197
Professional bodies, 4, 231
Professional commitments, 131
Progress control, 197
Promotion, 209
Promotional activities, 135–6
Proportional spacing, 13
Protocol, 137
Proxy, 146
Public relations, 133–9
  bureaucracy and, 138
  conferences, 150–5
  consumer relations, and, 134–5
  defensive activities, 136–7
  definition of, 133
  functions of, 133
  handouts, 134
  Institute of, 133
  promotional activities, 135–6
  protocol, 137
  references, 221
  sector, 174

Qualifications of secretary, 7
Quality control, 199
Quick reply letters, 31
Quorum, 144

Rank Xerox Ltd, 68–9, Plate 9, Fig. 7.2
Recall card, 63–4
Reception areas, 12
Recorded dictation, 40, 43
Records, personnel, 214–16
Recruitment, 207
Reference books, 218–22
  advisory services, 221
  conferences, 220
  consultancy services, 221
  correspondence, 218
  current affairs, 221
  English language, 218
  general, 221
  library, 222
  meetings, 219
  office equipment, 222
  people, 219
  Post Office services, 218–19
  press, 221
  public relations, 221
  trade and industry, 219–20
  travel, 220
References
  correspondence, in, 51
  personnel and, 209
Regional management centres, 211
Repeat keys, 13, 62
Reports, 35
  circulation, 143
  tabling, 143
Reprographics, 112–21
  AOD, 120
  centralisation, 112
  collators, 120

comparison chart, 118–19
  definition, 112
  diazo, 117
  dry, 117
  dual spectrum, 117
  dyeline, 117
  electrostatic, 117
  executive secretary, and, 112
  heat transfer, 116
  line selection, 116
  NCR, 115
  offset, 120
  plain paper, 117
  principles of, 113
  simultaneous, 114
  snap-apart sets, 114
  spirit, 116
  stencil, 115
  xerography, 117
Requests, 28
Return on capital invested, 198
Ribbon cartridges, 13
Roneo Neopost Ltd, 87

SCM (United Kingdom) Ltd, Plate 8, Fig. 7.1
STD, 72
Salutation, 52
Sasco Ltd, 127
Scientific management, 176
Screens, 9
Search and find facility, 65
Secretarial output, classification of, 64
Secretarial practice
  definition of, 1
  problems of, 1
Secretary
  business knowledge of, 3
  career prospects, 231
  command of English, 18
  communications centre, as, 122
  cooperation, instinct for, 20
  cost-effectiveness of, 22
  designation of, 6–7
  diaries and, 18
  dictation and, 42
  education of, 3, 4
  efficiency of, 21, 122
  executive, and, 16–23
  filing, and, 97
  functions of, 2
  organisational talents, and, 18
  personal qualities of, 3, 5
  priorities, sense of, 19
  skills of, 3, 4–5, 17
  telephone and, 71, 73–7
Selection
  consultants, 209
  personnel, of, 207
Shipton-Telstor Ltd, Plate 14
Short forms, 43
Shorthand, 4
Signatures, 56

Simultaneous copying, 114
Skills of secretary, 3, 4–5, 17
Slang, 26
Snap-apart sets, 114
Social functions, 156
  activities at start, 156
  follow-up activities, 158
  hostess duties, 156
Social responsibilities, 192
Space expand devices, 13
Span of control, 186
Spelling, 17, 49
Sperry Rand Ltd, Plate 8
Sperry Remington Kardex, Plate 4
Spicers Ltd, Plate 3
Spirit copying, 116
Staff
  agencies, 209
  development, 209–11
  relationships, 186
  selection, 207
  training, 209–11
Standard form
  letters, 32
  paragraphs, 65, 66
Standard Telephones and Cables Ltd,
  Plate 5
Statements, 28
Stationery, 13, 50
Statistical controls, 199
Statutory meetings, 140
Stencil copying, 115
Stock control, 198
Style
  correspondence in, 53–6, 58
  fully-blocked, 53
  house, 56
  indented, 55
  leadership, of, 178
  modified fully-blocked, 54
Subject headings in correspondence, 52
Succession planning, 207
Summaries, 36
Switchboards
  cordless PMBX, 75
  PABX, 73–7

Tabling of reports, 143
Tabulation, 67
Tape callmaker, 73, 78
Taylor, F. W., 176
Technical colleges, Management Centres
  in, 211
Telecommunications, 38, 80–3
  cables, 81
  datel, 83
  telegrams, 81–2
  telenotes, 37, 73, Plate 5
  Telex, 73, 82
Telegrams, wording of, 82
Telenotes, 37, 73, Plate 5
Telephone
  answering machines, 78–80

  card call-maker, 73, 78
  direct speech, 75
  facsimile copier, 73, 82
  index, 73
  intercom, 14
  key call-maker, 78
  lists, 163
  loud-speaking, 73, 78
  PABX, 75
  PMBX, 75
  requirements of secretary, 73
  STD, 72
  secretary and, 71, 73–7
  switchboards, 73–7
  tape call-maker, 73, 78
  technique, 71–3
  telenote, 37, 73, Plate 5
  Telex, 73, 82
  Terryphone, 73, 80
Telex, 73, 82
  answer-back code, 82
Terryphone, 73, 80
The Shannon Ltd, Plates 1, 15 and 16,
  108–9
Thesaurus, 26, 218
Thought-tank, 44
Tickler systems, 19
Trade Union and Labour Relations
  Act, 1974, 213
Training, 210–11
Training Services Agency, 210
Transcription
  art of, 48
  attention line, 52
  complimentary close, 52
  continuation sheets, 58
  corrections, 59
  date, and, 51
  distribution, 57
  enclosures, 57
  facilities for, 49
  internal address, 52
  layout, 50–9
  letterhead, 50
  mailing instructions, 51
  paper, and, 49–50
  preparation, for, 49
  references, 51
  salutation, 52
  signatures, 56
  styles, 53–6, 58
  subject heading, 52
Travel, 160–7
  address lists, 163
  agents, use of, 161
  checklist, 166
  climatic aspects, 164
  cover during absence, 165
  credit cards, 164
  display equipment, 162
  electrical equipment, 164
  foreign exchange, 164
  health aids, 164

Travel—*cont.*
  importance of, 160
  insurance, 163
  international driving licence, 163
  itinerary, 161
  objectives, 160
  passports, 163
  preparation, 161–3
  procedural routines, 162
  reference books, 161, 220
  sales literature, 162
  secretary's needs, 164
  spectacles, 164
  speeches, 162
  telephone lists, 163
  visit briefs, 162
  visiting cards, 162
Trays, 12
Twinlock Ltd, 11, Fig. 2.2
Typewriters
  automatic repeat keys, 13
  correction keys, 13
  correction ribbons, 62
  desirable features of, 13
  electric, 13
  Flexowriter, 62
  impression control, 13, 62
  justified margins, 13
  lift-off ribbon, 62
  mastery of, 5, 48
  proportional spacing, 13
  repeat keys, 13, 62
  ribbon cartridges, 13
  space expand devices, 13
  stroke storage, 62
  transcription and, 48
  typing element, 62
  word processing, 63–70

Underscoring, 67
Unitype Printing Co. Ltd, 34

Visible index, 101, 104–5, 217
Visit briefs, 162
Visiting cards, 162
Visitors
  introductions, 129
  reception of, 128
Visits, *see* Travel
Visual planner, 127
  Sasco Ltd, 127

Wages, 211
Warwick Time Stamp Co. Ltd, 87
Word processing, 63–70
  applications, 65
  automatic centring, 67
  automatic underscoring, 67
  buffer memory and, 63
  centring, 67
  conscious error correction, 64
  correction features, 67
  definition of, 63
  graphics and, 66
  input media, 67
  introduction of, 64
  line length adjustment, 67
  mandatory carriage return, 64
  master preparation, 67
  memory in, 69
  optional carriage return, 64
  pitch changing, 67
  pool typing, 66
  printing heads, 67
  Rank-Xerox 800, 68–9, Plate 9
  recall card and, 63–4
  repetitive typewriting, 66
  revision typewriting, 66
  ribbon changes, 67
  search and find facility, 65
  speed and, 67
  standard paragraphs, 65, 66
  tabulation, 67
  underscoring, 67
  work-flow systems, and, 65
Work area, 8–15, Plates 1 and 2
  access to, 8
  acoustics and, 9
  air conditioning and, 9
  blinds and, 9
  chairs, 12
  chat areas, 9
  conference areas, 9
  desk configuration, 9–10
  draughts and, 9
  furniture, and, 9–15
  lighting, and, 8
  situation, 8
Work flow systems, 65

Xerography, 117

Year planner, 19, 127